THE BILDUNGSROMAN IN A GENOCIDAL AGE

THE BILDUNGSROMAN IN A GENOCIDAL AGE

Ned Curthoys

BLOOMSBURY ACADEMIC
NEW YORK • LONDON • OXFORD • NEW DELHI • SYDNEY

BLOOMSBURY ACADEMIC

Bloomsbury Publishing Inc, 1359 Broadway, New York, NY 10018, USA
Bloomsbury Publishing Plc, 50 Bedford Square, London, WC1B 3DP, UK
Bloomsbury Publishing Ireland, 29 Earlsfort Terrace, Dublin 2, D02 AY28, Ireland

BLOOMSBURY, BLOOMSBURY ACADEMIC and the Diana logo are trademarks of Bloomsbury Publishing Plc

First published in the United States of America 2024
This paperback edition published in 2025

Copyright © Ned Curthoys, 2024

For legal purposes the Acknowledgments on p. viii constitute an extension of this copyright page.

Cover design: Eleanor Rose
Cover image © borchee / Getty Images

All rights reserved. No part of this publication may be: i) reproduced or transmitted in any form, electronic or mechanical, including photocopying, recording or by means of any information storage or retrieval system without prior permission in writing from the publishers; or ii) used or reproduced in any way for the training, development or operation of artificial intelligence (AI) technologies, including generative AI technologies. The rights holders expressly reserve this publication from the text and data mining exception as per Article 4(3) of the Digital Single Market Directive (EU) 2019/790.

Bloomsbury Publishing Inc does not have any control over, or responsibility for, any third-party websites referred to or in this book. All internet addresses given in this book were correct at the time of going to press. The author and publisher regret any inconvenience caused if addresses have changed or sites have ceased to exist, but can accept no responsibility for any such changes.

Library of Congress Cataloging-in-Publication Data

Names: Curthoys, Ned, author.
Title: The bildungsroman in a genocidal age / Ned Curthoys.
Description: New York : Bloomsbury Academic, 2024. | Includes bibliographical references and index. | Summary: "Explores influential historical fictions about the Holocaust that deploy narrative strategies of the Bildungsroman in which a perpetrator or complicit protagonist interrogates their own past and questions ideologies responsible for the catastrophic genocide and its legacy"–Provided by publisher.
Identifiers: LCCN 2023029905 (print) | LCCN 2023029906 (ebook) | ISBN 9798765103890 (hardback) | ISBN 9798765103883 (paperback) | ISBN 9798765103913 (pdf) | ISBN 9798765103906 (epub) | ISBN 9798765103876
Subjects: LCSH: Bildungsromans–History and criticism. | Historical fiction–History and criticism. | Holocaust, Jewish (1939-1945), in literature. | Holocaust, Jewish (1939-1945), in motion pictures. | Motion pictures–History. | LCGFT: Literary criticism. | Film criticism.
Classification: LCC PN3448.B54 C87 2023 (print) | LCC PN3448.B54 (ebook) | DDC 809.3/9354–dc23/eng/20230831
LC record available at https://lccn.loc.gov/2023029905
LC ebook record available at https://lccn.loc.gov/2023029906

ISBN: HB: 979-8-7651-0389-0
PB: 979-8-7651-0388-3
ePDF: 979-8-7651-0391-3
eBook: 979-8-7651-0390-6

Typeset by Deanta Global Publishing Services, Chennai, India

For product safety related questions contact productsafety@bloomsbury.com.

To find out more about our authors and books visit www.bloomsbury.com and sign up for our newsletters.

To Shino and Leo

CONTENTS

Acknowledgements   viii

INTRODUCTION   1

Chapter 1
MEMORY AS REINVENTION IN KAZUO ISHIGURO'S *THE REMAINS OF THE DAY*   15

Chapter 2
VISIONARY DISENCHANTMENT: ACCESSING SECOND SIGHT IN *THE KINDLY ONES*   37

Chapter 3
AN EXEMPLARY *BILDUNGSHELD*: BRINGING DIASPORA HOME IN *DANIEL STEIN, INTERPRETER*   53

Chapter 4
UNOFFICIAL EDUCATION AND THE PROMOTION OF ACTIVE READERSHIP IN TWO HOLOCAUST-THEMED NOVELS FOR CHILDREN: *HITLER'S DAUGHTER* AND *THE BOY IN THE STRIPED PYJAMAS*   71

Chapter 5
THE COUNTERFEITERS AS *BILDUNGSFILM*: ALLEGORIZING JEWISH HISTORY   91

Chapter 6
A PROTAGONIST FOR DARK TIMES: REPURPOSING MEMORY AND THE FUTURE OF CIVIL COURAGE IN MARGARETHE VON TROTTA'S BIOPIC *HANNAH ARENDT*   111

CONCLUSION   129

Notes   133
Bibliography   138
Index   149

ACKNOWLEDGEMENTS

Research for this book began in earnest while I was a visiting scholar at the Hannah Arendt Center at Bard College in 2018. My thanks to Roger Berkowitz and Samantha Hill for hosting me and for providing such a lively and stimulating intellectual community. I spent time while at Bard researching the book at the Stevenson Library.

I am immensely grateful for the love, support, advice, generosity, and invaluable assistance of Shino Konishi in preparing this book for publication. I thank Shino and my son Leo for inspiring me each and every day. My profound thanks to my parents Ann Curthoys and John Docker for reading drafts of this book and for their wise suggestions. Thank you to extended members of my family including Caitlan Markiewicz and Glenys Holley.

I thank my colleagues at the University of Western Australia for their interest in the book and support during the years in which it was not always easy to balance work and research commitments. My hearty thanks to the UWA writer's group that read and commented on drafts over a number of years and that was unfailingly constructive and encouraging. Particular thanks go to Tanya Dalziell, Tony Hughes D'Aeth, Daniel Juckes, Ethan Blue, Andrea Gaynor, and Dylan Lino who contributed timely comments at various stages.

Earlier versions of these chapters have previously been published. Chapter 2 first appeared as "Evaluating Risk in Perpetrator Narratives: Resituating Jonathan Littel's *The Kindly Ones* as Historical Fiction", *Textual Practice* vol. 31, no. 3, May 2017: 457–75. Chapter 3 first appeared as "Tarrying with the Impossible: *Daniel Stein, Interpreter* and the Politics of Translation", *Australian Literary Studies* vol. 28, no. 3, October 2013: 28–43. Chapter 4 first appeared as "The Construction of an Active Reader in two Holocaust themed novels for children: *Hitler's Daughter* (1999) and *The Boy in the Striped Pyjamas* (2006) as Bildungsroman", *Children's Literature in Education* 2021, vol. 52, no. 2: 253–70. Chapter 5 first appeared as "*The Counterfeiters as Bildungsfilm*: a Genre Study", *College Literature* vol. 48: no. 4 (Fall) 2021: 653–76. Chapter 6 first appeared as "Selbstdenken, Remembrance, and the Future of Civil Courage in Margarethe von Trotta's *Hannah Arendt* (2012): On the Pyschogenesis of the 'Banality of Evil'", *Screening the Past* 41 (December 2016).

INTRODUCTION

The supposition of this book is that the genre of the *Bildungsroman*, which is now an intermedial form that encompasses inter alia novels and films, long-form television, children's and young adult's literature, and graphic novels, continues to engage new readerships and reach new audiences because its structural features have been successfully adapted for the edifying and revisionist purposes of historical fiction. The genre's well-known thematic markers of an unformed protagonist leaving home and provincial circumstances, rejecting the dominance and negativity of the father by refusing or deferring a scripted social and professional destiny, and undergoing a testing set of experiences that 'educates' or leads them out of (*educere*) indoctrination and a constricted habitus, continues to provide historical novels and films with narrative strategies. In this book I will be examining four influential historical novels about the Second World War and the Holocaust, *The Remains of the Day* (1989), *The Kindly Ones* (2006), *Hitler's Daughter* (1999), and *The Boy in the Striped Pyjamas* (2006), and two philosophically minded historical feature films, *The Counterfeiters* (2007) and *Hannah Arendt* (2012). These historical *Bildungsromane*, I argue, represent significant contributions to the evolution of the genre as they seek to represent difficult histories while at the same time stimulating an engaged reader to think about how they might apply their enriched historical understanding to contemporary circumstances.

In discussing historical representations that combine historical fidelity with an invented or fictionalized protagonist it is important to rethink the critical function enacted by the contemporary *Bildungsheld*. By a *Bildungsheld* I will be referring to the protagonist of a *Bildungsroman* who can offer witnessing and testimonial functions as a result of their spatial mobility and restless curiosity. The protagonist of a historical *Bildungsroman* can assist the reader and audience in challenging ideological orthodoxies as a result of their diverse experiences. The reader can also be guided by the tendency of their heterodox, associative memories to repurpose our sense of the past and its legacies in the present. In adapting our analysis to the refunctioned protagonists of recent historical *Bildungsromane*, *The Bildungsroman in a Genocidal Age* will, nevertheless, be mindful of genre continuities such as the ungovernable intellectual curiosity of the *Bildungsroman*, in which a questing protagonist searches for meaning and seeks out a variety of interlocutors in order to discuss a range of perspectives and ideas pertinent to their historical context. The questions posed by and to the unformed *Bildungsheld* tend to animate, destabilize, and haunt the protagonist and by extension the text, assisting the reader to themselves engage in philosophical reflection and generative historical inquiry.

One pertinent feature of the historical turn of the *Bildungsroman* in recent decades is that in order to complicate and defamiliarize our sense of the past, novels and films often represent subjectivities complicit with a perpetrator culture who may enact or be a beneficiary of genocidal violence and colonial occupation. There are reasons for this tendency as it allows the reader or audience, quite often a younger demographic, to grasp the modalities of acculturation and indoctrination that normalize hegemonic ideologies and to ask themselves hypothetical questions about their own actions and decisions in similar circumstances.[1] At the same time, the protagonists of the *Bildungsromane* we will be discussing have by no means foregone a hermeneutically productive genre trait, a plasticity of personality and receptivity to phenomena that helps guide the reader towards an interpretively active reading experience as they perforce share the protagonist's geo-psychic wanderings, travails, and occasional epiphanies.

Martin Swales' description of *The Magic Mountain*'s Hans Castorp as 'undistinguished by any dominant characteristic, propensity, or quality' (Swales 1978, 119), still largely holds true of the multifaceted protagonists we are discussing, meaning that the impulse towards exploring ideas and the underdeveloped or symbolically representative characterology of the genre continues to be an important feature of its representational strategies. As Franco Moretti reminds us, the protagonist of Goethe's genre originating *Wilhelm Meisters Lehrjahre* (1795), Wilhelm Meister, figures the mock-epic hero of the novelistic *Bildungsroman* not because of his striking individuality but rather because he blends within himself the 'countless nuances of the social context' in his yet to be formed personality, willingly agreeing to be 'determined from without' in the sense that situation and plot will shape his narrative trajectory (Moretti 2000, 21). Moretti suggests that the temporality of the narrative of a *Bildungsroman* is heterogeneous and inclusive rather than linear, interpreting the *Bildungsroman* as that genre in which obstacle 'must be *incorporated*' rather than overcome, which means that Wilhelm Meister and his later avatars exist '*only* in the course of his "years of apprenticeship"' (Moretti 2000, 48). Returning to the stimulating problem of reading perpetrator characters who double as conduits for an enhanced awareness of the worlds they inhabit, it becomes apparent that we will need a versatile hermeneutics because, as Sue Vice reminds us of many fictional Holocaust representations, and which is especially marked in the *Bildungsroman*, 'meaning is constructed not by authorial fiat but by the clash of discourses' (Vice 2000, 11). As readers we can be piqued by the provocative arguments of unpalatable subjectivities while at the same time exploring the reflective space opened by the focalizing dexterity of protagonists who are always in the process of journeying beyond a complacent sense of identity and belonging.

While the interpretive challenges and diversity of the genre of the *Bildungsroman* have been recognized by scholars in numerous fields including feminist and women's writing, postcolonial studies, Victorian and modernist studies, and studies of the literature of the United States,[2] *The Bildungsroman in a Genocidal Age* seeks to rectify an inattention to the profound influence of the genre on historical fiction addressing the Second World War and the Holocaust over the last three decades. I would suggest that there has been dutiful recognition of Bakhtin's almost euphoric description of the *Bildungsroman* as a genre that offers a richly chronotopic image of human beings '*in the process of becoming*', but little close analytical work exploring its implications (Bakhtin 2010, 21). The genre of the *Bildungsroman*, a quintessential example of the representational innovation of the novel form, can provide such a rich image of human emergence, of the possibility of a 'new, unprecedented type of human being', only by assimilating 'real historical time' (21). Bakhtin feels that the 'organizing force held by the future' has a profound effect on the genre, as the threshold of the new throws up a variety of problems for consideration, of freedom and necessity, the realization of human potential, possibilities for creative initiative, and these problems remind us that the 'very *foundations* of the world are changing' and that human beings must change along with them (23–4).

The texts I will analyse also illuminate a dynamic historicity in symbiotic relationship with the possibility of what is yet to emerge. I am interested, in particular, in the manner in which a number of the novels and films adumbrate imaginative horizons that look beyond current geopolitical impasses and stagnant conceptions of national identity. In *Daniel Stein* and *Hannah Arendt*, for example, characters visit the ancient city of Jerusalem and experience idiosyncratic epiphanies that are displaced versions of the 'Jerusalem syndrome', enabling the reader and audience to rethink the imaginative cartography of the Israel-Palestinian conflict.

In order to perform explorative readings of the texts I have selected it will be necessary to restore an emphasis on the *Bildungsroman* as rewardingly reader-centred rather than focused on teleological narrative trajectories. Since the publication of Franco Moretti's classic study, *The Way of the World*, there has been a tendency to assume the developmental focus of the genre has various legitimating functions including the identification of the protagonist's eventual maturation with a recognition of the legitimacy of civil society, in which the irresolute wandering and possible self-destruction of the protagonist induces the 'individual to renounce with conviction the path of individuality' (Moretti 2000, 59). As another prominent theorist of the *Bildungsroman* Joseph Slaughter puts it: '*Bildung*'s more pedestrian work is to reconcile the perceived conflict between the natural inclinations of the human individual and the normalizing regulatory demands of society and the nation-state' (Slaughter 2009, 122).

Attempting to summarize a European genre awaiting postcolonial subversion, Maria Helena Lima informs us that the '*Bildungsroman* duplicates in literary form a cohesive cultural code whose primary function is to govern social integration in such a way that young men and women fit into society [...] the novel must convey a social order that appears legitimate' (Lima 1993, 434). The proclivity to describe the genre in teleological terms has been usefully dubbed a critical fetish for 'end-orientation'[3] which enables totalizing ideological critique but inhibits the articulations of the pleasures of reading texts with unresolved ethical perplexities and manifold rhetorical impacts. In the field of studies of the *Bildungsroman*, a lingering end-orientation has created the nominalist suspicion as to whether the genre really exists if the texts themselves do not capture a steady movement towards psycho-social maturity.[4] In addition the anxiety that the genre is originally predicated on a mobile, socially ascendant bourgeois male can invite a critical manoeuvre in which the resistant critic insists on the subversive or parodic qualities of their own preferred textual example which tends to minimize conversation with pertinent genre studies and underestimate the nuances and complexities that pertain to even the earliest examples of the genre.[5]

If we are to rectify this default end-orientation then it is worth returning to one of the keenest readers of Goethe's ur-text, *Wilhelm Meisters Lehrjahre*, Goethe's friend, interlocutor and collaborator Friedrich Schiller, who noted in a letter to him of 1796 that as a *Bildungsheld* Wilhelm Meister is necessary yet not 'the most important' character in the novel (cited in Moretti 2000, 20). Valuable because of his 'pliability', Meister is a character for whom everything takes place around but not because of him, surrounded as he is by people and things which 'represent and express energies' (cited in Moretti 2000, 20). One of the earliest proponents of the *Bildungsroman* in the early decades of the nineteenth century, Karl Morgenstern, was not long in taking up Schiller's suggestion, arguing that the representation of an individual in various phases of development, and in interaction with their environment, 'promotes the development of the reader to a greater extent than any other kind of novel' (Morgenstern 2009, 654–5). In a more recent discussion of the genre, the observant genre critic and Goethe scholar Martin Swales has argued that the ironic indeterminacy of Goethe's novel in which a shrewd narrator often subtly undermines or manipulates a callow *Bildungsheld*, repositions the reader to explore the constellation of persons, institutions, and communities that make up the world of the novel (Swales 2012, 133). Inescapably, as Swales puts it, the reader of the genre undergoes an 'open-ended process of *Bildung* in our hermeneutic relationship' to an elusive text (Swales 2012, 133) in which it is unclear if Wilhelm has ever controlled his own fate. As Martin Swales noted in an earlier study, the abiding ideal of the organic growth of the individual rarely receives 'unequivocal narrative realization' in the *Bildungsroman* (Swales 1978, 30).

The challenge for the reader is not only that the genre does not invite ready identification with the principal protagonist as it allows ample scope for other characters to tell their stories and mount their arguments, but also that it is a morphological hybrid. In recent decades there are numerous examples of studies of the genre that stress that no matter how far back we go, in the *Bildungsroman* we are dealing with an uncertain, polyvalent, and often experimental literary form that must be read carefully rather than rendered epiphenomenal of larger historical processes.[6]

A decoupling of the genre's literary manifestations from any univocal conception of its ideological underpinnings will, I suggest, allow for a more conjunctural reading of the 'hero' of the *Bildungsroman* as a character who, as Moretti reminds us, *belongs* to the episodic, often digressive, and fluid adventure-time of the text and who helps to focalize a series of existential potentialities that cannot be described as the narrative's destination or meaning. We might suggest that the reader is being continually reminded of Wilhelm von Humboldt's ideal of education in many of these texts, in which, as Kristin Gjesdal reminds us, education is not an accreditation or accomplishment, 'not a stage one leaves behind but a lifelong endeavour' (Gjesdal 2015, 704).

My study, sceptical of end-oriented readings that enforce coherence on wayward texts, owes much to Susan Fraiman's classic revisionist study *Unbecoming Women: British Women Writers and the Novel of Development* which voices a suspicion of the masculinist ideology of a literary genre, the Goethean *Bildungsroman*, whose somewhat phantasmatic appeal seems to be 'coextensive with the experience of the *Bildungsheld*', a central character 'whose movements are tracked, detectivelike, to the exclusion of other movements or meanings' (Fraiman 1993, 10). Fraiman would rather acknowledge an alternative tradition in Victorian female-authored novels of 'unbecoming' female protagonists who, like Maggie Tulliver in *The Mill on the Floss*, fail to leave home and relinquish social bonds and as such can be considered exemplars of a version of personal destiny that 'evolves in dialectical relation to social structure, historical events, and other people' (Fraiman 1993, 10). Fraiman helps establish a more stimulating version of the genre, inflected by contradictory impulses, that does not offer a dominant narrative for the reader to follow but various plotlines and alternatives in which 'development is not one, clear thing, but many, unsure, contested and changing things' (Fraiman 1993, 138). In the readings that follow I wish to augment her pluralistic conception of a genre that often challenges a normative conception of psychological and gender-related development while also suggesting that the genre's interrogation of a linear maturation process is inseparable from its rhizomatic and picaresque quest structure.

Towards an engaged indicative hermeneutics

According to the OED, indication is 'The action of indicating, pointing out, or making known; that in which this is embodied; a hint, suggestion, or piece of information from which more may be inferred.' It can also refer to a 'sign, token, or symptom; an expression by sign or token'.

My strategy of interpretation in this book is to evoke the indicative significance of the texts under consideration in the sense of drawing out certain hints and suggestions as to what unfolding processes and emerging character traits are becoming visible and worthy of affirmation by readers and audiences. With underdeveloped protagonists, intellectual breadth, and a latter-day negative capability that can abide in uncertainty, the historical fictions we are examining can be said to indicate, point towards, and organize inferences for a reader. They can do so because the ethos of *Bildung*, the desire for self-formation through mobility, obtained through manifold modes of social association and reflective immersion in the natural world, continues to offer guidance to the reader even when the protagonist themselves would seem to be pre-designated as an obedient servant, a committed Nazi, a betrayer, an insultingly naïve ingenue, a swindler, and parvenu. Which is to say that the reader, attuned to the pleasures of reading a *Bildungsroman* in all its capaciousness, can continue to think about the multifarious conditions for the emergence of a self-inventing personality.

These conditions, arts of living, and affective intensities might comprise an increasing unease with the law of the father, a restless proclivity towards mobility, the inability to let go of important questions, a salutary disenchantment with a given social order or constituted authority, and resilience and reorientation in the face of testing ordeals. As we move beyond end-oriented readings of the genre we can appreciate a protagonist who defers final outcomes and refuses univocal meanings, who lives and moves in the counterfactual space of the 'not yet'.[7] The reader, attuned to the theme of a dilated apprenticeship in which the protagonist is schooled by a multiform world, will also begin to perceive a struggle to work out a vocation that strives against the grain of normative development, the dismal outlook of careerism and professional duty, instead drawing on their loyalty to the fluidity and crystallizing experiences of childhood in the hope that a youthful mien can be transmuted into an ethos, a life's purpose.

The engaged hermeneutics of indicative inference that I propose will prove consequential in enabling transformative interpretations of the texts themselves. For as I have suggested we will need to forebear to prematurely determine our protagonists according to realist criteria and perhaps appreciate their ability to refresh our own perspectives. The butler Stevens, for example, in *The Remains of the Day* and the character of Maximilien Aue in *The Kindly Ones*, the protagonists of the first two chapters, are often prematurely repudiated as examples of the banality of evil in the former case and of the monstrosity and perversity of a bona fide Nazi in the latter. An indicative hermeneutic approach would, in its affinity with the genre, observe both characters' increasingly apparent and discursively generative disillusionment with their earlier worldviews. What is needed, then, is a willingness to think with the text itself as a varied journey, offering us a movement away from a safe location, enabling us to enter into an uncertain period of formation as readers and audiences.

Some of the readings I propose, for example, indicate the need for increased sensitivity to the metaphorical resonance of off-piste wanderings. In many of the texts we will encounter, and perhaps they nod back to masterful examples of the genre such as Ursula Le Guin's *The Wizard of Earthsea*, self-knowledge is predicated on a movement away from known cartographies towards the marginal and off-map. At an allegorical level we can read this off-piste mobility as figuring how memory may enhance candid self-assessment and mature independence if it wanders in the margins and explores a miscellany of seemingly insignificant or inconvenient recollections in order to challenge the occlusions of complacent national narratives or to query egotistical self-projections. Just as a traveller after a chance encounter will develop new interests and so begin to leave a predetermined route, many of our protagonists will begin to revise their worldview and fashion new perspectives under the pressure of circumstances, circumstances that they themselves may subconsciously seek.

I will return to a discussion of the memory work enacted by the texts I have chosen in a few moments but I would first like to suggest that in various ways the texts I analyse are *kairotic*, which is to say inspired by the rhetorical notion of the *Kairos*, the capacity to intervene in a discourse in a timely, urgent, and opportune moment. The texts I analyse represent protagonists who are urgently seeking understanding, willing to take the opportunities to dilate the possibilities of the present moment and address with some urgency the needs of their time and ours. We can say with one of the principal theorists of the term, James Kinneavy, that 'kairos adds a dynamism and value dimension to temporality' (Kinneavy 2000, 434), and that it returns us again and again to the concrete case, the particular situational context (Kinneavy 2000, 441). With Susan Wells we can talk of many of these texts as interested in opening up the present to a 'discontinuous future', the result of a 'kairotic refunctioning of the past' (Wells 2022, 255). The indicative interest of a *Bildungsroman* from the perspective of an inquisitive reader is precisely its ability to continue to interrogate the enriched possibilities of the now, to be poised 'between past and future',[8] a temporality that Hannah Arendt, the subject of our final chapter, felt was the necessary scene of political thinking after the Second World War, an unprecedented era lacking the guidance of theological and philosophical 'banisters'.[9]

The Bildungsroman in a Genocidal Age is about how recent instances of the genre of the *Bildungsroman* are *kairotic* interventions into our understanding of the past and our responsibilities in the present, as historical novels and films seek to edify and engage readers and audiences in light of what I am terming the Eichmann problematic. By the Eichmann problematic I do not want at this point to enter into lengthy discussions about the accuracy of Hannah Arendt's judgements on Adolf Eichmann but rather I refer to questions that arise when one resists occulting evil and diabolizing those who commit atrocious deeds, and instead examine perpetrators as human beings with 'everyday human mindsets' (Boswell 2012, 13).[10] In the wake of the possibility of evil's banality and superficiality, one needs to examine the perpetrator by exploring the role of ideological conditioning, 'language rules' or linguistic euphemisms, familial and institutional acculturation, and the normative gratifications of obedience, which Hannah Arendt has described as the pleasure that can be taken in 'functioning', of going along, the obverse of which is genuine action, an enjoyment of discussion, of collectively reaching decisions and taking responsibility for them (Arendt 2013, 44).

That Arendt's reports on the banality of evil, which are the subject matter of the film *Hannah Arendt* that I discuss in Chapter 6, continue to stimulate *kairotic* reflection on the possibility of evil and injustice in respect of our own societies is impressively articulated in a recent article that appeared in the topical online journal *The Conversation*. In an article as part of the periodical's literature review series 'The Book that Changed Me' that appeared in November 2022, Peter Christoff describes how disturbed he was by Hannah Arendt's epochal *Eichmann in Jerusalem*. Christoff reflects that Eichmann was indeed 'unique' and no everyman, 'yet his terrifying moral complacency was reflected in the lives of those around him, Germans of his generation especially'. The problem, Christoff feels, is that the 'desire to keep one's head down and not cause trouble, and to benefit passively or actively from small wrongs and larger evils, was not merely a matter for Germans in Nazi Germany'.

At the heart of the 'Eichmann problem', Christoff feels, and here he recalls a problematic explored in studies such as Zygmunt Bauman's *The Holocaust and Modernity* (2000), are 'larger questions about the nature of wilful blindness, and the sources of compromise, complicity, and collaboration with forms of evil in complex bureaucratic societies'.

> Arendt's underlying question about 'How should we behave?' became, for me, a question about how ordinary people – like me – can participate in awful things and contribute to terrible outcomes, sometimes knowingly, using exculpatory stories to salve their consciences. (Christoff, 2022)

The *ad feminam* invective generated by the Arendt controversy can obscure how generative her redescription of the nature of evil has been, stimulating psychological experiment, historical and sociological investigations, and artistic representation.[11] In its ascription of the commission of evil acts to philistine conformism and 'sheer thoughtlessness', Arendt's suggestive observation stimulated perpetrator research by voiding reassuring images of the Nazi genocidaire as atavistic barbarian, sadistic monstrosity, and ideological zealot, while querying a mono-causal explanation of the Holocaust as the inevitable outcome of an eternal and undifferentiated gentile anti-Semitism. We can also remark that the notion of the banality of evil complicates a ubiquitous presupposition of ethical and political discourse in Western societies, the 'symbolic geography of evil', as felicitously described by Zygmunt Bauman and

Leonadis Donskis in *Moral Blindness: The Loss of Sensitivity in Liquid Modernity* (2013). The symbolic geography of evil is an invested imaginary in which evil 'lives somewhere else' (Bauman and Leonidas 2013, 7). Malfeasance is no longer reckoned with as something to do with our civilization but diabolized, occulted, and existentially neutralized by giving it objective form and ascribing its provenance to a recognizable psychological or cultural matrix (Bauman and Leonidas 2013, 8).

If we return to the texts I will be analysing as haunted by the problematic of the banality of evil then it may be worth recalling that one aspect of Arendt's own ethical response to the banality of evil was her emphasis on talking in meaningful ways about the past by exercising our memory and engaging in narrative understanding that helps us to reconcile with reality.[12] The effort to engage in reflective remembrance by characters who are both insiders and outsiders to a particular cultural matrix is a notable facet of a genre that has increasingly taken a psychological and introspective turn.[13] Characters I analyse such as Max Aue, Stevens, Daniel Stein, Hannah Arendt, and Sally Sorowitsch find ways to repurpose their refractory memories for a range of personal and vocational ends. My study, therefore, is in conversation with the growing field of memory studies in which memory is a dynamic agent open to the needs of the present.[14] I stress throughout this study that an urgent dimension of the *kairotic* memory work we find in many of these texts is a curatorial impulse that serves as an antidote to the corrosion of reflective memorialization that Eichmann embodies, expressing a desire to recuperate that which may be repressed, forgotten, or erased. Guided by an indicative awareness of the capacious historiographical interests of contemporary historical fictions, the reader will attend to the curatorial memory work initiated by various *Bildungshelden* and recognize that this memory work is congenial with a genre tendency to undermine sanguine developmental narratives which stress maturity at the expense of an affection for childhood and its realms of imagination and play. As feminist critics have pointed out, the *Bildungsoman* has long voiced suspicion of versions of development predicated on masculinist autonomy and the rejection of relationality and pre-Oedipal childhood attachment to the mother.[15] Drawing on an indicative approach that can read the genre as interrogating development narratives more broadly, the reader can extrapolate when reading or viewing historical *Bildungsromane*, that the genre's anti-developmental animus extends towards a suspicion of a ubiquitous modern precept, the supercessionist conviction that a supposedly inferior or underdeveloped culture needs to be replaced with a more deserving civilization.

Unreliable narrative

The final innovation of *The Bildungsroman in a Genocidal Age* that I wish to discuss is its explorations of the convergence between the questing, *kairotically* motivated *Bildungheld* of recent historical fictions and what decades of narratology has fruitfully designated as the unreliable narrator. The convergence between two types of narrator-protagonist is initially surprising as the *Bildungsroman* still tantalizes its proponents and critics as an optimistic genre offering a developmental storyline journeying towards clarity and a coherent identity. Unreliable narrators, meanwhile, at least since Henry James' *The Turn of the Screw*, encourage labyrinthine interpretations that query the narrator's ethical probity and possible mental pathology. Textual signals discouraging empathy and credulity towards such a narrator are the very stuff of narratological taxonomies as we shall see when we discuss the character of Stevens in *The Remains of the Day*. Unreliable narrative seemingly acknowledges the subterranean world of the unconscious uncovered by psychoanalysis, dramatizing a subjectivity grappling with guilt and repression, self-deception and fantasy, illustrative of the dynamic falsifications of memory. In *The Art of Fiction* David Lodge suggests, for example, that 'the point of using an unreliable narrator is . . . to reveal an interesting gap between appearance and reality, and to show how human beings distort or conceal the latter' (Lodge 2011, 155). Thus the text's artful structuration and creative design would seem to hold sway in a manner that has rarely held true for a genre that has been difficult to disentangle from the promise of modernity and is now often extolled as a form congenial to emancipative self-expression by a range of marginalized and subaltern subjectivities.

Yet the increasingly nuanced and self-revising tendencies of recent genre studies of the *Bildungsroman* that we have been discussing can pave the way for serious attention to the convergence of the two types of protagonists. I would suggest that *Bildungsromane* increasingly resemble examples of unreliable narrative in encompassing the retrospective time of memory in which the protagonist may or may not be in the process of transformation as they reconsider their actions and decisions. Nor is the *Bildungsheld* what it once was in terms of self-understanding. Speaking of *Wilhelm Meisters Lehrjahre*, Thomas Jeffers has noted Goethe's attempts to free up 'the unconscious' intelligent, life favoring energies' and of the novel's suggestion that 'the unconscious can through trial and error find its own proper path to gratification' (Jeffers, 32). Martin Swales has reminded us that self-presence is not a hallmark of the *Bildungsheld* as they remain tentative in their educational progress and open to external determinations. As we shall see, Swales' comment that Wilhelm Meister 'learns and forgets, he is both seeing and unseeing' (Swales 2012, 132) can also be made of unreliable narrators with various narrative functions such as Stevens and Maximilien Aue.

There is also a feeling that even classic Victorian *Bildungshelden* are self-contradictory and retentive, exemplifying arrested emotional development, as reflected in Maynard's suggestion that in *Great Expectations* Pip 'embodies contradictory impulses to move up in class to great expectations and also to be loyal to the world of working class, petty bourgeois, or convict abjects'

(Maynard 2008, 283). In a similar vein Sarah Graham reminds us that Holden Caulfield not only expresses no interest in conforming to models of sexuality, aspiration, or material acquisition but spends considerable time in *The Catcher in the Rye* looking back to his younger deceased brother Allie, a 'loving innocent who valued poetry' (Graham, 'The American Bildungsroman' 2019, 141). The formative power of unconscious drives and influences in the *Bildungsroman* are allied to the genre's emphasis on the role of chance and opportunity in personal development and the impingement of complex environmental factors on one's life education. As Ellen McWilliams points out, 'everything that happens to us leaves its traces, everything contributes imperceptibly to our development' (McWilliams 2009, 257).

We stand, then, to gain much by now examining the *Bildungsroman* as a hybrid and absorptive genre that has expanded its narratological range and capacity to address mature retrospection and a whole variety of psychic and historical phenomena. This means that as the two character types overlap, we can note a compossibility of interpretive positions that one can take towards the protagonists of historical *Bildungromane*. Of course, there are functional considerations here also. The *kairotic* interest in the Eichmann problematic will require the reader to be tested, to be thoroughly immersed in discourses of perpetration, confronting an unstable or even incoherent *Bildungheld* who can be evasive, defensive, dogmatic, but also disarmingly confessional and capable of speaking truth to power. It is to this less coherent *Bildungsheld*, reconstituting themselves through memorial discourse but staring at the past as an unfathomable abyss, that we will need to attend to in the chapters to follow.

Chapter 1, 'Memory as reinvention in Kazuo Ishiguro's *The Remains of the Day*', analyses a novel which has tended to straddle either narratological interest in its unreliable narrator, for which it is a *locus classicus*, or a strand of ethical criticism that takes Stevens as an Eichmann like figure with a rigid ego ideal predicated on unwavering service to an idealized master. My approach is to incorporate Stevens within the genre of the *Bildungsroman* as a narrator-protagonist experiencing a mature awakening. Stevens' journey combines an off-piste drive into the west country which will parallel his winding exploration of memories of his period of service at Darlington Hall. Following the engaged, indicative hermeneutic I propose, I will evoke the gradual renewal and reconstitution of an effectively orphaned subject, now separating themselves from a patriarchal and constraining microcosm, and experiencing an equipoise of disillusionment and redemptive possibility. I suggest that Stevens' dedication to working on his vocation as a butler is closely related to his capacity for growth and moral independence as he uses the latent democratizing power of servants' discourse to question his masters and to deploy ruse, mask and disguise in order to interrogate Britain's imperial legacy and affirm social-democratic perspectives in the post-war era.

In Chapter 2, 'Visionary disenchantment: Accessing second sight in *The Kindly Ones*', I discuss the controversial narrator-protagonist Maximilien Aue, a Nazi SS officer who would seem to be devious, oleaginous, and equivocating in reflecting on his historical participation in Nazi crimes. I attend closely, however, to the novel's quest structure in which Aue demonstrates a tendency to wander in the periphery where, as a meditative *flâneur*, he will display a curatorial interest in Jewish diasporic history and begin to debunk the concept of 'race' and other myths of determinative origins. I then trace the development of Aue's capacity for a penetrative, derealizing 'second sight' after he is wounded at the Battle of Stalingrad. From that point forward Aue demonstrates an increasing detachment from the law of the father as he mocks Hitler's anti-Semitism as a paranoid projection of his own ethical nullity and moves beyond attempts to emulate the destiny of his fascist father. I propose an indicative, inferential exploration of Aue's mobile textual functions as detective figure, trickster, witness to the horrors of war, and, like Stevens, conduit for historical revisionism.

Chapter 3, 'An exemplary *Bildungsheld*: Bringing diaspora home in *Daniel Stein, Interpreter*', draws attention to the geopolitical resonances of the protagonist Daniel Stein's journey of self-formation as his syncretic attempts to combine Catholic and Jewish identities undermine a variety of supercessionist ideologies in which, for example, Zionist nationalism has negated the weakness of the Jewish diasporic condition. While clearly engaging in acts of rescue, Stein has nevertheless passed through a period of complicity serving as a translator for the Nazi and Soviet occupying powers which he will repurpose as a humanist critique of war and militant nationalism. Arriving in the Holy Land not long after the establishment of Israel in 1948, Stein wishes to articulate an anomalous identity as a Jewish man of the Catholic faith which I read as symptomatic of his lifelong vocational interest in translating between cultures and faiths, and embracing the land in which he lives as a religious, linguistic and cultural palimpsest. I suggest that Daniel's version of the 'Jerusalem Syndrome' is not the archaeological revelation of one's true and original identity but a stimulus to rethinking what the land he has arrived in may still become in light of an ethics of cohabitation.

Chapter 4, 'Unofficial education and the promotion of active readership in two Holocaust-themed novels for children: *Hitler's Daughter* and *The Boy in the Striped Pyjamas*' explores two influential historical fictions written primarily for children, *Hitler's Daughter* (1999) and *The Boy in the Striped Pyjamas* (2006). In both novels we follow inquisitive children, two of whom are growing up in Nazi Germany, who will come to interrogate the values and epistemologies of their homes, legible as sites of indoctrination, conformity, and the repression of intellectual curiosity. On the question of vocation, the protagonists of these stories begin to discern a life in which playfulness, imagination, and questioning and critique, can inform their choices and encourage them to oppose injustice. In the case of *The Boy in the Striped Pyjamas* the reader will need to think about the protagonist Bruno not just as a preposterously naïve son of an Auschwitz commandant but as self-educating through exploration, friendship, and conversation, eventually committed to cross-border acts of solidarity that allow contemporary readers to probe xenophobic and nationalist rationales for various forms of spatial segregation, while also rethinking what the rise of mass statelessness means for the rights of the child.

In Chapter 5, '*The Counterfeiters* as *Bildungsfilm*: allegorizing Jewish history', I argue that the Stefan-Ruzowitzky-directed film *The Counterfeiters* (2007) is a cinematic dramatization of the ethical and political significance of personal formation in dire circumstances. We watch as its resourceful *Bildungsheld* Solomon (Sally) Sorowitsch morphs from a detached and cynical spectator to a position of moral leadership. I read Sally as a searching protagonist affected by trauma, indeed on the precipice of nihilistic despair, who begins to reawaken an attachment to life and a sense of purpose as he assists the young and vulnerable in his midst and opens himself up to a variety of problematics including justifications for utilitarian approaches to ethics. Sally focalizes moral quandaries in the concentration camp system that can be extended to the responsibilities of the privileged in today's world, and, in a similar fashion to protagonists such as Daniel Stein who have refused or deferred identarian alternatives, encourages the viewer to reflect with generosity and understanding on the past, present, and future of the Jewish diaspora.

In Chapter 6, 'A protagonist for dark times: Repurposing memory and the future of civil courage in Margarethe von Trotta's biopic *Hannah Arendt*', I analyse the 2012 biopic *Hannah Arendt*, which depicts the civil courage of Hannah Arendt, one of very few female philosophers of her era. Arendt makes the brave but risky decision to embark on a difficult, possibly retraumatizing but ultimately edifying journey into the newly formed country of Israel, a journey which will double as a confrontation with her past as a victim of the Nazis and a stateless person. I argue that Arendt, as she thinks through her earlier beguilement by Martin Heidegger and is aware of the infidelity of her husband Heinrich Blücher, consistently enacts a relational mode of *Selbstdenken*, a way of thinking for oneself that is mindful of thinking as an exemplary and worldly performance. For Arendt *Selbstdenken* signified the demonstration of critical independence in the full face of the public gaze, as a way of caring for the plurality of the world in all its fragility. The cinematic character Arendt expresses her independence and relational care while she formulates and then defends her unprecedented characterization of Adolf Eichmann, one of the principal architects of the Nazi genocide of European Jews, as an unnerving example of the 'banality of evil'. While I agree with some of the scholarship that Arendt emerges in the film as unreliable in self-understanding, I suggest that the film draws indicative attention to a *kairotic* mise en scène, the presence and passionate investments of younger onlookers, including her secretary and friend Lotte Köhler, who wish to see public manifestations of independent thought and to interrogate manifestations of the banality of evil in their own society.

Chapter 1

MEMORY AS REINVENTION IN KAZUO ISHIGURO'S *THE REMAINS OF THE DAY*

Addressing the critical reception

This chapter suggests that the narrator of Kazuo Ishiguro's novel *The Remains of the Day* (1989), the butler Stevens, can be read as the fluid protagonist of a *Bildungsroman*, a character experiencing emotional development, and capable of adaptive self-fashioning and rigorous self-examination. My interpretation of Stevens might take some readers by surprise given the received image of Stevens as an emotionally repressed and self-deceived functionary clinging throughout most of the novel to a protective self-image of his professional rectitude. The reading I propose will entail points of difference with the numerous narratological readings that take the novel as a test case for advancing theories of unreliable narrative.[1] Readings of this kind tend to subsume Stevens' attempts to achieve greater self-understanding within a framework of interpretation that wishes to detect an implied author or constructive agent determining his narrative and establishing a knowing rapport with the reader. Such a reading will often take it for granted that the astute reader can discern significant limitations to Stevens' self-understanding and moral values. Sometimes taxonomic, these cognitively oriented readings, while growing in subtlety and sophistication as they have explored the challenges Stevens' narration poses to readers in a multicultural and postmodern age (Nünning 2005, 97), have remained wanting in attention to the generic hybridity of the novel. Narratological readings have been particularly deficient in heeding textual signals that hint at Stevens' characterological heritage, in which, as Bruce Robbins has argued, literary servants have long had the prerogative of provocation, the choric ability to address the audience and to challenge and renegotiate (Robbins 1986, 19) the discursive authority of the masters.

I will also critically engage with another subset of readings of Stevens that extend concerns with his unreliability to the indictment of his moral deficiencies, lamenting his complicity with the anti-Semitism and pro-fascist leanings of his master Lord Darlington. For these readers Stevens often resembles an Eichmann-like figure, an obedient functionary who can only engage us as a negative exemplar of mendacity and self-deception. In the words of David Lodge:

> the narrator of Kazuo Ishiguro's novel is not an evil man, but his life has been based on the suppression and evasion of truth, about himself and about others. His narrative is a kind of confession, but it is riddled with devious self-justification and special pleading. (Lodge 2011, 155)

While ethically engaged readings of *The Remains of the Day* have contributed to our understanding of the allegorical resonances of the novel as indexing the problem of culpability and complicity under modern, hierarchical social conditions, they often take the unimaginative decision to treat Stevens as a proxy for the subjectivity of the complicit perpetrator rather than a complex and contradictory fictional character with multiple textual functions. These condemnatory interpretations threaten to become sanctimonious and self-congratulatory. Indeed, subtly self-regarding readings of this kind can be ironically mimetic of the classist and dismissive attitudes towards Stevens displayed in the novel by aristocratic characters including Lord Darlington.[2]

Harking back to the supple and diverse theories of the *Bildungsroman* I explored in the introduction, I would like to emphasize other, productively indicative aspects of Stevens' character that encourage reader engagement and hermeneutic activity. I read Stevens' physical peregrinations and the rush of memories they enable as hinting at a searching internal dialogue, but one that can only be conducted by addressing a worldly readership beyond the confining environment he has heretofore experienced. To date, both narratological and perpetrator-oriented readings of Stevens have largely underestimated the creative mobility of his thoughts and memories and the possibilities for emotional development, reflective self-interrogation, and optimistic self-fashioning that arise from his emotionally charged, ambivalent recollections. As we shall see, far from presenting us with a rigid ego ideal or pre-cast subjectivity, the consummate professional who does not allow for spontaneity or admit affective motivation, in the novel a liminal, metamorphic protagonist emerges whose recollections bespeak explorative curiosity, suppressed anger, the pathos of missed opportunities, diverse sympathies, and a burgeoning enjoyment of the ludic and transgressive.

Stevens' expansive narrative, in allowing for leisurely rumination and careful introspection, can be considered a modality of *Bildung*, enabling a 'journey in', in the parlance of Abel, Hirsch, and Langland's classic volume dedicated to fictions of female development. Stevens' journey into the past *mirrors and is prompted by open-ended mobility and exploration* as he undertakes a testing but also uplifting journey away from his stultifying residence at Darlington Hall. On his journey Stevens will encounter the natural world as it contrasts with the artificiality of his own surroundings, meet people from a variety of social strata who hold different perspectives on important questions of the day, and experience a pleasing if destabilizing variety of situation that contrasts with his routine activities.

My point will be that Stevens can be understood as a character in the process of becoming other, a questing *Bildungsheld* who begins to respond to the ethical demands and *kairotic* urgency of the centrifugal journey he has willingly undertaken. He exists, one might say, for the sake of a reader who can appreciate a character engaged in a quest for understanding in a changing and increasingly complex world. I will also suggest that Stevens' transformational becoming entails a dialectical tension with various rich and suggestively indecorous modes of 'unbecoming' as the rather prim Stevens, used to deploying evasive circumlocutions, a form of canned speech that has colonized his psychic life, has his deepest assumptions challenged or mocked as he is continually exposed to the indecorous demotic speech and tendentious discourse of the vernacular world. Steven's decentred adventures, I suggest, can remind us of Bakhtin's enthusiasm for the emergent subjectivity depicted in the *Bildungsroman* as various ordeals 'test' the hero (Bakhtin 2010, 16), and where the compositional force of that testing allows the novel a combination of the 'keenly adventuristic' with the 'profoundly problematical and complexly psychological' (Bakhtin, 16). The hero of such a novel, as Bakhtin argues, is no longer a fixed point but in the 'process of becoming', for changes in the hero 'acquire *plot* significance, and thus the entire plot of the novel is reinterpreted and reconstructed' by the solicitous reader (Bakhtin 2010, 21).

While Bakhtin points out that the reader must consistently reconstruct the thematic significance of the psychologically piquant narrative of a *Bildungsroman*, along with Hamish Dalley we might suggest that Stevens is one of those characters of a historical fiction requiring an informed reading, as his peregrinations through a social geography 'can be read as representative of larger scale historical processes' (Dalley 2014, 10). Stevens' lack of determined social position and defined qualities, his continuing receptivity to a variety of phenomena, mark him as one of those middling or in-between characters who 'provides a mobile point of focalisation which can move between competing "historical-types"' (Dalley 2014, 22). These socio-historical types range in *The Remains of the Day* from aristocrats to servants and proto-feminist housekeepers, working-class agitators, rural petit bourgeois, cynical politicians, middle-class professionals constructing the welfare state, and representatives of the generations as Britain seeks redefinition after the Second World War.

If we are to complicate the perception of Stevens as a compromised and complicit Eichmann-like figure who idealizes obedience then we must draw attention to the adventurous Stevens as an indicative focalizer, a matrix for problematics of existence and uncomfortable narrative truth-telling that has considerable interest for the receptive and curious reader. At a time in which British history threatens to become reified as a nostalgic mythology of good vs evil or lapse into imperial nostalgia, Stevens draws on private memories and the networked historical knowledge of his fellow servants to challenge various forms of collective amnesia regarding pro-fascist sentiment in the period leading up to the Second World War, as well reprising war crimes committed in the era of British imperialism during the period of the Boer War. In contrast to certain readings which are preoccupied with Stevens' complicit obedience and his tawdry narrative of self-justification, I will suggest that Stevens' politically charged and revisionist discussions of the past, with a multidirectional testimonial function addressed to the post-war era, engage closely with the Eichmann problematic, and indeed can offer an antidote to the unreflective narcissism and grotesque triviality that Hannah Arendt detected in Adolf Eichmann's relationship to memory during the Jerusalem trial.

As Irene McMullin points out, an aspect of Arendt's befuddlement with Eichmann at his Jerusalem trial was that it became apparent Eichmann had no 'communal memory' and that 'what he remembered was almost exclusively specific to his own life narrative' (McMullin 2011, 104). His memory according to Arendt, was filled with 'human interest stories of the worst type', in which bowling with his superiors or his failure to gain a promotion came more easily to mind than his role in the mass deportations of Jews to the death camps (McMullin 2011, 105). By contrast, I would suggest that Stevens' acute consciousness of his audience bears the hallmarks of the kind of heteroglossic speech analysed by Bakhtin, in which the possible response of the sceptical and inquisitive interlocutor destabilizes, dialogizes, and ambiguates the significance of the narrative at every turn. As Bakhtin argues of the underground man in *Problems of Dostoevsky's Poetics*, we must ponder a character who is not an 'objectified image but an autonomous discourse', a character known only through his proliferating monologue: 'we do not see him, we hear him', for his 'consciousness of self lives by its unfinalizability, by its unclosedness and its indeterminacy' (Bakhtin 1984, 53).

If we are to read Stevens more generously, and within the context of the genre heritage discussed by Bruce Robbins, it is important to read his conscious and unconscious drives as cathected to his anomalous position as a butler who is uneasily situated between the ruling and working classes, who needs to perform the gentility of a 'gentleman' but whose precarious social status is purely dependent on his professional employment. As Karen Scherzinger points out, the butler, like the Victorian literary figure of the governess, is a figure of considerable 'hierarchical uncertainty', neither simply a servant, nor 'fully-fledged member of the family he serves' (Scherzinger 2004, 3). As we have discussed, an uncertain or liminal social position and its correlative in the ambivalent awareness of an undefined future is almost a prerequisite of the literary *Bildungsheld* as the explorative protagonist of a historical fiction. Such a character can be situated somewhere between parvenu and maverick picaro, attempting to integrate within the social order while exposing it to critique from the outside, desiring affluence while understanding the follies and corruptions of the powerful, perhaps alerting readers to the metanarrative that the entire social structure is predicated on performance and duplicity. Such a figure does not move in linear fashion towards a predetermined future but is schooled by the world and continues to interrogate the possibilities and opportunities for self-education offered by their liminal vocation, deferring and dilating the march of time. In Stevens' case we will encounter a character whose concerns, as his journey gets underway, are rarely narrowly 'professional' or careerist, as he eavesdrops on conversations, is preoccupied with relationships that are both vexing and emancipatory such as his entanglements with Miss Kenton, dwells at length on ludic and farcical moments, enjoys transgressive speech, and theatricalizes his confused interiority and submerged yearnings.

Returning to the indicative, reader-centred approach to the genre of the *Bildungsroman* mentioned in the introduction, I will offer a hermeneutically open reading of the ethical awakening of Stevens' character. If we follow the precept that the novel is a *Bildungsoman* that can affirm and render visible productive trajectories for self-cultivation, we will need to pay close attention to various aspects of Stevens' interrogative discourse, associative memories, and their close imbrication in the wayward and sometimes literally off-piste journey that he has undertaken. We need not place all our emphasis on the liberating effects of the journey either, since Stevens' desire for reflection and self-examination is hinted at in his enjoyment of solitude while at Darlington Hall, his eclectic reading, and his preference for the company of his peers in which all manner of topics pertaining to his profession can be discussed at leisure. Less dependent on his master for the simulation of learned sociability, Stevens is not unlike Henry James' autodidactic Brooksmith in the story of that name, curating his master's conversational gatherings so as to enjoy and learn from 'the talk', constantly 'mingling in the conversation' (James 1999, 762), 'perpetually present on a hundred legitimate pretexts, errands, necessities, and breathing the very atmosphere of criticism, the famous criticism of life' (763).

As we shall see in the next section, Stevens will indicate the importance of an awakening consciousness that spurs itself towards an increased independence from prior conditioning. We will need to pay attention to the manner in which Stevens' separates himself from a constricting hierarchical microcosm, questions the idealized law of the father, exposes himself to a democratizing post-war Britain, strenuously and rigorously *tests* his ideas, and is willing to dwell long enough in the reflective space of disillusionment for redemptive possibilities in the future to become apparent. Genre theory also assists us here in that we can also allow that the growth of Stevens is tentative and not always manifest in his actions or explicit level of insight. As Martin Swales reminds us, in the *Bildungsroman* we are often dealing with a text that hints and indicates, where the novel itself can only offer 'directions, implications, and intimations of the possible', expressing a certain scepticism about the law of 'linear experience' that means the novel will have no 'unequivocal narrative realisation' (Swales 1978, 30). Swales' caution is appropriate to *The Remains of the Day* as a sophisticated exercise in unreliable narrative which still retains its ability to provoke and redirect the reader in the name of unforeseen pathways of inquiry.

Turning points: Stevens' awakening

Stevens' relative maturity and lack of youthful vitality may be one of the reasons he is rarely discussed as the increasingly independently minded protagonist of a *Bildungsroman*. However, I think we can adapt some of the analysis of the nineteenth- and twentieth-century feminist novel of awakening to understand Stevens' predicament and the journey towards self-knowledge that he will undertake. First, we need to search for textual evidence that his character is undergoing a life crisis in the tradition of that genre of novel. Ellen McWilliams has suggested that the temporal parameters of the female *Bildunsgroman* can be 'drawn along moments of crisis so that change is prompted by turning points' (Mc Williams 2009, 20). In the case of the female *Bildunsroman* such moments would include puberty, imminent marriage, or the prospect of children leaving home. By transposition we can examine Stevens at the outset of the novel as now occupying a near-empty house, serving a new owner, and having lost important friendships and social connections. Stevens lives in changing times in which his former master's actions are now questionable, engendering the existential problem, perhaps transferred onto the long absent former housekeeper Miss Kenton, of a 'life that has come to be so dominated by a sense of waste' (Ishiguro 2021, 51), raising questions about whether one can regain a sense of purpose and hope for the period to come. Miss Kenton's letter to him, hinting at a possible separation and divorce from her husband and hopefully interpreted by Stevens as expressing nostalgia for her pre-war existence at Darlington Hall, may well be the turning point that crystallizes Stevens' yearning and pervasive melancholia. It well may be Stevens himself, and not Miss Kenton onto whom he projects a more forthright alter-ego who is now pondering 'with regret decisions made in the far-off past that have now left [. . . him] deep in middle age, so alone and desolate', unable to retrieve those 'lost years' that Miss Kenton alludes to (Ishiguro 2021, 50).

While Stevens is told early on in the novel by his new American master Mr Farriday that he looks like he 'could make use of a good break' (Ishiguro 2021, 4) the reasons for Stevens' weariness, and the cause of his seemingly trivial but increasingly frequent 'errors' (5) are ambiguous and overdetermined, to be clarified to Stevens' awakening consciousness and inferred by the reader over the course of the novel. That Stevens is deeply concerned with his pre-war actions and desires to 'retrieve' those lost years by getting away from his increasingly tiresome duties and denuded environment is arguably signalled by an early speculation that is more self-referential than it might appear once one has digested Stevens' later complicity in the dismissal of the Jewish maids and the caesura in his own career that the downfall of Lord Darlington represents:

> Who knows how many quarrels, false accusations, *unnecessary dismissals, how many promising careers cut short* can be attributed to a butler's slovenliness at the stage of drawing up the staff plan? (5, my emphasis)

That Stevens cannot quite place the speaker, whether it be Miss Kenton or Lord Darlington, who indicated that there is a 'larger significance' to the 'errors' (63) his father had committed, indicates not only an anxious preoccupation with recognizing the signs that led to his own father's rapid demise and early death but that he possesses an at least incipient desire to understand and address the symptoms of his own decline. This moment of crisis for Stevens maps on, as many critics have noted, to the Suez crisis of 1956 and its acceleration of Britain's imperial decline, and it will be a question for the reader as to whether the unfolding narrative is a defensive and nostalgic 'repression' (Thakkar 2017, 91) of the implications of that crisis or a recursive investigation of its significance.

In another moment of *kairotic* auto-suggestion that hints at the urgency of his situation, very early in his road trip Stevens is alerted to the need to actively reconstruct the remains of his day by the sudden, adventitious appearance of a 'thin, white-haired man in a cloth cap', in monomythical terms a messenger figure and quest announcer who desires him to enjoy a 'better view' (25), a broader prospect different from the literally obscure and hierarchically organized residence he has inhabited, for in another couple of years for the ageing Stevens it might be 'too late' (25).

One of Stevens' repeated refrains, not often touched on even by more sympathetic readers, is the waning of his friendship and connection with a fellow butler, Mr Graham, with whom, we are reminded on several occasions throughout the novel, 'sadly, I seem to have lost touch' (31, 179). The loss of companionship and mutual respect clearly weighs on Stevens, hinting that he does not simply mimetically identify with Lord Darlington in the manner of Brooksmith's desire for tutelage by Mr Offord, but misses 'debate' and lively discussion with other members of his profession. The desire for travel, encounter, the possibility of human warmth, answers, then, a potentiality of Stevens' character, just as Hans Castorp's dilated interregnum at a sanatorium in *The Magic Mountain* meets his fluid psychosexual development, speculative nature, and fascination with death. In undertaking his journey Stevens wishes to resume his innate need for relationality and human connection and wants a life narrative that reconnects him to worldly and historical time.

We might say with Susan Fraiman that *The Remains of the Day* offers an aspect of the genre to be found in fictions of female development, suggesting a pluralized strategy of reading that does not make the novel coextensive with the journey of the *Bildungsheld* to the 'exclusion of other movements and meanings', but, in the manner of Bakhtin's desideratum for the novel of ordeal, explores how 'personal destiny evolves in dialectical relation to historical events, social structures, and other people' (Fraiman 1993, 10).

Of course we cannot deny that Stevens may really believe, at least at times, that his journey has strictly professional motivations as he seeks to overcome a temporary melancholy through professional exertion and redeem his own life choices by recruiting the bereft Miss Kenton once more as a member of the household staff. As Franco Moretti has pointed out, the late *Bildungsroman* is a genre that in its modernist guise has proved capable of recognizing and composing with the creative forces of the (traumatized) unconscious, which brings it within touching distance of the fecund ambiguities of narrative unreliability. An embarrassingly humanist genre which might have seemed dedicated to the unity of the ego has come to encompass the role of the unconscious in the 'constitution of twentieth-century subjects, and in their socialization' (Moretti 2000, 236), 'in which unconscious psychic materials are no longer obstacles to but instruments of social integration' (Moretti 2000, 236–7). David James' has noticed a delicate poise in *The Remains of the Day* requiring the interpretive reconstruction of which Bakhtin spoke, the novel's liminal oscillation between cathartic confession and defensive apologetics, when he remarks that 'Ishiguro invites us to balance our sense of the way Stevens would prefer to tell his past and the force with which memories return unexpectedly to alter his priorities as a narrator' (James 2010, 57).

One aspect, then, of Stevens' awakening through travel and the combination of willed and involuntary memories that affect him, is a perhaps only partially recognized drive to leave an unfulfilling or controlling relationship with Darlington Hall and to question what he has been gaslighted to take for common sense, his master's by no means exceptional class conviction of the inferiority of mass democracies, the childlike ignorance of ordinary working people, and the superiority of authoritarian and fascist alternatives. What will assist Stevens' testing of this idea is that his own restless character inclines towards the classical conception of *Bildung* or self-formation through worldly intercourse. One of the most prominent Enlightenment proponents of the ideal of harmonious self-cultivation, Wilhelm von Humboldt, stressed that freedom, social intercourse, and variety of situation are the preconditions of *Bildung*, in which 'even the most free and self-reliant of men is thwarted and hindered in his development by uniformity of position' (cited in Wulf 2003, 245; see also Sorkin 1983, 58). Other needs will also inform Stevens' desire for an interactive and varied journey including the desire to defer ageing through the experience of novelty, escape artificial environs and see the real world of human struggle, and a willingness to explore inhibited sexual desire and romantic longing. If Stevens is to become other and see the world differently, however, he will need a sphere of social intercourse in which he can gain some critical perspective on the centrality of Darlington Hall to his sense of self and the baleful effects of the lingering *imago* of his father who in fact led a life of subordination and self-erasure. As Karen Scherzinger argues, Stevens' journey 'will place him and his firmly-held beliefs in crisis at the same time as grant him new and unexpected pleasures' (Scherzinger 2004, 6).

A movement away from the centre

What sort of firmly held beliefs are these? Stevens' desire for a picaresque or episodic journey that moves him beyond the precincts of Darlington Hall constitutes a self-willed journey away from an abode and a site of imaginative investment that has colonized his ego ideal and encouraged his introjection of hierarchical structures of authority. Stevens has, as we shall see, cathected his conception of the centrality of Darlington Hall to his somewhat desperate, reparative desire to fetishize and emulate the stoicism of his father.

Karen Scherzinger has paid considerable attention to the character of Miss Kenton as exemplifying a possible means of liberation and departure for Stevens, for whom the doorways of Darlington Hall represent both 'imprisonment and freedom' (Scherzinger 2004, 6), the possibility of intimacy and the internalization of surveillance. I want to defer a discussion of Miss Kenton for the moment, as she is of critical significance to Stevens' ethical growth, but one cannot miss the significance of Stevens, a character whose lexical choices and their repetition can indicate a preoccupation, revealingly describing his father's room in Darlington Hall as a 'prison cell' (67), analogous to his own room that is earlier observed by Miss Kenton as 'stark and bereft of colour' (55) and later also described as a 'prison cell' (174). While the actual episode is farcical, it is also true as Scherzinger argues, that Miss Kenton intensifies Stevens' suppressed desire for escape when, desperate to avoid the truth about his father's situation, Stevens contemplates a rather precipitous 'departure via the French windows' (60). The question for the acute reader then turns towards Stevens' rationalizations of his captivity. How, in the tradition of the servant character who resists erasure through exaggerated, verbally florid compliance, is one to lend oneself a certain dignity within a humiliating class system? One pillar of Stevens' need to misrecognize his situation is to construct Darlington Hall as a metonymy of England itself, thereby precluding the need for actual emancipative mobility:

> although we did not see a great deal of the country in the sense of touring the country-side and visiting picturesque sites, [those of our profession] did actually 'see' more of England than most, placed as we were in houses where the greatest ladies and gentlemen of the land gathered. (4)

It is of a piece that Stevens' rather huffy reply to his insouciant new master Farriday's early query as to why he has not seen more of England is to claim that 'it has been my privilege to see the best of England within these very walls' (4).

Later in the novel Stevens will use a continually rehearsed trope of England and the world it dominates as an imperial power as structured like a 'wheel', in which largesse emanates from a centre, in order to justify the limitations he experienced during his period of service:

the world was a wheel, revolving with these great houses at the hub, their mighty decisions emanating out to all else, rich and poor, who revolved around them [. . .] to have served his lordship at Darlington Hall during those years was to come as close to the hub of this world's wheel as one such as I could have dreamt. (122, 133)

There is a complacency, a feeble patrician nationalism, in this static, organicist, and increasingly anachronistic conception of the English class system, a trickle-down conception of the benefits of hierarchical decision-making which rationalizes away the need to actually experience one's own society or interrogate the decisions that are always already made for the benefit of the lower orders. The defensive nostalgia Stevens evokes in these passages is encoded in the wistful tones of the pastoral, as Stevens offers a self-referential characterization of a tranquil English landscape in terms of 'the very *lack* of obvious drama or spectacle that sets the beauty of our land apart'. The unique 'sense of restraint' this landscape evokes lends 'the feeling that one is in the presence of greatness. We call this land of ours *Great* Britain' (29).

As Molly Westerman suggests, Stevens sets up a metonymic relation between himself, the idealized English butler, and a mythic national character, that is uncomfortably xenophobic (Westerman 2004, 158):

> It is sometimes said that butlers only truly exist in England . . . Continentals are unable to be butlers because they are as a breed incapable of the emotional restraint which only the English race is capable of [. . .] it is for this reason that when you think of a great butler, he is bound, almost by definition, to be an Englishman. (44)

There is, as Westerman points out, an unmissable vanity in Stevens' homage in which Englishness itself is fixed in its meaning, butlers such as he can be made to 'stand for Englishness', and he keeps in order a house that takes on the meaning of England as such (Westerman 2004, 161). There is no doubt that in this pompous register the 'dignity' that Stevens is preoccupied with is 'given to him' by a hierarchical idealization of power and authority, as derivative, passive, and complacent in its conception as the borrowed clothes that he wears (Westerman 2004, 161).

Stevens cathects this image of an England that needs no further investigation or justification to a 'one-dimensional version of his father' (Westerman 2004, 162), a mythic father, the very figure of a paradigmatic butler that will enable him to avert his eyes from the real one (Westerman 2004, 162), with whom he converses 'less and less' (Ishiguro 2021, 66). Stevens' actual father suffered untold indignities, being forced to serve a war criminal general who contributed to the death of his son Leonard, Stevens' elder brother (41). The diminution of his actual father, the extraordinary humiliations he was exposed to, his father's own demonstrable capacity for violence as a barely controlled response to his own sufferings ('his dark, severe presence quite blotting out the effect of the gentle Hertfordshire scenery behind him', 40), are one of the reasons that Stevens, in the manner of the novel that 'tests' ideas, in which the adventuristic and psychological intimately interpenetrate, will not be able to let go of the problem of 'dignity' and its compatibility with a degrading life of unquestioning service.

One could say that the mythic father is upheld by Stevens in order to redeem the actual father who has been downtrodden and the family structure that has been fractured by the depredations of years of hard labour. Yet we might suggest that Stevens' always probing and unsettled discourse as he travels away from Darlington Hall, a conservative landed estate which seems central to his self-image, does not emulate the largely silent father or replicate a discourse of emotional restraint and knowledge of one's place. Stevens' spirited narrative, emboldened by travel and encounter, is more like a *dangerous supplement* in Derrida's terms, more likely than not to subvert and invert the metonymic chain he has constructed. On closer inspection Stevens' narrative participates in the anti-canonical spirit of *Bildung*, a drive for independent self-formation through manifold experiences that places significant critical pressure on what has been taken for the canonical and civilized.[3]

Which is to say that the discursive position of the loquacious Stevens, always thinking, reflecting, and essaying one topic after another, is not that of his gruff and downtrodden father who lacks the verbal resources to renegotiate his relationship to authority. Stevens' discourse, an expansive monologue with many byways, subtexts, and hidden corners, is addressed to the world and has something left over of the 'servant-narrated works of the picaresque tradition' (Robbins 1986, 37), including the necessary dissimulation of the poor when obliged to give an account of themselves. That intriguingly ambivalent discourse, never to be fully objectified as Bakhtin reminds us, will oscillate between the 'inadvertent admissions of a dehumanized victim [. . .] and] the contrivances of a mask-wearing trickster' (cited in Robbins 1986, 37).

What we will actually witness in Stevens' discourse are subtle disruptions to mythic images of the supposedly timeless English character and class system at every turn of his winding journey. Stevens supplements the silence of his taciturn father, a silence that on at least one occasion pondered violent outlets ('something so powerfully rebuking [. . .] about his figure', 40) to express its pain, with a stream of discourse exploring his humiliation and marginalization, thus lending his father voice and testimonial representation. Stevens supposedly models himself on his father's ideal of the self-effacing butler who quickly and efficiently shoots a malingering tiger under the table in time for the dinner service, embodying 'British dignity in the face of colonial disorder' (O'Brien 1996, 790). Stevens will not stop there though and will explore conceptions of dignity, exemplified for example in the remonstrations of Miss Kenton, that are not self-erasing in their smooth efficiency but disruptive and highly visible. It is Stevens himself who will not disappear into his professional role but experiment with his identity and appear deceptively in the 'costume' of his master throughout the novel, allowing him inter alia to gain a deeper understanding of how people now understand his master's activities before and during the Second World War.

In another sense Stevens' discourse represents an 'intervention in the story', the capability of arbitrarily interfering in 'plots devoted to the destinies of his or her superiors' (Robbins 1986, 41), for the reputational fate of his deceased English master now rests in his hands. If we look at an episode that has often been the main source of evidence for critics pointing at the functional obedience of his character, his failure to attend to his dying father during the 1923 conference,[4] then we might remark that we can only know of his father's sufferings, the sympathetic actions of Miss Kenton and other servants, and his own palpable devastation ('I say, Stevens, are you sure you're all right there?', 109), as we are provided with that information by Stevens' own narrative. Stevens' seeming narrative of a dedicated professional surmounting personal trials in the service of international diplomacy continually superimposes its angst-filled regrets and sense of injury on the retelling of an event, the 1923 conference dedicated to the repeal of the Treaty of Versailles. It is this event that should, ironically, serve as a prime example of benevolent power emanating from the centre of great houses. In its own artful manner, the time Stevens spends exploring the fate of his own father as a dehumanized victim of the class system has indicative value as a discursive example of the servant's non sequitur, the 'servant's refusal to follow' (Robbins 1986, 73).

Aware of an audience that it also beseeches to understand and sympathize, the discourse of Stevens partakes of that 'audience-directed and self-assertive' (Robbins 1986, 75) servant's speech that Robbins has alerted us to, which projects out of a dialogue of unequals and towards an expressive, ungovernable monologue. While the events captured seem to indicate the servant's dutiful response to orders, the audience and its democratizing impulse is a dangerous supplement to this unequal encounter of the classes, a 'second and sovereign master' that attunes the reader towards rhetorical impact rather than surface dialogue (Robbins 1986, 75).

Thus, for Stevens, the projected centre does not hold, it awaits deconstruction and historicity, and this is because a certain ideal of the butler has not protected his father, or himself, from devastation, injury, and humiliation. In freeing himself from domination by the English country house and all its mythic and conservative associations, Stevens will rehabilitate his own father in sympathetic recollection and reflective discourse while transcending the reproductive, paternalistic law of the father.

The question of vocation

The fate of Stevens' father also poses the question of vocation, of how his profession can be redefined, worked on, teased apart from subservient labour,

1. Memory as reinvention in Kazuo Ishiguro's The Remains of the Day

and investigated as to the opportunities for self-improvement it may offer. In his narrative, addressing an audience that wishes to get to know him, Stevens can resume the always interesting discussions he held with Graham and other butlers in the heyday of Darlington Hall. In the tradition of *Bildungshelden* such as Frédéric Moreau, as analysed by Franco Moretti, there is apparent in Stevens a will towards procrastination, mediation, the preservation of 'psycho-social indetermination' as the deferral of finality and univocal meaning (Moretti 2000, 177). As Scherzinger argues, his position as a butler is 'predicated on the imitation and enactment of the gentleman', infinitely deferring his complete possession of the identity of the gentleman or gentleman's gentleman (Scherzinger 2004, 16). It is that very gap, and Stevens' ineluctable role-playing that enables speculation, hypothesis, and testing. It is not merely a pun to say that Stevens 'waits' by professional inclination; on his travels there will be an opportunity for dialogue with the flesh and blood perspectives of other men and women that he has lacked in a confining environment with repetitive duties. The temporality in which he evaluates and reflects is also liminal and heterogenous as he moves towards an uncertain future while seeking to make sense of and actively respond to a catastrophic past. There is a question in the novel of the degree to which his professional life has been that of imitation, of borrowed clothes and borrowed gravitas, of whether being a butler is 'like playing some pantomime role' (43), of whether Stevens is 'mock' (129, 130) through and through ('Why, Mr Stevens, why, why, do you always have to *pretend*?', 162). Yet, and this is where disdaining critics have been rather precipitous, perhaps as Robbins mused prone to sneer at the servant figure as stock entertainment rather than unsettling commentator (Robbins 1986, 73), there are also genuine opportunities for autodidacticism, for mingling in different company, for engaging in various modes of self-fashioning in a profession whose standing does not consistently refer to class origins, in which its more polished practitioners can accrue some of the complex associations of the parvenu as rogue operator, trickster, subversive imitator, and resourceful bricoleur.

As Thomas Jeffers comments of Wilhelm Meister, he may lack visionary talent but having avoided a life of bourgeois dedication to the calculus of business, he can find opportunities in theatrical performance, direction, and criticism to work on 'his vocation' (Jeffers 2005, 16). As Jerome Buckley notes in *Season of Youth*:

> childhood, the conflict of generations, provinciality, the larger society, self-education, alienation, ordeal by love and the search for a vocation and a working philosophy – answers the requirements of the Bildungsroman as I am here seeking to describe and definite it. (McWilliams 2009, citing Buckley, 13)

As we know, Stevens continually revisits the question of 'dignity' in light of his desire to revisit his own period of now compromised service to Lord

Darlington, reflect on differences between his own and his father's generation, perhaps in search of broader perspectives on a problematic of comportment that in the post-war world pertains to the upholding of freedom and human rights. Despite the suggestion that dignity is merely a professional mien that allows no private self, throughout this novel of ideas Stevens does not allow any simple resolution to the question of dignity and remains open to its variety of inscription. Part of Stevens' ordeal will be to have his more derivative ideal of dignity as performing one's role or station continually challenged by democratizing perspectives. Stevens will need to consider whether his professional 'triumph' at the 1923 conference was in fact the abject surrender of his autonomy and moral responsibility. He will need to question, as he reviews his past in memory, whether his 'professional' demeanour was a mask for arrested emotional development and led to the abandonment of the possibility of a loving relationship with Miss Kenton. As Scherzinger notes, terms 'such as "dignity", "professionalism", "greatness" [. . .] are persistently presented within inverted commas', making these terms objects of curiosity in their own right (Scherzinger 2004, 15). They are problematic, to be supplemented by yet another discourse, consideration and anecdote as they arise in the adventure-time of the novel.

I agree with David James that Stevens avoids the 'concrete instantiation of what dignity might involve in workaday life' (James 2010, 58) but I doubt that Stevens instead simply favours 'abstract claims or recycled maxims' (James 2010, 58). I would suggest instead that Stevens' discussion of his vocation, his interest in the opportunities for self-education that it affords, is a prophylactic against the threat of being an 'anachronism: the most conspicuous surviving type of preindustrial dependency' (Robbins 1986, 42). Rather, Stevens' ruminations on his profession, his love of 'discussing every aspect of our vocation' (Ishiguro 2021, 18) is ever mindful of contemporary conditions in which the cash nexus has created a landless class that can now voluntarily sell its labour and choose its employer free of the assumption of 'mutuality, and paternal care' (Robbins 1986, 42). Thus Stevens, the mobile professional, willingly serves the American Mr Farriday and demonstrates a capacity for intelligent adjustment to circumstance as he continually reflects on the significance of witty 'banter' as a new and potential interesting professional duty. It is a modernizing and pragmatically inclined Stevens, who rejects out of hand the elitist and 'outmoded understanding' (119) of the Hays Society and its attempts to arbitrate 'standards in our profession' (33), or to snobbishly reject any butler associated with new industrialists and the rising middle-class such as the new master he now serves.

In the course of discoursing on his vocation, of making it a site of free inquiry, other mentors and advisers also become possible. They include Mr Graham, Miss Kenton, and the wisdom dispensed in his rather improbable encounter with a former butler at the close of the novel. I would suggest that 'dignity', then, emerges in the novel as posing a transcendental question, a problem of existence, in that one must continually and energetically rethink how dignity is to be attained and defended within systems of inequality and social domination. Thus the function of citing these terms in quote marks may well have something to do with an attribute of servant speech noted by Bruce Robbins, in which the speculative, disruptive speech of the servant looks past any particular interlocutor and towards social hope and utopian possibility (Robbins 1986, 47, 84). As Stevens himself remarks, 'it is surely a professional responsibility for us all to think deeply about such things so that each of may strive towards attaining "dignity" for ourselves' (45).

The indicative importance of travel

We do need to analyse the way in which the horizons of adjustment and reconciliation to the present moment that vocational inquiry suggests are prompted by Stevens' travels:

> As I say, I have never in all these years thought of the matter [what constitutes a 'great' butler] in quite this way; but then it perhaps in the nature of coming away on a trip such as this that one is prompted towards such surprising new perspectives on topics one imagined one had long ago thought through thoroughly. (123)

One of the reasons that Stevens relishes the opportunity for travel, for discovering new perspectives through social intercourse, is precisely the pressure of maintaining a role at Darlington Hall. In the post-war world, as a butler, he may turn out to be a purchasable commodity who is required to offer a humiliating, anachronistic performance whenever there are visitors: 'And you're a genuine old-fashioned English butler, not just some waiter pretending to be one. You're the real thing, aren't you? That's what I wanted, isn't that what I have?' (131). It is important, then, to 'lose' oneself through travel in order to find oneself, perhaps to shake off the creeping fatigue and resentment that is affecting one's welfare and self-regard.

As Martin Swales has written of Hans Castorp and the significance of his escape from practical existence:

> Outwardly, Hans Castorp is swallowed up without trace; inwardly, he has the distinction of trying to know himself more strenuously than the practical world of the flatlands would ever have permitted. (Swales 1978, 128)

The artificiality of Darlington Hall, in which he is both a performative disciplinarian and an entertaining spectacle, in his own right encourages Steven's desire for a return to more natural surroundings as Scherzinger notes:

Steven's journey is notably a journey of freedom from the Hall and a quiet celebration of nature and biological rhythms – so much so that the Mortimer's Pond section suggestively recalls Thoreau's Walden, and thereby, in turn, invokes the long, Romantic tradition of the deep and vital connections that inhere between nature, the self, and the imagination. (Scherzinger 2004, 14)

Both Stevens and Thoreau respond to the natural phenomenon of the pond or lake, Scherzinger suggests, by transforming the smooth surface before them into a 'reflective mirror of the soul' (Scherzinger 2004, 14).

Scherzinger's illuminating analysis is devoted to whether Stevens' journey can be understood as a pilgrimage, in which pilgrims experience a separation from a fixed state of life and social status, passing into a 'liminal or threshold phase' in which the previous rules of their duty-bound social existence do not apply (Scherzinger 2004, 7), which would explain the vertiginous exhilaration with which Stevens approaches the early stages of his journey:

> I had gone beyond all previous boundaries [with a sense of] unease mixed with exhilaration ... The feeling swept over me that I had truly left Darlington Hall behind, and I must confess I did have a slight feeling of alarm – a sense aggravated by the feeling that I was perhaps not on the correct road at all, but speeding off in totally the wrong direction into a wilderness. (24)

It is noteworthy that Stevens will undertake that journey, suggested by his new American master, in an iconic symbol of American capitalism and in presentiment of the liberating effects of the American road trip genre, a Ford.

We should also note another facet of Stevens' journey, and that is the lack of realism that typifies its adventitious character, in which linearity of plot often gives way to symbolically patterned recurrences so that characters appear and reappear in a remarkably providential way congenial to the needs and future horizons of the *Bildungsheld*. As Marianne Hirsch notes, the society of the classic German *Bildungsroman* 'has universal and symbolic rather than particular significance. It embodies the ideal experiential field for the growing individual' (Hirsch 1979, 303). As Scherzinger points out, Stevens does encounter, 'at regular and important intervals, unfamiliar figures who appear apparently out of nowhere to guide him towards new geographical and existential vistas' (Scherzinger 2004, 10), and these include the white-haired man in the cloth cap, never to be seen again, who wishes him to pause and to have a broader prospect of the English countryside, the 'young woman in an apron' who affects Stevens, so used to artifice and indirection, with the simple kindness of ordinary people (Scherzinger 2004, 11), and the quest assisting batman who directs him down 'narrow, twisting lanes', away from the idyllic and picturesque and towards Mortimer's Pond where, as Scherzinger notes, he can explore the 'troubled depths of his own calm surface' (Scherzinger 2004, 12). Of course, one point to make about these providential and surprising encounters, germane to the genre, is, as Scherzinger observes, a 'reaggregation into the community with new (self) knowledge' (Scherzinger 2004, 8). The desire for the unpredictability of social intercourse is hinted at in a more productive 'trivial error' of Stevens' that inverts the earlier signs of cognitive decline: 'I allowed the Ford to run out of petrol' (Ishiguro 2021, 168), a prelude to meeting the Taylors, in which, by disguising himself as an aristocratic gentleman, he will find out more about the meaning of dignity in the changing post-war world he inhabits. As Scherzinger argues, Stevens' failure to rectify the impression he is a gentleman with the Taylors is a manifestation of the ludic spirit of play and enjoyment of variability and new discoveries that inhabits the dedicated traveller (Scherzinger 2004, 14). It is this commitment to experimental play and performance, an active recuperation of his objectification as a simulacrum of a fantasized England, that gestures towards his own unbecoming, the collapse of his prized professional identity and the emergence of new possibilities.

Stevens' unbecoming in memory

Another aspect of Stevens' travels is that he can ponder the present and future with more clarity, allowing him to 'keep one's attention focused on the present; to guard against any complacency creeping in on account of what one may have achieved in the past' (148). He can now understand the way the class system is perceived by ordinary working people and to glimpse a nation emerging from the devastation of war. He enjoys and is tested by unvarnished human intercourse, which, it is true, provokes painful memories that cast him and his period of service in an inglorious light. Yet as he journeys towards a decisive meeting with her he will recall the true value of Miss Kenton as confidante, guide to warmth and intimacy, provocateur, romantic antagonist, and fondly remember dialogues that bear all the hallmarks of romantic comedy, dialogues that came considerably closer to 'banter' than restrained and respectful conversation between household staff.

As Susan Fraiman suggests, what can prove so unbecoming in the narrative of a *Bildungsroman*, a narrative that at the outset Stevens may have envisaged as devoted to his ascendant professional development and his unimpeachable service to the ideals of his first and only real master, is that the genre can turn on its dominant narrative, allowing for antagonistic plotlines, counternarratives, alternative destinies, ideological confusion, and 'the building of solidarity' rather than the 'scaling of an intellectual summit' (Fraiman 1993, 10, 11) hinted at early in Stevens' narrative when he talks confidently about his knowledge of England and the true meaning of professionalism. It turns out that Stevens will not be able to understand himself or his decisions without thinking through his most important relationships and the impacts of his actions on others. If we trace the contours of Stevens' narrative carefully, as punctuated by his experiences while travelling, we can observe that his willingness to mask himself and take certain risks in self-presentation, eliciting unguarded pro-democratic sentiments, now permeates his narrative, which becomes something other than self-justification, no longer respecting class hierarchies and the official narrative of the Second World War that pits a united, democratic England against a pitiless and evil foe. Here we recall Bruce Robbins' reminder that the servant's 'sense of a primal injustice' in her or his condition may enter into the narrative (Robbins 1986, 106), that a certain 'duplicity is typical' of the servant's speech as it proves capable of turning on its master or mistress (Robbins 1986, 119).

The luminous presence of Miss Kenton is critical in this respect as she has balanced robust independence with professional acumen, has provoked and prodded his self-regard, asked him to reveal his better self, and assaulted, in the humiliating idiolect of romantic comedy, his now shopworn conception of 'dignity' at every moment. As Scherzinger argues, recalling us to the various enabling characters present in quest narratives, Miss Kenton can be understood as a spiritual guide for Stevens and a catalyst for his journey (Scherzinger 2004, 5): 'Miss Kenton is an agent of propelling volition in the novel: she crosses thresholds with relish, offering the obdurate Stevens the dangerous example of transgression' (Scherzinger 2004, 5).

Stevens was and is clearly drawn to the rebellious and passionate Miss Kenton and this is in part because he wishes to come undone, to become other to who he was, and it is she who emboldens him to enact his belated rebellion against the aristocrats who have diminished his agency and denied him a more fundamental experience of human dignity.

Let us reconsider the searing episode in the novel when Stevens, the consummate professional, interprets the firing of two Jewish maids as ordered by his master Lord Darlington, who in the 1930s has become a Nazi sympathizer, as a troubling but necessary duty. While Stevens remarks to the reader that his 'every instinct' opposed the idea of the maids' dismissal (156) he nevertheless regarded this display of 'personal doubts' at the time as 'irresponsible' (156). In the teeth of the housekeeper Miss Kenton's impassioned opposition at the time he sets about the commission of what he describes as a 'difficult task' in as 'concise' and 'businesslike' a way as possible (156) in his instructions to Miss Kenton. It is clear that Stevens would like to conceive of the lack of empathy for the fired maids he continues to demonstrate even in subsequent private conversations with the aghast Miss Kenton as a mark of his 'dignity', his ability at all times to suppress his own personal inclinations in favour of a higher ideal or purpose that he is privileged to enact.

However, the 1956 journey is a dangerous supplement to this professional rectitude. Stevens comes to realize that the choices he has made, and the conception of professional conduct that he has clung to, are mistaken, futile, and liable to have grievous consequences for himself and others. We are in the midst of a disenchantment that is profound, in which the trial of his character is at its most meaningful, as he is close to being reduced to a nullity ('I can't even say that I made my own mistakes. Really – one has to ask oneself – what dignity is there in that?', 256).

What emerges from Stevens' guilt, despair, and disillusionment in the present is the possibility of the rebirth of the self, a self that is capable of surviving a severe trial of character and working towards its own reinvention in altered circumstances. One aspect of this reinvention is that Stevens refuses, in Hannah Arendt's conception of the term as signifying the evasion of one's responsibility to remember one's actions and activate one's conscience, to become 'lonely'. On his journey Stevens will seek out company and he will keep himself company; in moments of solitude he will remember and reflect on those memories to a projected audience. In sympathy with Hannah Arendt's conception of conscience as an energetic internal conversation ('I am my own partner when I am thinking, I am my own witness when I am acting', Arendt 2003, 90), the task of lucid consciousness rather than an innate faculty, we can say that Stevens is divided into two selves who conduct a tense but ethically rewarding conversation with each other, an internal dialogue between different selves refracted through a candid address to the reader; the Stevens of impersonal officialese and canned speech who protests his inviolate professionalism and the rectitude of his record of service and the Stevens who recognizes his fallibility and acknowledges that the claims of others both past and present will now require the recalibration of his tailored life narrative and the reconstitution of his personality as requiring inventive and intelligent adjustment to his contemporary circumstances. We can say that through this conversation Stevens is working towards his final meeting with Miss Kenton. She is no longer, in the teleological sense, a fantasized prize that will succour his battered ego and redeem his decisions. Overtaken by his journey, Stevens will reflect on Miss Kenton as a friend and mentor, and he will finally meet with her as a fellow human being living in the present who has made her own difficult but necessary adjustments to circumstance. Before that encounter, Miss Kenton's constant presence, her solicitude and care, will also guide the thread of his memories.

One can remark that even in the notorious episode in which Stevens has to fire two Jewish maids on Darlington's orders, Stevens vividly records and is clearly shocked by his master's anti-Semitic remarks and his association with Oswald Mosely and his 'blackshirts' (146), drawing sustained attention to the willingness of many English aristocrats to entertain Herr Joachim von Ribbentrop, Hitler's Machiavellian foreign minister. While Stevens continues to profess his unerring admiration for Lord Darlington and defends his loyalty to him, he records every sleight Darlington has ever made against him, including an appalling episode in which Darlington and his associates mock his ignorance of world affairs in order to prove the absurdity of the democratic franchise (205–6). Of course, Stevens' mounting charge sheet against Darlington doesn't stop there since Stevens' entire journey combats Darlington's fascist elitism by dwelling at length on the perspectives of ordinary people including the democratic agitator Harry Smith, who rebukes Stevens' derivative and merely performative conception of professional dignity by suggesting that 'Dignity isn't just something gentlemen have. Dignity is something every man and woman in this country can strive for and get' (195). Robbins reminds us that 'nothing is more faithful to comic tradition than a sudden involuntary stumble from the heights of praise into a pointed disservice' (Robbins 1986, 66). Citing Dixon in Gaskell's *North and South*, Robbins points out that 'it is often when the servant's opposition is most loyal, when it emerges neither into consciousness nor into the plot, that it makes its most radical statements', reaching in the case of Dixon to 'extremes of class complaint' (Robbins 1986, 68).

Stevens' recollection of being insulted, taking place as it does so soon after his meeting with Harry Smith, suggests his earlier version of dignified behaviour is unravelling. In terms of his swirling affective life, the Stevens who pretends that even moments of harrowing personal loss such as the death of his father actually constitute a professional triumph is contradicted by the Stevens who remains profoundly loyal to and models his professionalism on his father, cries later and is clearly devastated at his passing, and, as we pointed out, continues to express his own sense of waste and futility while projecting those feelings onto the absent Miss Kenton. The anachronistic Stevens, who projects the superiority of a stoic conception of Englishness increasingly gives way to the incipiently xenophilic Stevens, who embraces the breezy humour and informality of his new American master Mr Farriday. Just as he secretly enjoyed the mocking, affectionate Miss Kenton, the novel closes with Stevens recommitting enthusiastically to developing his bantering skills as a way of participating in the human warmth that has long been denied him.

Hopefully we have gone some way towards thinking of Stevens as a candidate for a mature *Bildungsroman* in which a character only experiences an ethical awakening after playing a socially prescribed role that was meant to be fulfilling. For it seems that it is only by reflectively playing out roles that are unbecoming for an old-fashioned, anachronistic English butler that Stevens achieves moral insight:

> As I say, the happiness with which the pleasure-seekers gathering on [. . . Weymouth] pier greeted [. . . the turning on of the pier lights] would tend to vouch for the correctness of my companion's words; for a great many people, the evening is the most enjoyable part of the day. Perhaps, then, there is something to his advice that I should cease looking back so much . . . and try to make the best of what remains of my day (256) . . . Listening to them now, I can hear them exchanging one bantering remark after another (257) . . . After all, when one thinks about it, it is not such a foolish thing to indulge in – particularly if it is the case that in bantering lies the key to human warmth. (258)

The Remains of the Day: Political allegory and future horizons

The analysis so far has been dedicated to demonstrating the rhetorical impact upon the reader of Stevens' narrative as we begin to discern various counternarratives to his proud self-possession and mythic construction of an all-consuming professional identity. The complex functionality of the *Bildungsroman* as it intersects with the requirements of an engaging historical fiction also enjoins the reader to be attentive to aspects of the novel that constitute proximal witnessing, testimony, and associative private memories that can rewrite national narratives. As David James has reminded us, it is the 'candid medium of testimony that makes *The Remains of the Day* so compelling' (James 2010, 55). Stevens' increasingly complex reaction to the demise of the British empire signified by the Suez crisis, as he willingly journeys beyond previous boundaries into Britain's varied communities and away from its constructed centre of imagined identity and political power, may indicate there is a geopolitical and allegorical significance to his journey. Stevens perhaps has something of the allegorical significance of Margaret Hale in Elizabeth Gaskell's great historical novel *North and South*, a character clinging to the past but, as Patricia Johnson suggests, needing to 'come to terms with a changed reality', to mature into new responsibilities (Johnson 1994, 2). In thinking about his responsibilities Stevens has perhaps remained 'preoccupied' with the young Mr Cardinal's accusation of his incuriosity on the political manoeuvring surrounding him, asking him how he can 'just let all this go on before you and [...] never think to look at it for what it is' (234).

Stevens' journey into post-war Britain takes more time to truly 'look' at the world as it is, challenging a mythic 'Englishness' based on the inherited wealth of landed estates and attentive to the activity required to ensure human equality and the preservation of freedom. His timely journey is also an attempt to remind readers of a national past that is repressed and threatens to be forgotten. Reviewing his implication in Lord Darlington's pro-Nazi agitations has complicated a complacent national narrative and reminded Britain of its considerable pro-Nazi and anti-democratic elite sympathies in the 1930s and its associations with a legacy of imperial violence, the desire to exploit, rule over others, and to subjugate rebellion and disorder. Stevens' internal hybridity and sly civility point towards the discursive function of the servant to disturb this regnant ideology and offer an alternative 'social vision' (Robbins 1986, 23).

Stevens' support for empire early in the novel has been complicated by the suggestion that his own family's servitude has analogies to the fate of colonized peoples. Stevens' willingness to deconstruct ideologies that legitimize hierarchy and dependence signals a willingness to enter into and be transformed by the creative horizons of historical time. As Løvlie and Standish recognize, 'Bildung is a desire to participate in the world's transformation' (Løvlie 2003, 4).

What remains for the indicatively engaged reader are threads to unravel. Harry Smith may have impressed upon him that your 'born free and you're born so that you can express your opinion freely' (196) but he conflates that right with the privileges of being English and doubts the wisdom of Britain abandoning its remaining empire (202). Smith protests that you can't have 'dignity if you're a slave' (196) but he is projecting a possible future under the Nazis rather than reflecting on the British empire's long history of slavery, a legacy it is still confronting while avoiding meaningful reparations. Stevens' willingness to keep the question of dignity alive and his recognition that a crucial aspect of defending human dignity is the ability to reckon with the past can, then, speak to a contemporary readership who may question whether postcolonial recognition of British slavery and the reparations to follow are now an aspect of a dignified future for colonized peoples. That reader will appreciate that the varied social intercourse, intellectual curiosity, and diverse mentors that have guided his independent *Bildung* have enabled him to acknowledge and move beyond an arrested development, to embrace ethical and political problematics, and transcend a childlike model of 'filial devotion' (O'Brien 1996, 790) that masks class stratification and service to the empire.

Chapter 2

VISIONARY DISENCHANTMENT
ACCESSING SECOND SIGHT IN *THE KINDLY ONES*

> A new understanding of the past gives us at the same time a new prospect of the future, which in turn becomes an impulse to intellectual and social life.
> (Ernst Cassirer 1944, 178)

In this chapter I argue for an interpretation of Jonathan Littell's historical novel *The Kindly Ones* (2010), originally published in French in 2006, as both ironically and yet sincerely participating in the genre of the Bildungsroman. Such a reading, I suggest, can help us to appraise the ethical implications of its fictional perpetrator Maximilien Aue, a first-person narrator who neither apologizes for nor consistently seeks to minimize his culpability in the commission of mass murder and other genocidal atrocities. I will also suggest that the ethical significance of this novel partially resides in various historiographical arguments it wishes to make about the Holocaust as a European project, and about anti-Semitism as the externalization and failed extirpation of undesirable traits in the subject. Locating these historiographical and psychoanalytic prisms will help us push back against a strain of criticism, prominent in early reviews of the novel, that suggested, along with Dominic LaCapra and Julia Kristeva amongst other commentators, that the novel's focus on a perpetrator narrator invites the reader's complicity with perpetrator subjectivity and does not afford the reader enough critical distance from Nazi ideology. In a 2011 review essay, LaCapra expresses strong reservations about the ethical dangers of reading the novel. He fears that Aue 'engages the reader in a dialogic relation from the very outset, or rather a manipulative, pseudo-dialogical relation' that is primarily aimed at generating 'complicity and subordination rather than critical exchange' in the manner of the Nazis' coercive policy of establishing collaborative Jewish councils (LaCapra 2011, 73).

Responding to LaCapra's widely shared anxiety about the novel requires a discussion of the novel's indicative hermeneutics in which the reader of a *Bildungsroman* need not be preoccupied with identifying with the protagonist as a biographical subject but can develop an abiding interest in the picaresque dimensions of their journey and the more desirable characteristics that the protagonist displays along the way. As we have discussed a reader who followed Stevens' journey could discern an inclination towards the off-piste and the deferred rather than the linear and instrumental, a continual desire for variety of situation, a restless intellectual curiosity, and the need to seek advisers and mentors so as to converse about important values and ideas.

We can more easily, I would suggest, ascertain the indicative temporal and geographic trajectories and character traits in this novel if we read it as loosely structured by the requirements of a *Bildungsroman* in which we can infer three distinct phases. The first phase requires us to read *The Kindly Ones* as a historical novel in which the character's travels encompass a geographical and historical panorama such that the Nazis' genocidal colonial project of erasing other civilizations including that of the Jews is gradually displaced by Maximilien Aue's off-piste wanderings, curatorial interests, commitment to a quest for meaning, and tendency to question every deterministic account of origins and provenance. As Orit Troupin argues, 'Aue's quest for an ecstatic origin is subverted and ironized several times in the novel' (Troupin 2020, 319).

The second phase, highlighted in more recent discussions of the genre, is that of Aue's disillusionment, in which certain ideals, fantasies, or assumptions are tested by experience, harking back to the genre's indebtedness to the epic motif of trial by ordeal. Here I will mostly focus on Aue's development of a kind of 'second' sight generated by his traumatic experiences at the Battle of Stalingrad. Aue's prophetic disillusionment can be compared to Stevens' struggles with the legacy of his father's *imago*, as Aue's drive to imitate his father's identity as it would have been fulfilled in the Nazi movement is profoundly disrupted by the shattering reality of his wartime experience. Aue's disillusionment, commingling with a range of other character functions and so requiring vigilant attention by the reader, is expressed in numerous ways but I will particularly focus on Aue's increasingly cynical appraisal of Hitler, who, it is intimated, has been interpreted by the youthful Aue as a kind of fantasized surrogate father figure capable of redeeming his father's fascist vision.

The third phase, which needs a degree of reader inference alert to the narrator's performative contradiction of their residual Nazi world view, is that the protagonist now has a different and refreshed perspective, undergoing a tentative ethical awakening and a renewed sense of purpose, suggesting a possible vocation in intelligence work that can translate some of his capacity to defer, dilate, and curate into concrete action on behalf of the Jewish people. I will argue that Aue is double-coded after Stalingrad as an avenging detective, a 'trickster figure' who bonds with the reader in his deployment of ruse and disguise, a strategy enabling him to intervene in the fate of the Jews and document unspeakable crimes. As Zoë Roth argues, Aue moves from being a transparent spectator – 'I observe and do nothing, that's my favorite position', to acknowledging his complicity in events – 'I consider that watching engages my responsibility as much as doing' (Roth 2017, 84).

All these features of the genre will help us to understand the varied functionality of Aue's character as observer, trickster, avenger, (inspired) madman, and picaro. It will also assist in the discussion of the novel's narrative strategy as offering a complex species of unreliable narration in which the reader can experience both bonding and estrangement with Aue since his identity as a perpetrator of unspeakable crimes is overlaid with genre markers that stress his fluidity and avidity for concrete experiences. As a *Bildungsroman*, *The Kindly Ones* affords us a variety of indicative reading experiences so that we do not forget that, as Debarati Sanyal argues, Aue is a polymorphous character who is continually reconstituted by the 'jostling demands of historical fiction, testimony, Greek tragedy, *Bildungsroman*, picaresque, kitsch, satire, archival documentation, and philosophical rêverie' (Sanyal 2015, 199). In the final section I will argue that as a protagonist of a historical *Bildungsroman* written to stimulate a contemporary readership, infused with the ethos of multidirectional memory, Aue throws up a bewildering array of evanescent images, reflections, and aperçus that constellate with our own precarious circumstances. As Zoë Roth argues, the novel creates an 'alternative archive that brings together the Holocaust and WWII, colonialism and imperialism, and contemporary events' (Roth 2017, 82).

My genre-influenced reading of the novel occurs within a critical context in which the novel is criticized or celebrated as a *locus classicus* in perpetrator fiction with responses veering between reading it as dangerous or salutary, in other cases attempting to work out the historical and ethical implications of its aesthetics of excess. As Eric Sandberg has argued, the novel's 'encyclopaedic scope and exhaustive length imply a different aesthetic which responds to the historical suffering of the period with an overwhelming excess of narrative' (Sandberg 2014, 238). As Daniel Mendelsohn comments in his sympathetic review in *The New Yorker*, *The Kindly Ones* has been 'both extravagantly blessed and hideously cursed' (Mendelsohn 2009, 15). Some interpreters have failed to accept the challenge posed by its narrator, Maximilien Aue, a former high-ranking officer of the SS, who addresses the reader in the present day as an affluent bourgeois proprietor of a lace factory who wishes to give an honest account of events. Aue initially solicits the reader's sympathy as a fellow human being who found himself in circumstances that were not of his making, but then goes on to detail his active support for the Nazis' genocidal crimes and expatiate at length on his extravagant psychosexual proclivities, including his fatal erotic love for his twin sister Una; a German critic in *Die Zeit* (2008) sums up many critics' feeling of revulsion with the novel's scatological fixations when she questions why she should read a book 'written by an educated idiot who writes badly, is haunted by sexual perversities and [has] abandoned himself to racist ideology and an archaic belief in fate'. Littell's novel has, on the other hand, been more enthusiastically analysed inter alia by proponents of Holocaust 'impiety' such as Mathew Boswell (2012), Erin McGlothlin (2021), and Debarati Sanyal (2015) as an unsettling instance of the 'taboo thought-work' that can be achieved by perpetrator fiction (Boswell 2012, 16). This is a fruitful approach but I will have a very mild criticism towards the end of the chapter as to whether it privileges the disruptive ethics of reading above practical attention to the novel's discernible historiographical observations, and genre markers that would mitigate psychologistic approaches to reading the text, knowing aspects of the text that encourage us to ponder its holistic rhetorical impact as we sought to do for *The Remains of the Day*.

LaCapra's critique of *The Kindly Ones* hinges on whether there are textual markers or procedures that provide the reader with 'critical distance' from, rather than complicity with, Aue as the entreating 'first-person narrator'. LaCapra concludes that such markers of critical distance are rare, partially because Aue is presented in dehistoricized fashion as an 'everyman' who closes off other perspectives while the persecuted other, the Jewish victim of Nazi violence, remains silenced, obscured, or obfuscated (LaCapra 2011, 76). LaCapra's concern about the seductive effects of reading *The Kindly Ones* is symptomatic of an entrenched reluctance by some critics, haunted by the prospect of recidivism, to concede that imaginative access to a Nazi perpetrator can have any critical or ethical interest as an alternative to much needed victim-centred accounts of the Holocaust. Walter Benn Michaels is correct in suggesting that criticism of the novel fears the 'imposition of a morally obnoxious . . . subjectivity' in place of 'unpretentious objectivity' and thus dutifully protests against a seeming obscenity, the 'emergence of the narrator's or central character's relation to these events as the primary object of interest' (Michaels 2013, 919).

It is clear that LaCapra simply blanches at the unacceptable discursive power of Aue as the narrative focus. He confines discussion of characters to a single footnote who, after the dialogical fashion of *Bildungsromane* such as Thomas Mann's *The Magic Mountain*, engage in animated disagreement with Aue including his forbidden love Una, her husband von Uxküll, and the race debunking linguist Voss. The reasons for this diminution of the text's polyphony are not hard to find. LaCapra wants to affirm Julia Kristeva's alarmist review of the book, quoting her claim that the novel's absence of distance between the narrator and the perspective of the perpetrator makes it 'difficult, if not impossible, to locate the least distance in relation to the anti-Semitic and nihilistic universe' of the novel, a conflation which ultimately mimes the 'grip of Nazi ideology on the reader' (Kristeva 2007, 76).

At this juncture, we might seek to draw on Jenni Adams' valuable suggestion that we need to think about the 'variety and range of functions' (Adams, 2013, 3–4) Aue might serve as a slippery narrative focus. It is important to examine the implications of Aue as a self-divided unreliable narrator, a dynamic and peripatetic focalizer of events who observes more than he can psychically incorporate and struggles to rationalize that which he experiences; a figure whose fallibility and discordant perspectives may be orchestrated by an implied author or constructive agent, someone beckoning us to read between the lines, to think carefully about what Aue's observations are really communicating to a reader who is in some respects themselves in formation and engaged in a quest to understand the meaning of events that continue to disturb the present. Readers of *The Kindly Ones*, perhaps preoccupied with Littell's daring, unprecedented attempt to render the interiority of a bona fide 'Nazi', and perhaps analysing the novel as the apotheosis of Gillian Rose's desideratum for a Nazi *Bildungsroman* that will engineer a crisis of identification, have sometimes overlooked the narrative theorist Seymour Chatman's deceptively simple observation on creative design, that a 'narrative text . . . contains within itself, explicitly or implicitly, information about how to read it' (Chatman 1990, 83).

Some defenders of the suasive significance of unreliable narrative are confident that initially bewildering texts can quickly 'train' their readers to distrust the narrative surface and search for other ways of understanding the referential structure and ethical import of the text. One approach is to treat unreliable narrative as a satisfyingly edifying process of reading otherwise than according to the narrator's account of events. This involves focusing on the 'narrator's limited knowledge, . . . personal involvement, and . . . problematic value-scheme' (Rimmon-Kenan cited in Nünning 2005, 94). A related narratological prism, more pertinent to our analysis, is less interested in establishing just the right amount of dubiety about the narrator's objectivity and trustworthiness and instead filters its interpretation of the narrator as a flexible construct or 'mobile focalizer' (Dalley 2014, 22) of our attention and interpretative energies. Such an approach invokes a heuristic character typology, pertinent as we have seen to Stevens, which may include the 'naïve narrator, the hypocrite, the pervert, the [madman] and morally debased narrator, the picaro, the liar, the trickster, or the clown' (Riggan 1981, 94).

More recently, there has been a shift away from relying on a normative intentionalist model of unreliable narration in which, as Kathleen Wall complains, an 'implied author and an implied reader silently nudge one another in the ribs at the folly and delusion of the narrator' (Wall 1994, 26). Wall's influential article has helped to inaugurate a shift from classificatory schema addressing how a narrator's perception and values conflict with epistemic or social 'norms' to the study of interior conflicts that may manifest themselves in unreliable narration including disassociation and 'split subjectivity' (Wall 1994, 38). James Phelan and Mary Patricia Martin, seeking a middle way between formalism and reader-response theory, have productively argued that texts with unreliable narrators have a variety of registers, sometimes guiding our inferencing by clear textual signals they send to the audience, sometimes transferring the responsibility of disambiguation or ethical response to the reader (Phelan and Martin 1999). In a more recent essay, Phelan suggests that carefully distinguishing between different personae in unreliable narration can enable us to distinguish between *estranging unreliability* that increases the moral and cognitive distance between narrator and authorial audience and *bonding unreliability* which reduces that distance (Phelan 2008). At the latter end of the spectrum, we often encounter what Phelan usefully calls 'mask narration', a 'rhetorical act' in which an implied author uses a character-narrator to endorse certain ideas or increase their appeal or persuasiveness (Phelan 2008, 10).

The *Bildungsroman* aligns with this aspect of contemporary theories of unreliable narrative in that both narrative modes ask the reader to be attentive to discrete moments of focalization that can have engaging and alienating effects, rather than treating the narrator as an already-known psycho-social subject. So as genre-sensitive readers acknowledging that the historical fiction we are reading is intent on interrogating the relationship between subjective desire and memory, we sense when, as we remark Stevens' obscure origins, social ambition, and self-inventing energies, we are scrutinizing a parvenu, when we are interested in the observational power of the narrative, when alert to the conjunction of disillusionment and social critique, and when incipient ethical growth is intimated but not always consciously acknowledged or fulfilled in narrative trajectory.

Phelan's rhetorical distinction between the bonding and estranging effects of reading unreliable narrative, an underestimated dimension of the contemporary *Bildungsroman*, helps us to read *The Kindly Ones* in view of narratology's oscillation between reading the unreliable narrator as communicative by virtue of its careful construction by an intentional agent, an 'implied author', and the recognition that unreliable narratives address a pluralist age and thus need to be regarded as drawing attention to their own artifice or as engaging the judgement of the reader (Nünning 2005, 97). Both strategies are in play when Aue trains the reader's attention to ponder significant historiographical themes and ethical questions while also challenging the residual desire of any historicism to prevent the past from bleeding into the present. Observing the venerable story/discourse or showing/telling distinction we can read Aue as a beguiling and mendacious Sophist whose initial bonding discourse as a victim of circumstance worthy of pity is undermined by the cumulatively estranging effects of the extraordinary, patently culpable story that he tells us. On the other hand, with astute interpreters such as Susan Suleiman, we can examine Aue as double-coded, a seemingly estranging perpetrator whose observational gifts and analytical abilities combined with his presence at many of the key sites of the Holocaust, allow us to 'bond' with his observations to a certain degree by inferring that his character, in the mould of Stevens, has a more familiar narrative function as a 'reliable historical witness' to Nazi crimes (Suleiman 2009, 5, 11).

We can also draw on and extend Riggan's character typology as it intersects with the various strategies of the novel as a capacious historical fiction and *Bildungsroman*. Thus, Aue is naïve enough to report events accurately and continually ask pertinent questions ('my question wouldn't let go of me') about the rationale for the genocide of the Jews and the potential consequences of the war (Little 2010, 109). He is deranged or debased enough to help us focus on the nihilism, frenzied eroticism, and morbidity of genocidal violence. Aue is an idealistic and argumentative theoretician of Nazism, so a questing figure who drives the intellectual obsessions of the novel with its partial genealogy in Menippean satire. He is also in part a curatorial figure, deferring definitive outcomes and engaged in a project of memorialization, an ethnographically and historically curious 'picaresque *flâneur*' idling behind the lines of the advancing zone of occupation, a meditative figure who engages our interest in the bewildering cultural and linguistic complexity of the Caucasus at a historical moment in which the Nazis would eradicate or segregate perceived races and cultures in the name of a purified modernity; and at times Aue also seems to be a trickster and detective figure who begins to investigate and expose hypocrisy and injustice.

First phase: Aue as mobile focalizer in a historical novel

In Maximilien Aue, we have a fictional narrative protagonist who is bifurcated between a substantive self, a historical witness and perpetrator of verifiable historical atrocities, and, as Boswell, Adams and other interpreters have argued, a metafictional device, a philosophically curious 'critical interpreter' or 'reader' of events who enables the novel to take a 'self-conscious tour of the literature and theory of the Third Reich' (Boswell 2012, 16). In addition to its unflinching, sometimes sickening depiction of genocidal and homicidal violence, the novel presents us with the quandary of a narrating character engaged in a quest for meaning, someone who is highly educated and cultivated, analytical, ruminative and often lucidly self-aware. Max Aue is present at or actively participates in the Nazis' wartime activities while continually querying their ultimate objectives and the ethical and historiographical significance of the events he witnesses. He both participates in and records the killings conducted by the Einsatzgruppen behind the front lines of the Wehrmacht on the Eastern Front, culminating in the massacre of more than 33,000 Jews at the Babi Yar ravine on the outskirts of Kiev in late September 1941. He is subsequently shot and badly wounded at the Battle for Stalingrad. Later in the novel Aue serves as a functionary on Heinrich Himmler's staff seeking to maximize the productivity of slave labour by visiting and reporting on conditions in the Auschwitz and Bergen-Belsen death camps. He is present while Adolf Eichmann condemns the Jews of Hungary to what Samuel Moyn has described as a 'massive paroxysm of death' in the space of a few months in 1944 (Moyn 2009, 32). He finds himself in Hitler's bunker as the Soviets invade, memorably biting the Führer on the nose in a moment of pure burlesque. Aue is also in all likelihood a matricide who has had an incestuous relationship with his twin sister and spends the latter half of the novel engaged in a state of hallucinatory derangement while describing morbid autoerotic activities and incestuous desires and fantasies in extraordinary detail.

While too ideologically committed to the *Weltanschauung* of Nazism to be a pure Lukacsian 'middle character', nevertheless we can interpret Aue along with Dalley as a 'mobile point of focalisation', a type common to historical fiction, a figure whose lack of an assured position in the world helps us to move freely through social space. As a capacious metafictional character Aue is in part a choric voice guiding an ethical response to events as they unfold but also a devious individual, a post-war apologist, and machinating intriguer who threatens to corrupt our understanding of events in order to draw us into the mire of complicity. Aue is both insider and outsider to the Nazi movement which means his sympathies and engagements can align with both centre and periphery, orthodoxy and heterodoxy, as the narrative progresses. Both participant and observer, Aue is initially motivated by a bitter and intense identification with a revanchist *imago*, an idealized German father, a former member of the proto-fascist Freikorps who left when he was eight. Aue is also of Alsatian French heritage on his mother's side, thus bilingual and bicultural, an immigrant and slightly suspect foreigner in Hitler's Germany; he is a dedicated SS ideologue straight out of Zygmunt Bauman's *Modernity and the Holocaust*, a 'rationalist' committed to eliminating social 'problems' but also a watchful, covert homosexual who despises bourgeois morality and cherishes the homosociality and pederastic educational philosophy of the ancient Greeks. He is an introspective, freethinking intellectual who nevertheless loathes the spiritual vapidity of bourgeois liberalism and insists on the importance of a cohesive *Weltenschaaung*. Aue's bifurcation between singular and more generalizable referents makes him an interesting indicative index, if also parodic travesty, of perpetrator rationales. Inducted into the security forces of the National Socialists by his university mentor Otto Ohlendorf, the historical former head of the Inland SD, Aue draws attention to the extensive support lent by German academics to the Nazi movement. As the narrative progresses, Aue articulates the motivating force, for those who joined, of misanthropic *ressentiment*, careerist ambition, utopian fantasy, adventurism, nihilism, sadism, and libidinal urges of all kinds.

Second phase: Aue as disillusioned historical witness

Some interpretations of the novel have looked beyond its scandalous premise towards its artful technique and treated Aue as double-coded, such that the contemporary reader can reasonably infer the novel's historiographical and ethical intentions as the more traditional animus of bearing witness not only to Nazi crimes but also to the mendacity of anti-Semitism. Susan Suleiman makes much of Aue as a homophone for 'eye' in French. As a reporting observer nominally engaged in intelligence work Aue is uncannily present at all the major events of the Holocaust and the decision-making processes that attended them. As Eric Sandberg points out, when Aue becomes a participant-observer of mass murder during the massacre of the Jews in Lutsk, Poland in the early stages of the war, Aue's meditations on the reality of death represents the 'first fissure in the rational, calculated and impersonal detachment with which Aue observes and narrates his observations' (Sandberg 2014, 242.). He is in the audience and writes a detailed account of Himmler's Posen speech in 1943 in which Himmler notoriously professed elation over the genocide of the Jews, and declared the Holocaust a page in history that 'will never be written', a moment anxious readers of this novel sometimes fail to miss is imbued with dramatic irony. As a reflective intellectual at a remove from the machinery of power, and thus sometimes invisible to the military hierarchy, Aue is in a perfect position as a 'reflector character' to debunk self-serving collective memories simply by letting perpetrators incautiously speak for themselves. As Klaus Theweleit argues, Littell's first 300 pages can be read as the obituary of the legend of the 'innocent Wehrmacht' (Theweleit 2009, 29). Consider the following pointed denunciation of the Wehrmacht's hypocrisy by Aue's immediate superior Blobel, who is disgusted with an order from Erich von Manstein, the Commander of the Eleventh Army in the Crimea, a real historical figure who is partially responsible for the myth of the clean Wehrmacht:

> It is dishonourable for officers to be present at the executions of Jews. Dishonorable! Those assholes. As if what they were doing was so honourable ... as if they were treating their POWs with honor! ... those little Wehrmacht shits. They want to leave the dirty work to us [...] What would he say, when AOK Eleven asks its Einsatzgruppe to liquidate all the Jews of Simferopol before Christmas, so the officers can have a judenfrei holiday? (181)

On his way to his next assignment as a functionary on Himmler's staff Aue presages, and debunks, the claim that the concentration camp archipelago was sequestered from civilian populations. Note in the following quote that the detailed accumulation of quotidian activity in the midst of appalling suffering has just a hint of suppressed rage:

> I had thought that the camps of the Einsatz were set up in uninhabited areas, difficult to access; but this one was right next to a little town swarming with German settlers and their families; the main railroad linking Galicia to the rest of the CG, on which civilians and soldiers travelled daily ... all these people, trading, travelling, scurrying in one direction or another, chatted, argued, wrote letters, spread rumours, told jokes. (587)

Aue also reports a telling observation of his hedonistic friend Thomas Hauser, a dedicated career Nazi who reinforces the historiographical focus on the consensual and popular dimensions of National Socialist rule when he celebrates the depth of its support amongst the German people and its potential resurgence even after the calamity of defeat and humiliation:

> It's striking how much people know about the so-called secrets, the euthanasia program, the destruction of the Jews, the camps in Poland, the gas, everything

... But what's encouraging is that despite all that people continue to support the Party and the authorities, they still have faith in our Führer ... Which proves what? [That] ... the National Socialist spirit has ... penetrated into the most obscure recesses. And so even if we lose the war, it will survive. (549)

Aue's eye for detail soon encourages the confidences of Adolf Eichmann. A boastful technocrat, Eichmann reminds us of the energetic collaboration of Vichy France and thus gestures towards the Holocaust as a collaborative 'European project' that, in the words of Dan Stone, cannot be confined to the more 'clichéd images of industrial mass-murder' under German supervision (Stone 2010, 22):

[T]he French showed a lot of understanding, also thanks to the assistance of the French police, without which we could have done nothing, of course, since we don't have the resources ... so the aid of the French police was a vital element, since they're the ones who arrested the Jews and transferred them to us, and they even overdid it, since we had only officially asked for Jews over sixteen – but ... they gave them all to us, even the orphans. (558)

Pertinent in regard to the novel's focus on collaboration, redolent of Arendt's caustic overview of the various European sites of the Holocaust in *Eichmann in Jerusalem*, is the novel's attention to the Austrian background of many of the Holocaust's protagonists, from Auschwitz Commandant Odilo Globoknic to Adolf Eichmann and of course Hitler himself, an attentiveness that reads as a pointed rebuke to Austria's ongoing reluctance to confront its embrace of Nazism and anti-Semitism before and after the Anschluss.

The disillusionment of a true believer

Yet if Aue is in some respects the naïf who simply reports what he sees without imposing a jaundiced prism of interpretation, it is equally significant as a bonding narrator that he shares the 'idealism' of the butler Stevens in Kazuo Ishiguro's *The Remains of the Day*, a focalizing narrator that seems to have inspired Littel as a multifaceted textual construction. Analogous to Stevens' loyalty to his former master Lord Darlington, Aue remains a true believer in Nazism, even if ruing its leadership's betrayal of his youthful ideals. At the novel's outset he explicitly refuses the Nuremberg defence of ignorance or coerced subordination in despising the slavish Prussian obedience of the 'Knecht'. Aue is clear-sighted enough to recognize that Nazism will live and die by the sword, that only as long as it is successful will it be able to redefine truth and justice as pertinent only to the destiny of the German Volk (161), after which its representatives will need to assume responsibility for their actions. Thereafter, the worm will turn with savage consequences. As an idealistic intellectual who feels betrayed by his movement's leadership, Aue's disgust with the apologias and evasions of former Nazis such as Albert Speer reminds us that a stirring indictment is often more piquant, and certainly less estranging than a hackneyed excuse or mendacious evasion, when it comes from a disillusioned subordinate. Comparable, as we have discussed, is Stevens' attempts to defend Lord Darlington for collaborating with the Nazis when he sternly rebukes the post-war British aristocracy that has conveniently forgotten that it was more than happy to entertain Hitler's foreign minister Ribbentrop in the 1930s during a period in which an Anglo-German détente was a real possibility. The following passage has an exasperated Aue bristling at Speer's attempts to distance himself from the genocidal policies he assiduously served:

> Speer, as all the specialists now affirm, gave at least two extra years to National Socialist Germany, more than anyone he contributed to prolonging the business, and would have prolonged it even more if he could have, and certainly he wanted victory, he struggled vehemently for victory, the victory of this National Socialist Germany that was destroying the Jews, women and children included, and the Gypsies too and many others besides, and that's why I permit myself, despite the immense respect I have for his accomplishments as Minister, to find his oh so very public post-war regrets somewhat indecent. (67)

The corrosion of Aue's belief system also serves to position the novel as a *Bildungsroman* of disillusionment followed by emerging ethical autonomy as Aue's initial theoretical commitment to a 'redemptive anti-Semitism' that will emancipate the spiritual capacities of the Aryan race is quickly betrayed by the sordid reality of a corrupt, schismatic, grasping Nazi officialdom and derealized by the sadism, greed, and destructive lunacy that he witnesses. As Theweleit argues, the novel itself is a powerful rejoinder to racist ideology, as Aue's experiences confound projections of an Aryan 'New Man' emancipated from the calculating self-interest of bourgeois modernity.

> Every SS man who gains even one Reichsmark from Jewish assets will be ruthlessly shot'. As if . . . Mountains of files documenting just such breaches pile up around Aue, ordered by Himmler's own investigatory commission . . . SS officers behaved like the Nazis' projection of the Jews; they stole, they embezzled, they took bribes, they enriched themselves. (Theweleit 2009, 27)

Third phase: From blindness to insight

To pursue further the novel as *Bildungsroman* that draws on the inferential hermeneutic energies of unreliable narrative we would need to think about the point at which Aue experiences a significant transformation following a moment of traumatic and existential crisis after he is seriously wounded by a bullet to the head at Stalingrad. Thereafter he develops a kind of second sight, a forensic and prophetic 'third eye', that is internally 'directed at the darkness', gifting Aue the Dionysian power of looking at the 'bare face of death' (443). As Erin McGlothlin has argued, 'Aue's altered mode of seeing and the hallucinations it causes allow for a fresh perspective from which we can regard the Holocaust' (McGlothlin 2021, 245). It is this 'pineal' third eye that helps Aue recognize Hitler as the very incarnation of the lying and parasitical 'Jew' that he despises. After Stalingrad, Aue is subsequently less motivated by vicarious curiosity, a quest for pristine origins, and subservience to a metaphysical cause; the spectral presence of the many Jews he has been complicit in killing sparks something of a Hamlet complex as the *imago* of the father seeking proxy vengeance against a feminized and degenerate polity comes into question and he instead meditates ruefully on a corrupt universe and turns his attention to agents of the established regime. As Troupin suggests, 'Aue's quest for his original fascist lineage and identity by recourse to the memory of his father, a cruel Freikorps commander, brings only a mirage' (Troupin 2020, 319).

I think we can take quite seriously Auschwitz commandant Odilo Globocnik's claim after Aue arrives to nominally examine the 'degraded' conditions at Auschwitz, that Aue is indeed 'one of those bores who want to save the Jews under the pretext that we need labor' (579). Reverting to Riggan's character typology, Aue is double-coded after Stalingrad as an avenging detective, like Stevens a sometimes 'trickster figure' who bonds with the reader in his deployment of ruse and disguise, a strategy enabling him to document unspeakable crimes.

Resonances: Aue as provocateur

'Closing your eyes is never an answer'. (cited in Troupin 2020, 322)

In some respects, no interpretation of the novel can begin at the beginning since Aue's attempts to destabilize the reader in the opening section 'Toccata' can only be evaluated in light of the tragic, ironic, terrifying, absurd, and edifying arc of the narrative as a whole. In other words, the bonding and estranging effects of the narrative persona require considerable discernment and careful judgement when that narrative character is both disarmingly honest and cunningly oleaginous. As Sanyal suggests, the narrator begins by ushering us into a 'familiar textual regime of complicity' – 'Oh my human brothers, let me tell you how it happened' – that resonates with *Lolita*'s Humboldt, *A Clockwork Orange*'s Alex, *La Chute*'s Clamence and Baudelaire's 'hypocrite lecteur' in *Les Fleurs du Mal* (Sanyal 2015, 191). Aue makes an argument for fate as ruling human lives:

> In most cases the man standing above the mass grave no more asked to be there than the one lying, dead or dying, at the bottom of the pit (17) ... I am guilty, you're not, fine. But all the same you ought to be able to say to yourself that you might also have done what I did (20) ... nearly everyone, in a given set of circumstances, does what he is told to do; and, pardon me, but there's not much chance that you're the exception any more than I was. (20)

The narrator goes on to suggest that if you live an affluent life in a liberal democracy you might be 'luckier than I, but you're not a better person', and if you have the 'arrogance to think you are, that's just where the danger begins' (20). A plaything of fate, a perpetrator only in extremis under the conditions of total war, the narrator can confidently appeal to empathetic recognition: 'I am a man like other men, I am a man like you. I tell you I am just like you!' (24).

While LaCapra understands a passage like this as trite and dangerously deceptive, generalizing historically specific conditions by presenting Aue as an everyman, the rest of the novel goes on to amply demonstrate Aue's psychosexual singularity and ideological obsessions, even if the force of Aue's jeering at the serenity of the affluent liberal moralist retains a certain unsettling power. Perhaps we can infer that *The Kindly Ones*, which dramatizes a character's pursuit by the remorseless 'Furies' as agents of justice, undeterred by the 'fog of war', is sympathetic to Hannah Arendt's claim that there is no such thing as mere obedience, that the felicitous function of a legal trial such as that of Adolf Eichmann in Jerusalem was the cumulative, heuristic exposure of an individual; not a cog in a machine but someone who had already made a decision to 'support' a regime, ideology, or constituted power (Arendt 1994, 278–9).

Still, even if we read *The Kindly Ones* as a historical novel that uses a variety of narrative techniques to engage our interest in the extant historical record by establishing meaningful connections between verifiable knowledge and inventive representations (Dalley 2014, 19) it is also the case that experiencing the novel as a historically motivated *Bildungsroman* with indicative pathways for geopolitical reflection allows the reader considerable latitude to connect those representations with resonant issues in the present. In the opening sally to the reader in 'Toccata' Aue reminds us that it is the victors who get to decide what counts as legitimate military operations and what as 'atrocities' carried out by sadists and psychopaths, a point reinforced when the bombing of Berlin is ironically described in outraged terms as 'Luftmorder' by Himmler, who then promises war crimes trials following the *Endsieg*. When Aue computes the unimaginable number and frequency of deaths during the Second World War the narrator reminds us that it is the victors who determine what counts in Judith Butler's term as 'grievable life':

> I obviously am not including the Vietnamese dead; since you never speak of them, in your books or TV programs, they must not count for much to you. Yet you killed 40 of them for every single one of your own dead, a fine effort even compared to our own, and one that certainly speaks for the value of technical progress. (16)

Now of course one can read this arch admiration for the 'efficiency' of the American war machine as an equivocating argument designed to deflect the singularity of Nazi crimes. The German Historikerstreit was a struggle over whether German history could be brought back from the abyss by comparing Hitler's crimes to Stalin's. It is not hard, however, to see why Jenni Adams celebrates this passage. It reminds us of the amnesia and deliberate historical erasure of more recent imperial violence, such as the West's relative indifference towards the death toll of Vietnamese, Algerians, Afghans, and Iraqis, and the torture of prisoners detained without trial in Guantanamo Bay and Abu Ghraib (Adams 2013, 36).

There are also moments in which the reader must decide, according to their own lights, whether the novel's enunciations are specific to narrative context or more disjunctive and allegorically resonant. One such instance is when a delirious Aue, having putatively endured a journey into his own heart of darkness, complains bitterly to his ingenuous 'intended' Hélène of the syndrome of the 'good German' who refuses to know anything about death camps or the violence and expropriation of goods and labour on the colonial periphery. Perhaps giving full cry to his earlier muted fury at German civilians and colonizers socializing in the midst of death and suffering, Aue screams at her that 'no one knows anything, except the ones doing the dirty work' (816), a remark that could be directed at consumers of cheap clothing or iPhones who disdain awareness of the supply chains and labour practices affording them such congenial consumer goods. As we have pointed out, the novel confounds anti-Semitic logic at every point, deriding Hitler as the quintessential embodiment of the lying, corrupt, parasitical phantasmatic Jew he despises, and insisting that 'baseness, spinelessness, avarice, greed, thirst for domination, and facile malice are fundamentally German qualities' rather than Jewish vices (875). There is, however, an unsettling moment of prospective anxiety, when Una (who may be a creation of Aue's delirium, continuing the theme of auto-suggestion in unreliable narrative) worries that if Germany collapses and the Jews survive, they will 'forget what the name Jew means, they'll want to be more German than ever before'. For if the name of a Jew still signifies these days, it means 'Other, an Other and an Otherwise that might be impossible but that are necessary' (875). This is an ironic commentary on the Zionist project to normalize the Jewish people and rescue it from its alterity as a stranger amongst the nations, which constitutes a negation of a history of Jewish diasporic interaction with Christian and Muslim cultures. Arguably Una's warning about the threat to Jewish ethical traditions posed by the ethnocentric imperatives of territorial Zionism needs to be juxtaposed with much earlier episodes in the novel where Aue's *Volkisch* yet supposedly scientifically informed anti-Semitism (predicated on tropes of urbanized Ashkenazi Jews as rootless and parasitic on host cultures) is badly shaken by his wandering in the polyglot Caucasus where indigenized Jewish peoples such as the Bergjuden have mingled for many centuries with Christians and Muslims. Following Isabelle Hesse we might suggest that in bringing forth these prophetic epiphanies, Littell is implicitly reminding us of the ethical and cultural fertility of Jewish diasporic identity, a theme we will discuss further in Chapter 3, in order to 'critically engage with Zionism and the occupation of Palestine and the concomitant image of the Israeli Jew as a colonizer and oppressor' (Hesse 2016, 6).

In her reading of *The Kindly Ones* Jenni Adams makes the important point that the novel disrupts personal or national identification with 'morally safe victimhood' (Adams 2013, 37). She goes on to say, I think more problematically, that the novel encourages ethical responsibility and questions of complicity through the 'ethically taboo invitation to accept commonality with the perpetrator' (Adams 2013, 37). I hope to have indicated that reading the novel's narrative as 'deploying a radical ethics of encounter' with Aue's disturbing consciousness does not entirely satisfy either in its anthropomorphizing of a textual construct or in its modernist, anti-cognitivist preference for a vertiginous reading experience. I think we are better off approaching the novel as a densely mediated narrative artifice with diverse critical and artistic affinities, as risking some opprobrium in order to enrich and renew the politics of memory. It is no accident, indeed a hallmark of contemporary historical *Bildungsromane*, that the novel's most appreciative readers tend to be younger, more willing, as Dirk Moses recommends, to loosen themselves from *parti pris* ethnic identities and embrace comparative approaches to historical analysis. These readers are aware, suggests Moses, citing Eva Hoffman in *After Such Knowledge* (2004), that a fruitful historical consciousness 'translates backward' from an 'international, cross-cultural, or culturally intermingled perspective' (Moses 2016, 336). Such productive memorialization of historical atrocities is only possible, the novel encourages us to recognize, in an unfettered public sphere that encourages intellectual freedom, plurality of perspectives, and cosmopolitan human solidarities.

Chapter 3

AN EXEMPLARY *BILDUNGSHELD*
BRINGING DIASPORA HOME IN *DANIEL STEIN, INTERPRETER*

In this chapter I propose a number of reasons for thinking of Ludmila Ulitskaya's challenging philosophical novel *Daniel Stein, Interpreter*, first published in Russian in 2006, as participating in the genre of the *Bildungsroman*. One recognizable trait that we have already encountered in the characters of Stevens and Aue is that in this novel the fluid protagonist heralds a possible future that moves humanity beyond the perpetually damaging nation-centred nexus of people, faith, and territory. The novel, a fictional biography of the Jewish priest and Holocaust survivor Oswald Rufeisen, evokes an intimate relationship between biographical and historical time, reminding us of Bakhtin's enthusiastic suggestion that in the *Bildungsoman*:

> [The hero] emerges *along with the world* and he reflects the historical emergence of the world itself. He is no longer within an epoch, but on the border between two epochs, at the transition point from one to the other. This transition is accomplished in him and through him. He is forced to become a new, unprecedented type of human being. The organizing force held by the [. . . historical] future is therefore extremely great here. [. . .] It is as though the very *foundations* of the world are changing, and man must change along with them. (23–4)

Bakhtin's suggestion that the *Bildungsroman* links its protagonists' emergence to historical change, and articulates historical dynamics and creative future horizons through its interest in biographical time, aligns with Løvlie and Standish's point that *Bildung* is a restless dispositional drive, a desire to 'participate in the world's transformation', in which the 'education of the self is undertaken with the transformation of contemporary culture in tandem' (Løvlie 2003, 4). In this chapter I will suggest that Daniel's own unique journey, as a Jewish survivor of the Holocaust who converts to Catholicism in order to interpret his tumultuous near-death experiences, will contribute, practically and symbolically, to a broken world that now lacks the guidance of religious and philosophical tradition. The disenchanted situation Daniel enters is described by Ulitskaya herself, who emerges as a choric commentator in the novel. She wants us to understand that 'with the whole of his life', Daniel raised a

> heap of unresolved, highly inconvenient issues which nobody talks about: the value of a life turned into mush beneath one's feet; the freedom which few people want; God for whom there is ever less room in our life; efforts to extricate Him from archaic words, all the ecclesiastical garbage, and life which has closed in on itself. (108)

In reading this novel's protagonist as responding to the difficult questions 'Ulitskaya' poses in the novel, we can take our bearings from Jed Esty's suggestion that since the late nineteenth century the *Bildungsroman* often functions as a national or geopolitical allegory with an increasingly 'unstable frame of social reference' (Esty 2012, 6), as an increasingly modernist genre began to explore youthful characters affected by uneven development in the colonial periphery whose relationship to national destiny or temporal logics of development are shaped by dissonance and disillusionment. In respect of the novel's historical implications and sense of the future, I will be arguing that Daniel Stein's mature self-formation, as a confessional Catholic Jew who leaves a Europe in ruins for the emergent nation of post-war Israel, is bound up with the subversion of a narrative in which the fact of Israel's establishment negates or overcomes the Jewish diasporic condition, a point I will illustrate in reference to the work of Judith Butler in *Parting Ways* (2012).

If we take the *Bildungsroman* to be a genre interested in the significance of the layers of lived experience that enrich and problematize the task of memory, hinting, as discussed in the previous chapters, that this vital mode of understanding assists character development, then, as Marja Sorvari indicates, we should note that the novel is an exploration of historical and spiritual experiences that take place in concrete episodes of biographical and historical time outside of institutional religious spaces and places like churches or masses (Sorvari 2017, 282). Sorvari points out that one of the reasons for Daniel Stein's controversial conversion to Catholicism after escaping from the Gestapo during the Second World War is his idiosyncratic conviction, after picking up a Catholic magazine detailing the apparitions of the Virgin Mary at Lourdes, that his own salvation after narrowly escaping being shot had 'also been a miracle of this kind' (quoted in Sorvari 2017, 282). Stein, as Sorvari explains, thereby explains his renewed sense of faith through his 'close interaction with the surrounding world, in a specific historical time and place' (Sorvari 2017, 282). A scene of both existential crisis and willed self-formation at a moment of unparalleled crisis, Daniel's highly personal conversion to Catholicism pertains to the needs of 'his own historical reality, his lived experience' (Sorvari 2017, 282) and is exemplary in its connection to his own 'lifeworld' (Sorvari 2017, 282). Daniel's epiphany, creatively leaning on the force of insurgent memories, refuses guidance by the 'bannisters' of any philosophical or religious tradition. The novel's subsequent probing of his conversion, and the reasons behind it, stimulates the novel's dialogical interest in the lived experience, vernacular religiosity, and existential interrogations of its diverse characters, who are also presented in 'historical and subjective terms' as biographical subjects grappling with difficult life choices in a changing world (Sorvari 2017, 282).

We can also understand *Daniel Stein* as a meditation on one's vocation or purpose, an attempt by Daniel to find his place in the world while honouring his early experiences in the manner of a Maggie Tulliver, Pip, or Holden Caulfield.[1] I will argue that we can understand Daniel Stein as a *Bildungsheld* searching to retain and remediate his wartime experiences of the benefits of linguistic and inter-cultural translation and interpretation in such a way that his religious vocation in a specific time and place, that of contemporary Israel, can become visible and meaningful in its ethical and political effects. Stein's chosen activity as a roving Carmelite monk recalls the hallowed classical Enlightenment conception of *Bildung* in that he will refuse monastic seclusion and demand 'variety of situation', recognizing that he could be 'thwarted and hindered in his development by uniformity of position' (Wulf 2003, 244–5). As described by Margarita Levantovskaya, Daniel becomes a 'trickster translator' (Levantovskaya 2012, 100) who transmutes the artful and strategic practice of translation learnt through dialogical encounters with non-Jewish societies into an abiding interest in potentials for coexistence in the land in which he lives. He embodies an ethos of cohabitation with difference that is singularly appropriate to the religious, ethical, and political challenges that have confronted the state of Israel since 1948.

As a translator and therefore a willing intermediary between cultures, languages, and religions, Daniel Stein also resembles Franco Moretti's depiction of the determined *indecision* of the protean protagonist of the classic *Bildunsgroman* who delays and defers maturity or development if it means the resolution of fluid alternatives and the reification of identity. As with Frédéric in Flaubert's *Sentimental Education*, or Hans Castorp in Thomas Mann's *The Magic Mountain*, Daniel Stein 'holds back' plot rather than accelerating it. He is the champion of mediation', someone who like Frédéric postpones the moment of separation and exclusion (Moretti 2000, 175). Where Moretti understands Flaubert's ironic novel as representing the attempt by a post-Napoleonic youth in an age of reaction to preserve possibility in the face of the prosaic reality of finance capitalism, Daniel Stein is a traumatized subject reluctant to accept nationalism and the isomorphism of a people and a territory as a solution to the quandaries that he encounters. Daniel perhaps articulates the kind of fluid and non-sovereign identity Marianne Hirsch theorizes in *The Voyage In* where she discusses an anti-Oedipal protagonist who resists a 'social reality that violates their psychological needs, defined by separation, discontinuity, alienation, and self-denial' (Hirsch 1983, 27). Here we might also transpose Sarah Graham's suggestion made of the refractory protagonists of American *Bildungsromane* that we are dealing with a subject who evokes their resistance to the world's established order by refusing to 'undertake the rituals that signify the end of youth' such as marriage and accepted forms of professional employment (Graham 2019, 120).

Daniel's creative disdain for normative development as either a model Jewish Israeli citizen or an appropriately domiciled Carmelite monk cannot be distinguished from the work of the novel form as alerting us to the transformative power of memory; as Lukacs put it, 'only in the novel and in certain epic forms resembling the novel does memory occur as a creative force affecting the object and transforming it', in which the 'living present has grown from the stream of [. . . the protagonist's] past life dammed up within his memory' (Lukács 2006, 127). Indeed Daniel Stein's commitment to the benefits of applying complex memories to unprecedented situations and his aligned autodidactic enthusiasm for historical research pose a challenge to James Baer's contention that 'Daniel Stein himself changes little. His fundamental character is fixed; there is nothing "fluid" about him'. For the remainder of this chapter I shall take issue with Baer's contention, citing Jasmina Vojvodić, that Stein 'remains essentially identical to himself' (Baer 2014, 255).

My reading of the novel (perforce in translation), by contrast, enlarges on Levantovskaya's point that the novel's eponymous hero Daniel Stein 'finds a way to bend the limits of his inherited identity through a series of actions that embody metaphorical and literal processes of translation' (Levantovskaya 2012, 98). In making these arguments, I draw on Judith Butler's *Parting Ways: Jewishness and the Critique of Zionism* (2012) to suggest that the innovative, hybridizing hermeneutic practices of Daniel Stein can be theorized as a form of diasporic self-formation, an intervention into the politics of memory with considerable ethical and political potential. I am interested in the way that Daniel's various 'translations' of his diasporic experiences upon arriving in his new homeland, the state of Israel, can help us to re-imagine the significance of Jewish identity and Judaism in the post-Holocaust era. Thus, I argue for Daniel as an optimistic incarnation of the over-determined literary figure of the Wandering Jew. Daniel Stein, or 'Brother Daniel' as he is known after his conversion to Christianity, is no longer the Wandering Jew as accursed exile and rootless cosmopolitan, but a diasporic wanderer returned to the Holy Land in order to be a translator and mediator between schismatic identities and opposed historical narratives.

Daniel Stein, Interpreter tells the story of the Polish-Jewish resistance hero Daniel Stein, a wartime convert to Catholicism. The events of his life, as Ulitskaya informs us in the foreword, 'coincides almost entirely' with the biography of Oswald Rufeisen (1922–98) (5). Rufeisen, or Brother Daniel as he was known, was born in a shtetl in southern Poland. He received a secular, German language education in an elite culturally mixed Polish school once his academic potential became clear. When Poland was occupied in 1939 he escaped with his older brother to Lithuania and then to Belarus. The novel relates how in 1941 Stein organized the escape of three hundred Jews from the Emsk ghetto (a fictionalized version of the Mir ghetto), managing to send nearly all of the Gestapo and local police on a wild-goose chase after non-existent partisans, just before a 'liquidation' of its Jewish population was due to take place. He hid in the surrounding forests and then in a nearby convent, an experience that stimulated his interest in the New Testament and provoked his sudden conversion to Catholicism. After Belarus was liberated by the Red Army, Brother Daniel served as a translator for the NKVD, the Soviet secret police and security apparatus. He subsequently joined partisans in the Belorussian forests and was recognized as a war hero by the Soviet Union and Israel.[2] In 1959 Brother Daniel emigrated to Haifa, Israel, in order to become a Carmelite monk. Resisting a life of seclusion in the Stella Maris monastery, he earned his living as a tour guide and soon became deeply involved in the struggle to reconcile warring faiths by insisting to various bemused or hostile audiences that he was a Jewish Christian just like his Master, the 'Galilean Rabbi' Jesus Christ.

Much of this extraordinary novel explores Daniel Stein's heterodox attempts to recreate an ecumenical Catholic community in Israel modelled on the Church of St James, the first Christian Church in Jerusalem, before Judaism's schism with Christianity. Brother Daniel is a portrayal of a man who, in the author's words, sought to promote 'understanding and reconciliation' between peoples and faiths (Ulitskaya 2011, 5). Ulitskaya's sometimes hagiographic portrayal of Daniel, who leaves none of the lives of people he encounters untouched, encourages us to think of him as a kind of tzaddik in the Hassidic tradition, a charismatic spiritual leader and righteous man, renowned for his saintliness and ability as a mentor. In Hasidic writings the tzaddik is a 'channel' or 'conduit' through which divine grace flows to bring blessings to his followers in particular but also to others with whom he comes in contact.[3] As is appropriate to a charismatic and saintly figure, Daniel is only occasionally a homo-diegetic narrator; more often represented by the testament of others, his character and beliefs are illuminated through letters, transcribed interviews, archival documents, newspaper letters to the editor, talks given to German school children, diaries, correspondence, academic lectures, and his heterodox liturgies. Nonetheless, this is also a classically polyphonic novel: Daniel's views and particularly his decision to convert to Christianity do not go unchallenged.

Following Bakhtin we can think of 'Ulitskaya' the author as an arranger of conflicting discourses and perspectives rather than as an omniscient presence. She appears as a character at the end of each section in the novel, explaining her joy and frustration to her publisher at the progress of the novel, but also the bewilderment accompanying her attempts to understand her paradoxical subject. In the tradition of the contemporary historical novel, which claims epistemological responsibility because, and not in spite of, its imaginative inventions,[4] the author proclaims that the documents used in the book relating to Rufeisen are a blend of the 'authentic' and 'fictitious', since the intention has been to 'allow the truth of literature to transcend the truth of mundane reality' (5). What has been retained, the fictionalized author 'Ludmila Ulitskaya' tells her publisher at the conclusion of the first section, is the Brother Daniel of exemplary or '"non-private" significance' (108).

Reminding us of Maximilien Aue, Daniel Stein poses the ethical and existential challenge of the revenant, the traumatized survivor of inconceivable horrors who returns to question those habitual mores and behaviours undergirded by collective memory and organized faith. However many of the book's Anglophone reviewers have been less troubled by the novel's representation of Brother Daniel's quest to find the true 'kernel' of faith, than the challenge his conversion to Catholicism poses to normative conceptions of Jewish identity.[5] The novel received an antagonistic reception in the English-speaking world from critics who are resistant to its central episode of Christian conversion and wary of the novel's implicit criticism of Israeli policies. This criticism is itself unsurprising: since the rise of political Zionism, an ideology predicated on the rebirth of the Jewish people in a sovereign Jewish state, Jewish identity continues to be aligned with support for the state of Israel. Moreover, as an ethno-nationalist movement prioritizing cultural survival and Jewish renewal, Zionism remains deeply wary of the aggressive universalism of Pauline Christianity and its perceived secular avatar, the post-Enlightenment liberal state incapable of accepting Jewish difference.

Given the burden of this history, some reviews of the novel were vehemently critical of Brother Daniel's conversion to Christianity, while more or less ignoring his post-conversion insistence on his Jewish identity. In *The Washington Post* Melvin Bukiet reads Daniel's conversion as a barely camouflaged millenarian Christian fantasy with anti-Semitic implications:

> the book becomes a wish-fulfilment fantasy of the conversion of the Jews. Worse is the background against which these conversions occur. Lord knows, Israel is no paradise and Israelis no angels, but Ulitskaya dwells on the ugliest aspects of the place and its people [. . .] *Daniel Stein, Interpreter* genuflects to Jewish suffering while diminishing it at every opportunity. (Bukiet 2011).

Similarly Ruth Wajnryb, reviewing *Daniel Stein, Interpreter* in *The Sydney Morning Herald*, reads Daniel Stein's conversion to Catholicism as facile and self-negating, an opportunistic abrogation of Judaism in its darkest hour. Wajnryb goes on to suggest that the success of the book in Russia is only explicable as the pandering of a deracinated and assimilated Russian author, a Jewish convert to Russian Orthodoxy, to her domestic audience:

> My main quibble, though, concerns the level of meaning in the Jewish-Christian motif. Like her hero, Ulitskaya is a Jewish convert to Christianity

and the affinity is palpable. It can't be accidental that Jews in the story do little to warrant praise and a lot to attract opprobrium . . . In Russia, *Daniel Stein, Interpreter* was hailed as a significant literary event and became a bestseller. As Melvin Bukiet remarks: 'Maybe nations listen to what they want to hear.' (Wajnryb 2011)

Wajnryb's is by no means an isolated response to Daniel Stein's fusion of seemingly inimical identities.[6] In this strand of hostility to the novel, with its *ad feminam* critique of Ulitskaya the convert, there are echoes of political Zionism's hostility to diaspora Jewry, a diaspora whose complex accommodations to non-Jewish host societies have been vehemently condemned as assimilationist and self-hating.[7]

In a sense the novel's more hostile reviewers have taken it upon themselves to reinforce the contentious 1962 decision of the Israeli Supreme Court portrayed in the novel, in which a majority rejected Oswald Rufeisen/Daniel Stein's application, as a Holocaust survivor and Jewish refugee, to become a Jewish citizen of Israel while simultaneously proclaiming a Catholic confessional identity. By more or less identifying Brother Daniel as a traitor to Judaism, despite his claims to Jewish nationality, reviewers betray a certain degree of defensiveness about the state of Israel's inability to resolve a problem interrogated by the novel, that of Jewish identity and continuity in dispersion. As the improvised and contested ruling of the court made clear, Jewishness remains a dynamic and interstitial identity that conjoins but is irreducible to religious, ethnic, cultural, and political categories (Levantovskaya 2012, 94–5). It is important to note, as Levantovkskaya points out, that the decision of 1962 defied Jewish Halakhic law based on the long-standing rabbinical position that a Jew remains a Jew despite conversion. Levantovskaya suggests that in its argument for the 'acceptance of the evolutions of the diasporic Jewish self' *Daniel Stein* challenges both the rabbinical view that Jews do not submit to conversion and Zionism's investment in the historically antithetical relationship of Judaism and Christianity (Levantovskaya 2012, 94).

I suspect that critics of the novel intuit that Daniel Stein's claim to Jewish nationality calmly rejects political Zionism's legitimizing claim to be the transformative negation of Jewish exile or *galut*, the triumphant renewal of Jewish religion and culture from the ashes of murdered European Jewry. Standing ready to 'build' the land of Israel after a formative period in the wilderness (299), the hero challenges a dominant narrative of rebirth or achieved national maturity in which Zionism alone is the saviour of a scattered, politically passive, psychologically demoralized and culturally disoriented Jewish diaspora. As one of the foremost theorists of Zionism, Jacqueline Rose, has written of the imaginative investments of the state of Israel, 'This is a nation which desires its exiled potential citizens, diaspora Jewry, to come home, with as much fervour as it banishes the former occupants of its land from their own dream of statehood' (Rose, *States of Fantasy*, cited in Said 2003, 59). Drawing attention to Zionism's 'messianic roots', in *The Question of Zion* Rose suggests that in the minds of its supporters, the state of Israel is the heroic protagonist in a 'national drama of redemption' that will purify a millennial history of endemic anti-Semitic violence (Rose, 2005, 37, 40).

Given the serious charges made against the novel and its author in some reviews, it is important to register Ulitskaya's novel as an unresolved and intellectually passionate *Bildungsroman*, that is as a novel engaging with pressing ideas of an ethical, political, and theological nature. Filtering its explorations through Daniel Stein's marked effects on the characters he meets, I read the novel as a contribution to a sanguine body of theory that has sought to recover the creative possibilities of diaspora as a liminal space of cross-cultural exchange, hybrid forms of life, and varied perspectives on both the projected 'homeland' and host society.[8] As a *Bilduingsheld* with exemplary or indexical functions Daniel Stein embodies and enacts Judith Butler's suggestion in *Parting Ways* that 'there are Jewish resources for the criticism of Israeli state violence' that are religious, ethical, and political. Butler maintains that these resources derive from a diasporic ethos of cohabitation with the non-Jew that she reads in performatively essentialist terms as 'part of the very ethical substance of diasporic Jewishness' (Butler 2012, 1). Embarking on a discussion of Jewishness as a form of translative self-fashioning under diasporic conditions, Butler argues tellingly that for a so-called 'Jewish' resource to be politically and ethically effective it must be translatable, that is, transposable to new contexts, a deceptively simple remark that can be applied to Daniel's ongoing efforts to apply aspects of the diasporic lifeworld he has inhabited since childhood to the unforeseen circumstances he encounters. Butler's theorization of the ethical importance of diaspora as a translatable historical experience of cohabitation can help us to examine Daniel as a *Bildungsheld* in the novelistic tradition. Daniel's character maturation depends heavily upon an understanding of others beyond the familiarity of his locale as he remains highly mobile even within the state of Israel, thus continuing a life of exilic movement, and is committed to a practically inclined ethical orthopraxis rather than doctrinal adherence, emblematizing Butler's point that a 'tradition' is always in some sense a departure from sanctified origins and communitarian frameworks (Butler 2012, 8).

Playing on the metaphor's literal signification in the context of the Zionist linkage of national redemption and land, Butler remarks that 'it is only by "ceding ground"' that an ethical resource from the past can thrive elsewhere and anew, in the 'midst of converging and competing ethical claims' (Butler 2012, 8). The point of Butler's paradoxical intervention is to dispute the 'Zionist monopoly on Jewishness' by theorizing diaspora Judaism as a vital and creative translative activity, one that exceeds identarian frameworks which define Jewishness according to a variety of religious-genealogical, communal, or territorial predicates. These predicates usually refuse an individual's capacity to judge their own complex affiliations to an inherited identity. In a dialectical twist, Butler argues that from the perspective of diaspora theory *galut* or the long period of Jewish exile should no longer be considered a fallen realm that needs rectification and restoration through return to the homeland; rather the 'idea of diaspora', in all of its multiple ways of being, should be 'brought back' to Israel/Palestine as a way of thinking about cohabitation, binationalism, and the critique of state violence (Butler 2012, 15). To bring the ethical principles of the Jewish diaspora back to a homeland imagined as the rectification of diasporic exile would not, according to Butler, be a supercilious secular and liberal prescription for redressing Israel's oppression of the Palestinians, criticisms typically dismissed as anti-Semitic or anti-Zionist. Rather the return of diasporic modes of existence to Israel/Palestine would be a way of recognizing that despite Zionist hegemony, diasporic ideals *already function there* as a sub-national ethos capable of bringing peoples with tragic and entwined histories into a conciliatory conversation (Butler 2012, 15, my emphasis).

Using Butler's prism of interpretation, the character of Daniel Stein can be interpreted as a diasporic Jew and protean *Bildungsheld* questioning the determinative power of genealogical origins in the manner of the ethically maturing Maximilien Aue, someone 'constantly in a state of self-departure' and thus affirming his Jewishness as newly meaningful by virtue of his passage through heterogeneous diasporic circumstances, including, almost impossibly, his own conversion to Christianity.[9] How does he do this?

Well, Daniel transmutes the various interpretive practices and ethical inclinations of his diasporic Judaism, some below the threshold of conscious conviction, into his heterodox ethico-religious creed. In his own person Daniel reinvigorates the possibility of a Jewish Christianity that complicates identarian assumptions. Daniel's simultaneous capacity to bear witness to the birth of a new nation, and to record the process of dispossession and exclusion that national formation entails, is neither expressed in the sanctimonious vocabulary of rationalist secular critique nor does it emanate from a secure Jewish subject position. Rather Daniel's quest for a reconciled Judaic Christianity is an interpretive translation of his polycultural diasporic formation. In an Israeli context in which a majoritarian ethno-national state has recently come into being, Daniel's demand for recognition as a Jewish Christian can be interpreted as the 'ethical movement of responding to the claims made by those who are not fully recognizable as part of the "nation"' (Butler 2012, 18).

Returning to the distilled fictional 'truth' of Daniel Stein as a literary character, we can identify a representative figure whose syncretic geographical and cultural origins, subsequent wanderings, and conversion to Catholicism are not simply adventitious or biographical-historical events. We can also remark Daniel's story as a microcosm of the expulsions, enforced and chosen conversions and assimilations, and subsequent cultural liminality of the post-biblical Jewish diaspora. A figure of the multiplicity of Jewish history, Daniel incarnates the existentially layered or palimpsestial protagonist of the *Bildungsroman*, reminding us once more that 'everything that happens to us leaves its traces, everything contributes imperceptibly to our development' (McWilliams 2009, 7).

In the first third of the novel, Ulitskaya's Daniel Stein is something of a Lukacsian middle character and observer-narrator in the sense that his loyalties and affiliations are plural and indeterminate. He is also a mixed or liminal character like Stevens and Aue, poised between worlds and commitments, as his wanderings traverse the complex cultural geography and internal boundaries of diasporic Jewry. Born in a poverty-stricken village in 1922 that once belonged to the Austro-Hungarian empire, has been part of the Principality of Galicia, and is now situated in Poland, Daniel is the son of a déclassé petit bourgeois Polish-Jewish mother and an aspirational Germanophile Austrian-Jewish father, a former soldier for the Austro-Hungarian empire who considered himself Jewish, attended synagogue, but was also loyal to Central European culture and the German language.

Daniel Stein, given the German name 'Dieter' by his father, must navigate complex cultural co-ordinates, including the tension between the traditionalism of Yiddish-speaking East European Jewish culture and the more urban, acculturated and upwardly mobile post-Haskalah Judaism of central and Western Europe (Ulitskaya 2011, 45).[10] In Daniel's formative years a cleavage emerges between the pragmatic motivations of Jews emigrating to countries like the United States, and those 'enthused by Zionism' who go to Palestine (45). Retracing the religious heterogeneity of Ashkenazi Judaism, in 1939 the seventeen-year-old Dieter Stein leaves occupied Poland and finds himself in Wilno, as Vilnius was then called, a traditionalist or Mitnagdim city that was then 50 per cent Jewish. However, Jews in his home country of Poland on the whole belonged mainly to the Hassidic tradition, which put great store by Kabbalah and expected the imminent advent of the Messiah. As a 'covert Jew' (145) or converso and then a serving Catholic priest in Poland and Israel, Daniel straddles a variety of cultures – Polish Catholic, Yiddish Jewish, German-speaking Central European, and Hebraic Israeli – while belonging exclusively to none of them.

In his work as a translator and cultural intermediary for the Gestapo and NKVD, Daniel is both victim and perpetrator, a trickster-messenger who survives his journey with Odyssean guile. Bearing in mind Daniel's allegorical condensation of recent Jewish history, and his mediating function as a *Bildungsheld*, I read his conversion to Catholicism through a literary prism as indicative of a curatorial and 'quixotic' desire to continue his own fluid, picaresque adventure of Jewish identity without succumbing to the ethnic nationalism that has inflicted genocidal violence upon his people and destroyed the polyglot world he once knew. Like the Scheherazade figure 'Nathan the Wise' in Lessing's famous Enlightenment play of the same name (*Nathan der Weise* 1779), when confronted with the chilling question of the one true faith, Dieter's conversion is not a decision in favour of a particularist identity but the prolongation of his Jewish self as a Marrano, a mediator and astute critic inside and outside the house of Judaism. In converting to Catholicism Daniel retraces and idealistically affirms a diasporic history of pragmatic accommodation to host cultures, like the many Converso and Marrano Jews of Spain and Portugal in the late fifteenth and sixteenth centuries who converted to Christianity under threat of death or expulsion but maintained a cryptic Jewish identity. In the Marrano tradition Daniel reveals a scepticism towards the central tenets of both Judaism and Christianity, denies the pivotal Jewish doctrine of the unique election of Israel, and rejects all religious particularism. He thus reaffirms a tradition of comparativism and critical detachment that culminated in the epochal philosophy of Spinoza (Gerber 1992, 20).[11]

Within the novel some of the Jewish characters, including Daniel's own brother and a former friend in the Zionist youth group Akiva, read Daniel's conversion as nonsensical or a betrayal. The secular Jewish partisan who saves his life, Isaak Gantman, interprets his initial withdrawal to monastic life as an escapist impulse, originating in a traumatized refusal to 'accept the kind of actions he had observed' (80). I think more revealing is the pre-conversion 'Dieter' Stein's prophetic observation, upon accepting the position of interpreter for the Belorussian police, that the 'opportunity of mediating gave me self-respect, and it was only by doing something for other people that I could salve my conscience and retain my integrity' (92). Later, while working for the Gestapo as a translator of Polish and Belorussian into German, Dieter Stein affirms his desire to '[work] with the local population' and to exploit opportunities for intervention through (mis)translation, including deflecting suspicion from those seen to have links with the partisans, as a counterbalance to his feelings of 'complicity' as an employee of the perpetrators (148). As a Jewish Christian, Daniel continues the converso tradition of combining Christian rites with Jewish fideism, of deriving spiritual succour and intellectual sustenance from his Jewish heritage while departing from a conception of Jewish identity defined in religious, communal, or national terms. Brother Daniel tells his nephew Alon, a militaristic young Zionist, that having come into contact with many soldiers, 'German, Russian, Polish, all sorts, [. . .] in all these years the only thing that gladdened me was that I was an interpreter. I was at least enabling people to reach agreement between themselves and I was not shooting anybody' (55). Echoing Levantovskaya and Butler's articulation of diasporic Jewishness as a translative activity that ethically metaphorizes the quotidian work of linguistic and cultural translation, Brother Daniel's commitment to his Jewish identity can only be expressed in its dissemination, by abandoning its orthodox religious beliefs and identarian predicates while simultaneously retaining Judaism's dynamic psychic life. This psychic life includes messianic longing and passionate idealism, and a language and text-centred sensibility that engenders enthusiasm for the unfettered interpretation of canonical theology, a commitment to creative translation that can serve the diverse needs of his community, broadly conceived.

Brother Daniel's translation of his Jewish origins into his Christian faith is powerfully expressed in the novel's pivotal conversion episode. Having witnessed untold atrocities Daniel realizes he can no longer believe in a conception of divine justice. However, in reading the stories and parables of Jesus in the New Testament Daniel's Jewish faith is paradoxically strengthened and revitalized, as he realizes that the 'God suffering together with the Jews was my God' (187). Jesus, the Jewish Jesus, reveals to Daniel that the problems dealt with in the Gospels were 'Jewish problems' associated with the land for which he 'was so homesick'; for Daniel the Cross of Christ is not a punishment from God but the path to salvation and resurrection, which he identifies with the 'cross my people bears and with all I had seen and experienced', an understanding of suffering that he also finds in the Jewish religion (187). As Levantovskaya comments, in this passage Stein's interpretive 'crossing' between Judaism and Christianity is ultimately unclear in terms of temporal precedence or spiritual hierarchy since Jewish suffering is read through Christian iconography and the rhetoric of corporeal suffering while the Christ figure is incorporated within the Judaic narrative of the Messiah, in the style of the Synoptic Gospels (Levantovksaya 2012, 101).

What is most remarkable in Daniel Stein's idiosyncratic translation of the Jesus of the Gospels into a Jewish discursive idiom is its transgressive historicity, its embrace of an entwined Jewish Christian history in the Holy Land and the interpretive problems thereby engendered, including that the real faith of the Jewish Jesus predates Pauline Christianity. In his self-forming attempts to understand the Jewish background of his master Jesus Christ, Daniel, and his faithful disciple, a young Catholic German woman named Hilda Engel, who wishes to atone for her grandfather's Nazism, take a deep interest in Professor Neuhaus and his innovative investigations in Judaic studies at the Hebrew University. Neuhaus' lectures, as reported by Hilda and other characters throughout the novel, explore the complexities and ironies of Jewish interpretive traditions in diaspora, including the tension between narrative-based Haggadah and Jewish Law, and between Judaism's strict monotheistic iconoclasm and its rich visual traditions. As Neuhaus explains, 'the immense vitality of Judaism' is founded on two contradictory principles: the strict regulation of Jewish behaviour found in the *Mitzvah* (commandments) and their subsequent codification in Rabbinic Halakhic Law (247); and the principle of 'complete and totally unfettered freedom of thought . . . effectively a total absence of prohibitions on intellectual investigation' in which everything is open to discussion and 'there is no dogma'. In Judaism, 'heresy, if not wholly absent, is nevertheless very diluted and blurred' (248).

Daniel, an interpretive bricoleur, the improvising autodidactic protagonist of a *Bildungsroman*, seeks to apply the two principles of Judaism, the quotidian-regulative and the Midrashic-hermeneutic, to his understanding of Jewish Christianity, and he does so with a cheerfully argumentative disregard for the dangerously heterodox implications of his interpretations. On the one hand he is profoundly interested in the Jewish Christ as a practitioner of Jewish Law. He identifies with a 'primal Christianity' that has 'inherited Judaism's attitude towards orthopraxis', stressing observance of the commandments and 'dignified behaviour' (289), thus rejecting theological speculation and asceticism since Daniel refuses to accept the distinction between 'life on a higher and lower, a spiritual and material plane'. He embraces Christ as a 'Jewish teacher' who said nothing unknown to the world before his coming and thanks to whom the 'commandments of the Torah were made known to the rest of the non-Jewish world' (214). As an adherent of the Jewish Christ, Daniel does not recognize Christian dogma since the Nicene Council: he refuses to accept the Holy Trinity or the cult of the Madonna which, as a Jewish monotheist, he considers later impositions of Greek rationalism and classical Paganism (285). He condemns the Catholic Church as a Greek-influenced, imperial institution that has fatally rejected its Jewish influences and thus its initial pluralism, a critique of the legacy of Pauline Christianity that reprises the philo-Semitic views of thinkers of the 'radical Enlightenment' such as John Toland (1670–1722).

Because his time in a Zionist youth group has inculcated a profound love of the land of the Bible, Daniel exclaims that Christ cannot be found in 'Church doctrines which appeared one thousand years after his death' but only 'here!' in the Holy Land as mediated by the profound narrative imagination of the Gospels (270). Rejecting the Christian logic of the New Testament as superseding Judaism's pharisaic legalism, Daniel avers that it is a matter of deep regret that Greek-inspired Pauline Christianity has repudiated Jewish influences, meaning that the Jewish emphasis on strict monotheism is 'more evident in Islam' which Daniel views inclusively (in the spirit of Toland and liberal Jewish thinkers such as Abraham Geiger, 1810–74) as a 'kind of interpretation of the Jewish Christian religion' (135–6). On the other hand Brother Daniel's commitment to the universalist 'Jesus [who] opens hearts' (392) and his desire to belong, like the Renaissance humanist Desiderius Erasmus, to a 'catholic' diaspora signifying 'unity, all-inclusiveness, global reach' rather that fealty to Rome, augurs an equally critical response to the exclusivist imaginary of political Zionism which has produced a secular version of Jewish election (289) and which seeks fealty from the Jewish diaspora. His own ecumenical 'catholic' community offers succour to a range of people whose complex affiliations leave them alienated or bereft in the newly founded Jewish state, including Polish Catholic women married to Jewish Israeli men, baptized Soviet Jews and other Orthodox Christians, and Christian Arabs.

As a near impossible identity, a 'Jew and a Christian', Daniel comes to Israel in 1959 in a quest to reprise a repressed history of entwined religious genealogies. He soon finds himself in a state of enthusiastic agitation known as the 'Jerusalem syndrome' which affects 'believers of all faiths when they first come to Israel' (77). Brother Daniel's Jerusalem syndrome is not, however, excitement at a primordial return to his Jewish origins, but a humanist moment of phenomenal wonder and archaeological curiosity about the extraordinary geographical and spiritual diversity of an ancient land, since 'everything was born here' (181), and 'the history of humanity is concentrated in this place' (363). Daniel's observations about the Holy Land that he will spend his life exploring continue to be imbued with, indeed to creatively translate, a diasporic Jewish experience of mobility and cohabitation with the other. Again we note that deferral of identity (his epiphany is not a mature realization of his authentic but artificially repressed identity as sought by many an emigrant to Israel) and the reluctance to embrace a defined cultural or social position is a hallmark of Daniel as a receptive and inquisitive *Bildungsheld*.

Once more, but now in a cultural and political rather than theological register, Daniel's interpretation of the situation in which he finds himself risks the opprobrium of the majority since his detailed interpretive mediations refuse to affirm a particular ethnocentric subjectivity or nationalist imaginary. Suggesting the insufficiency of the Zionist framework of Jewish emigration to Israel as a 'return' to a homeland, Daniel Stein comments to his fellow Polish priest Wladylsaw Klech that 'the picture I had in mind of the country I so loved from afar bore absolutely no relation to reality' but what 'I have seen has greatly exceeded my expectations' (77–8). As a Jewish Christian Daniel is impressed by the extraordinary diversity of spiritual forms and liturgical practices he encounters (94). Brother Daniel's 'Jerusalem syndrome' also entails a rejection of political Zionism's hostility to the Palestinians, Arabs, and other minority communities in the land of Yeretz Israel. Now embracing the ethical possibilities of his wanderings, his heretofore contingent trajectory, in which his own survival and that of his Jewish brethren owed so much to language acquisition, and having befriended a number of Arab Christian and Druze communities who afforded his small parish the ability to continue worshipping Christ, the chameleonic Brother Daniel is delighted at the possibilities of further adventures in linguistic and cultural translation. He is in raptures when he meets a local French-Catholic monk and linguist, Julien Sommers, who is compiling a Hebrew-Arabic dictionary (77). Embracing the possibility of translating his picaresque mobility into a meaningful form of living, Daniel eschews ascetic monasticism and becomes a tour guide, with detailed knowledge of the botanic and archaeological history of the region. Translating his own upbringing in a polyglot empire into an interest in the diverse cultural geography of his adopted land, Daniel is delighted to find, for example, that his Arab Christian friend Musa's grandfather designed the Persian Gardens of the Baha'i Temple in nearby Haifa (133).

When Daniel takes an interest in the local Druze who 'conceal their true views and adapt externally to the morals and religion of those around them' and who 'have no homeland except their doctrine', he does so mindful of Judaism's creative and resilient post-expulsion history. He explains to Hilda that Druze's adaptive faith in dispersion is how it should work for Christians too, 'that is what was intended, only it didn't work out' (113). Once more, and in the spirit of demotic interaction that drives Stevens and Aue, by working with 'local populations' as an intermediary between the Israeli state, the Hebrew-speaking majority, and the Roman Catholic Church, Daniel's Jewish origins and his contemporary difficulties as a Jewish Christian spurned by both Jewish and Christian communities allow him to appreciate the challenges of assimilating to a national culture. Like him, his Catholic parishioners are 'people displaced from their homes', some of them ill, crazy, their 'children disoriented' (103).

Much of Daniel's time in Israel entails him working through and re-animating his exilic and cosmopolitan heritage in order to bear witness to the complexity and fragility of the Holy Land. The affinities and observations that result are provocative but also profoundly humanizing when transposed to an Israeli context. For example, as a reminder of his Central European origins, Daniel clearly enjoys living in the vicinity of Haifa, a polyglot cosmopolitan city with a large Arab minority, a locale he finds preferable to Tel Aviv, the historical centre of the Zionist project. Anxious about Israel's vulnerable situation, he reiterates Israeli Jewish fears that Israel will be 'inundated' by the Arab world (55). However, his protégé Hilda also notes that the family of a Catholic Arab botanist named Musa used to own the plot of land where there is now a 'prison for Palestinians [the Damun prison] who are fighting the Jews in all sorts of illegal ways' (125). A reader interested in indicative reflection might note that this ironically tinged discussion of Palestinian incarceration on what was once Arab land may be a comment on the supposed illegality of Second World War partisan activities and Daniel's own periods of internment in Nazi-occupied Europe.

Daniel, like Maximilien Aue, transmutes his traumatic experiences into a heightened awareness of the horrors of war that necessarily touches on the cycles of retribution that characterize the Israeli-Palestinian conflict while refusing an interpretive framework that privileges Israeli 'security' and an ontology of Jewish victimhood. As someone keenly aware of the dehumanizing effects of violence, having worked intimately with perpetrators who destroyed their own souls in the process, Daniel cannot accept any conception of just or righteous warfare. Hence, he warns his nephew Alon against becoming a commando in the Israeli Defence Forces:

> [there is] nothing more vile and unnatural in this world than war. How it perverts not only life but even death – Death in war is bloody, full of animal fear, always violent, and what I was obliged to witness – mass murder, the execution of Jews and partisans – was fatally destructive also for those carrying out the atrocities. (120–21)

After the 1967 war annexing East Jerusalem and the West Bank, Daniel, like his friend Musa, understands through the experiential prism of failed, costly historical conquests that Israel has become a 'hostage to fortune'. Seizing territory has not resolved the issue but 'complicated it' (129).

In a reply to a letter in the *Haifa News*, responding to an outraged Israeli Jewish citizen upset by the presence of a small congregation of Jewish Christians, given the 'war, persecution, and death' Christianity has visited upon the Jews, Brother Daniel, now the director of the Association of Jewish Christians, affirms that it was Christ who preached forgiveness as well as many things familiar to Jews from the Torah (214):

> The land of Israel is a place of great holiness not only for the Jews who live here today – By Christians and Jewish Christians it is venerated no less than by Jews who profess Judaism, to say nothing of our brother Arabs who have settled this land, lived here for a thousand years, and whose ancestors' bones lie side by side with those of our own ancestors. When our land withers and is rolled up like an old carpet, when dry bones arise, we will be judged not by the language we prayed in but by whether we found compassion and mercy in our hearts. That is all our organization has been set up to achieve. It has no other aim. (215)

What is noteworthy is that in response to an understandable yet problematic grievance, Daniel translates and reformulates his palimpsestial fascination with the Holy Land as the birthplace of the three monotheisms, into a suggestively idiosyncratic political vision that transcends schismatic identities. As a dynamic translator who has literally found a 'common language', Hebrew, for his ecumenical liturgy with polyglot practitioners, he metaphorically discovers a common ethical vocabulary, and a series of shared memories in which attachment to the Holy Land can be articulated beyond communal frameworks, and insular religious traditions. As a figure of sympathy, compassion, and love, the Jewish Jesus examples ethical orthopraxis as a matrix for dialogue between the three monotheisms. Daniel/Christ's belief that the most important thing in human behaviour is not to do evil to one another and to show sympathy and compassion installs the ongoing and experimental process of achieving human coexistence rather than canonized articles of faith as being at the very core of character formation, of his personal *Bildung*.

Daniel Stein, as I have argued, is a reprise of the figure of the Wandering Jew in the guise of a cultural intermediary, a hero for our times who imaginatively translates the significance of his diasporic experiences into an ethos of cohabitation that might yet offer a salve to the religious, ethical, and political challenges confronting the state of Israel. The novel offers an irenic vision of coexistence in a land in which the historical logic of supersession, in which an inferior people or religious belief is supplanted by a superior, has finally been repudiated by a compassionate response to the claims of others present and past. As Jed Esty points out, the *Bildungsroman* as a historically motivated genre 'can and usually does project an array of overlapping chronotopic possibilities' (Esty 2012, 56). Daniel's diasporic vision of the Holy Land, as a palimpsest of historical communities, envisages a land in which supercessionist violence can no longer be enacted by Christians towards Jews, or militaristic Zionists towards Palestinians; implicitly Daniel's vision of historical and future coexistence also rejects an Islamist interpretation of Jews as mere intruders and sojourners in Muslim lands.

Daniel's prophetic political vision of humane coexistence, derived from his imaginative linguistic, cultural, and theological practice of translating against the grain of communitarian frameworks of interpretation, resonates with the 'translation zone' of literary comparativism discussed by Emily Apter. Indebted to Benjamin's seminal essay 'The Task of the Translator' Apter enthuses that the translated text is always something more than a reproduction of the original: 'Cast as an act of love, and as an act of disruption, translation becomes a means of repositioning the subject in the world and in history' (Apter 2006, 6). In order to achieve a re-conception of what might be possible in a fractious age of warring identities, Daniel reprises many of the classic precepts of *Bildung* as an ethic of self-cultivation and associative life, in which the 'first law is cultivate thyself and the second is: influence others by what thou art' (cited in Castle 2006, 40).

Chapter 4

UNOFFICIAL EDUCATION AND THE PROMOTION OF ACTIVE READERSHIP IN TWO HOLOCAUST-THEMED NOVELS FOR CHILDREN

HITLER'S DAUGHTER AND *THE BOY IN THE STRIPED PYJAMAS*

In this chapter I argue that two significant recent influential historical novels about the Holocaust, *Hitler's Daughter* (1999) and *The Boy in the Striped Pyjamas* (2006), reprise the genre traits of the *Bildungsroman* or novel of development and can be regarded as remarkably effective in engaging a younger readership. Both novels, intended for children and younger adolescent readers, are focused on initially sequestered child protagonists from a perpetrator culture who are unable to fully understand their circumstances but undergo formative experiences by leaving 'home', legible both as a physical domicile and a site of indoctrination and repression. As they journey away from a limited conception of biological family the novel's protagonists are able to reject constricting modes of social conditioning that repress authentic self-expression, curiosity, and impartial ethical judgement. In both novels the protagonists transform their perception of their circumstances by becoming resourceful bricoleurs, unearthing imaginative possibilities in their immediate environment that allow them to forestall emotional isolation and the dehumanization of designated 'Others' such as the Jews. While *The Boy in the Striped Pyjamas* has been read as reinforcing the myth of German innocence, I will suggest that its typological representation of a 'dangerous family' and its implied affirmation of Bruno's explorative instincts, empathetic capacities, and commitment to friendship, helps to foster the moral character and compassionate value system of the younger reader while affording them greater recognition of the 'banal ideologies and institutions occupied by the perpetrators' (Rider 2013, 65). Given the polarizing reception in particular of *The Boy in the Striped Pyjamas*, in the interpretation to follow I will remain mindful that the texts under analysis are not attempts to straightforwardly represent the past. Rather they encourage an energetic hermeneutics of indicative inference in which the unorthodox or 'unofficial' education of the protagonist points the reader towards the importance of asking difficult questions, challenging conventional mindsets, refusing the poisonous rhetoric of binary differences, and prolonging the fluidity, play instinct, and receptivity of youth as a life calling rather than a symptom of immaturity.

But first some context as to why these two novels and other children's fiction dealing with the Second World War and the Holocaust attract so much scrutiny. Scholars and educators are still grappling with a series of interrelated problems in teaching the events of the Holocaust and other violent and traumatic histories to children. How can children be taught about historical conflicts involving genocidal atrocities and other crimes against humanity in such a way that their understanding and capacity for ethical agency is enhanced rather than overwhelmed? In various disciplinary areas including museum studies, there is a conversation as to whether sorrow and empathy for the suffering of historical victims are sufficient to recognize the dynamic and therefore less readily legible subject positions of perpetrator, accomplice, and bystander in contemporary geopolitical contexts. As will become clearer, there is also a sometimes heated discussion about whether the purpose of children's historical fiction is to accurately edify children about the past or to stimulate the civic virtues and ethical awareness necessary to promote a contemporary human rights culture that might assist in combating authoritarianism and mass conformism.

In this chapter I will suggest that the *Bildungsroman* as a genre that helps to 'educate [...] the reader by portraying the education of the protagonist' (Hirsch 1979, 298) can help to mediate these alternatives. This polymorphic genre, which is congenial to both adventure-time and the more leisurely discussion of ideas, has been reinvented by children's authors as a genre of historical fiction that can create resonances between violent pasts and present-day geopolitical contexts. I would suggest that in the hands of authors such as Jackie French and John Boyne, the *Bildungsroman,* with its focus on the ongoing and transhistorical task of coming of age, proves adept at elucidating the travails of young people and their quest for self-formation in the absence of reliable ethical norms, supportive social structures, and educational institutions capable of catering to their psychological needs. A reconceived notion of the genre as dedicated to the incomplete but ethically rewarding journey of a younger protagonist confronted with social oppression in a range of historical contexts, can, as we've discussed, help the reader to unpick unhelpful categorical distinctions between totalitarianism and liberal democracy, and civilization and barbarism.

We can now extend our discussion of the contemporary historical *Bildungsroman* as a species of problem fiction by examining its contribution to an important pedagogical problematic surrounding historical literature for children, the need on the one hand to 'get the facts right' no matter what the genre (Gray 2014, 123, citing Cesarani) and on the other to demonstrate how the Holocaust is relevant to our era both globally and locally, a capacitating knowledge which Geoffrey Short argues to be the 'necessary condition of successful Holocaust education' (cited in Gray 2014, 123). Teaching students how to evaluate historical representations that can make oscillating claims to be both faithful to the documented past and ethically rewarding by virtue of symbolism and metaphor alerts us to the fiercely contested status of historical fiction for children. Valerie Tripp, for example, defends historical fiction for child readers as a mode of emotional socialization, arguing that good historical fiction for children 'exercises a child's imagination through a vicarious experience. It leads children to use themselves and their own lives as comparisons to the characters that lived long ago and often, far away, to reflect on their own experience, to ask their families questions. It awakens awareness, perks up perception, sparks conversations' (Tripp 2011). Lydia Kokkola by contrast, worries about texts that are politically correct but historically inaccurate, that 'spare the child' distress but are therefore misleading (Kokkola 2013, 305), a sceptical posture that informs the vituperative reaction to *The Boy in the Striped Pyjamas*. The important variable for Kokkola in assessing children's historical fiction about the Holocaust is not the text's accessibility or its creation of an active reader, but rather the prevalence of Holocaust denialism. For Kokkola, the dangers of the political context urge the precept that a fiction about the Holocaust for children has a 'greater moral obligation' to be historically accurate than fiction dealing with other catastrophic events (Kokkola 2013, 18).

A related problem in evaluating children's literature about the Holocaust is the barely traversable differences in expectation by invested reading communities including professional historians, educators, child readers, and other lay audiences. There is a mostly scholarly conversation that tends to examine Holocaust-themed literature and film through the prism of what has been deemed 'Holocaust etiquette', protocols of interpretation that emphasize historical accuracy, fidelity to survivor testimony, the paramount danger of denialism and anti-Semitism, and recognition of the uniqueness of the Holocaust (Teo 2015, 7). As Sue Vice argues in her important book *Holocaust Fiction* (2000), many people still feel that imaginative fiction about the Holocaust is in danger of making a 'fiction of the Holocaust' (Vice 2000, 6). In practice this defensive wariness, which tends to assume a child reader who lacks formal awareness and is passively awaiting indoctrination, has made applying immanent criteria of aesthetic judgement, including the insight of genre studies that literary form has its own narrative strategies and intertextual frames of reference, extraordinarily difficult to apply.

As a contribution to Sue Vice's emphasis on immanent practical criticism rather than moralistic strictures, and as a response to the literary ecology that now confronts us which includes genre fiction such as children's and YA literature, historical fiction blended with popular romance, and multimodal forms such as the graphic novel, in this chapter I will reprise Valerie Tripp's endorsement of the role of historical fiction for children in starting searching conversations about the relationship of past and present, and ponder the narrative strategies that are proving fruitful in engaging children and young people who might otherwise be distressed, bewildered, or even vicariously traumatized by the enormity of historical events such as the Second World War and the Holocaust. I have chosen to focus on two prominent, highly regarded works of the Second World War and Holocaust-themed children's fiction, Jackie French's *Hitler's Daughter* (1999) and John Boyne's best-selling 'fable' *The Boy in the Striped Pyjamas*, originally published in 2006. Both novels share the traits of the *Bildungsroman* including an emphasis on trial by ordeal, and the story of a young protagonist weathering difficult and varied experiences. Both novels, I would suggest, also attempt to avoid the supposedly jejune dimensions of that genre described by Franco Morretti in his analyses of Victorian examples of the *Bildungsroman* such as *Jane Eyre* and *Great Expectations*, where, as in a fairy tale, childhood wish fulfilment sees the protagonist achieve ripe maturity and social position, and where the world has meaning '*only if* it is relentlessly divided into good and evil' (Moretti 2000, p.187).

Many critics feel that French's novel, with its embedded narrative structure which generates a heuristic conversation between past and present, and its metafictional focus on the importance of storytelling in witnessing injustice and making sense of shared experiences, is much more successful as a pedagogical text and carefully researched historical fiction than Boyne's unlikely and to some readers outrageously false depiction of a German boy ingénue who understands next to nothing of Nazism, anti-Semitism, and the function of the concentration camps. I will suggest, however, that Boyne's hugely popular but much-derided novel is pedagogically defensible and aesthetically rewarding in that it gently but effectively introduces children to the banal ideologies and ordinary mindsets that are enabling contexts for the commission or at least toleration of crimes against humanity while, contrastively, indicating the need to cultivate an active character that questions and interrogates accepted truths while affirmatively prioritizing sociability and friendship. I will argue that through the resonant curiosity of nine-year-old Bruno, *TBSP* construes a young reader who can turn their attention to contemporary political questions including the political legitimacy of fences and borders and the importance of play and mobility as fundamental human rights.

My suggestion is that both novels draw on the tropes of the *Bildungsroman* as an indicative genre which, as we have seen, affirms movement through social space, keeping in mind that as a capacious literary form the *Bildungsroman* has an affinity to the quest narrative (Golban 2018, 118). As we have seen the *Bildungsroman* is predicated on the need to leave home and forge unusual fellowships in the search for understanding; its guiding intuition derived from its Enlightenment heritage is that human beings are edified by relational encounters and variety of experience. In these narratives, we are inducted into the adult world through the initially innocent and sequestered but increasingly inquisitive perspective of a child protagonist who resists the naturalization of social hierarchies and the linguistic reification of other human groups. While the child's journey towards mature understanding of the historical situation they find themselves is ongoing, the questing child protagonist develops a probing orientation towards the claims of adult authority figures and, in the manner of Stevens and Aue, becomes a resourceful picaro, a self-forming personality who rejects a developmental logic of adulthood as requiring psychic repression and disenchantment as regards the feasibility of one's ideals. Preserving a sense of wonder, the child protagonist desires emotionally authentic modes of relating to the natural and social worlds in their phenomenal diversity. It is important to note, as theorists of the female-authored novels of development have done, that the *Bildungsroman* has been profoundly affected by feminist standpoints so that in many of its literary manifestations it does not represent a linear progression towards functional citizenship, hegemonic masculinity, and submission to the reality principle but instead inclines to defer predetermined outcomes and reprise the fluid imaginative creativity and pre-Oedipal attachments of childhood. For questing child protagonists in these novels such as Heidi, Mark, and Bruno, this deferral suggests a significant degree of resistance to differentiation as a sovereign and individuated subject with diminished relational sympathies (Abel et al. 1983, 27).

Both novels work adroitly as edifying historical fictions as they do not take the malignant evil that overdetermines most representations of the perpetrators as an established fact. The child protagonist does not find themselves immediately at the mercy of evil and incomprehensible forces since they themselves are born into a perpetrator culture that has prosaic rhythms and is present to them initially as a form of unquestioned common sense. Instead the narrative begins with the gradually maturing protagonist experiencing a more localized and even mundane discord with an increasingly 'dangerous family'.[1] In both novels an intensifying disagreement with adult authority figures in the family encourages the questioning child protagonist to reject an oppressive patriarchal *imago* whose rhetoric is closely associated with the mendacity of nationalist discourses. Having left 'home', a crucible for social conditioning, the questing child subject of the *Bildungsroman* can then deconstruct the aura of the patriarch as a symbolic figurehead who insists on emotional repression and naturalizes hierarchies in general. The beginning of critical autonomy for the child is not increased knowledge as to the total situation which remains obscured, but the ability to review and evaluate 'an extensive repertoire of experiences, expressions, and emotional practices' (Frevert et al. 2014, 8) that define permissible affective interaction and self-expression within the family, which were once learnt uncritically. The process of emotional (un)learning allows the child subject to question the belief systems perpetrated by repressive authorities, celebrate their own instinct for explorative play, performance, and disguise, construct alternative imaginative worlds, value friendship as a transcendental prerogative, and enjoy the pleasures of thinking and reflection. As Sara Ahmed reminds us, emotions imbued with reflexivity are transformative as they 'open up futures, in the ways they involve different orientations to others' (Ahmed 2014, 202).

The novels

We begin with the first novel in what is now known, with the publication of *Goodbye, Mr Hitler* (2017) as her 'Hitler Trilogy', *Hitler's Daughter* (1999) by Jackie French, a hugely successful Australian children's author. French has authored over 140 books and many have won national and international awards in a range of categories. The internationally lauded *Hitler's Daughter* won the Children's Book Council of Australia's Book of the Year (2000) for younger readers and more recently *Pennies for Hitler* (2012) won the NSW Premier's Young People's History Prize in 2013. *Hitler's Daughter* (1999) is about four schoolchildren in contemporary rural Australia. One day they decide to play 'The Game' of storytelling while waiting for a school bus. Anna starts telling the story of Heidi, the secret daughter of Adolf Hitler, who is known to her as 'Duffi' in the novel, a reminder of his avuncular status with the German people. Heidi has been brought up in seclusion on Hitler's country estate by her governess Fraulein Gelber, and her cook Frau Mundt, during the critical years of the Second World War. This is not only because she is Hitler's illegitimate child but because she is a source of shame, 'small like him, and dark', with a limp and unsightly birthmark. Banished and excluded, Heidi does not represent the perfect specimen of the 'Aryan race', the fantasy of tall children with blue eyes and blond hair (French 1999, 12). While the children listening such as Mark and Little Tracey assume the demonic Hitler was incapable of love, Anna, a surrogate for an implied author who wants to edify rather than condescend to children, prefers to preserve the enigmatic layers of her suspenseful story, remarking only that it was unclear whether Hitler loved her or not, but that Heidi 'always hoped he did' (French 1999, 12). Over time Heidi comes to realize that her evasive father will not acknowledge her because of her perceived defects. She cries at night over the fact she doesn't resemble the dolls with long blond hair brought to her by her father, since they are beautiful and she is not.

She also gleans various historical facts, however piecemeal and unwittingly, from working-class Germans appointed to her care. From her cook Frau Mundt she learns that many Germans supported Hitler because he promised the unemployed jobs and that he would restore German national pride. Hitler didn't rule by terror alone, he had mass support even before and after his rise to power; as his motorcade passed by in 1932 Frau Mundt remarks that her younger self was a member of the cheering crowds enthralled by his charisma: 'it was so wonderful – thousands of people, oh, so many people cheering' (French 1999, 29). As the war drags on and the fortunes of the German military wanes, she gathers from her poorer carers that young Germans are dying in large numbers on the front, that the Nazis are killing the physically and intellectually disabled, that the Jews are in concentration camps but that some Germans, such as a Herr Henssel whose daughter married a Jewish draper, are willing to hide them at great personal risk. There is a pivotal moment after visiting her father in his bunker in Berlin that she realizes that 'Duffi', her father Hitler, is a vicious man, a betrayer who rejects and despises her, banishing her to possible death in Berlin under siege by Allied forces.

Heidi's abandonment after remaining loyal to her father for so long points us to Hitler's contempt for German civilians memorably depicted in historical feature films such as *Downfall* (2004).[2] As someone treated as an outsider Heidi comes to sympathize with the mistreatment of the Jews and indeed prepares a place in her garden to hide them. She begins to wonder, 'What were Jews like?', and realizes that no adult has yet been 'able to tell her' (French 1999, 98), a moment of bathetic realization indicative of the phantasmatic dimensions of a racial discourse that has become central to the national imaginary. As an outsider herself Heidi rejects the insistence that Jews are a despised Other and instead tries to understand their difference in more sympathetic terms. A resourceful bricoleur, fashioning 'a picture of Jews in her mind' from available figural materials, Heidi imagines that they are like her and that they have red marks on their faces and one leg shorter than the other. Like her the Jews are a 'different people, who had to be hidden away' (French 1999, 98) for a time given the hostility and ignorance of the wider society that she has also experienced. Heidi makes a plan, watching out for any Jewish people in need of help that might come her way who are to be hidden in the old henhouse in the orchard. Tellingly, Heidi begins to steal supplies for her intended Jewish beneficiaries from the cellar, a sign of her increasing independence in judging right and wrong that can now encompass acts of civil disobedience and 'illegal' resistance to unjust uses of power.

After her rejection by Hitler in the climactic bunker scene Heidi matures further, eventually escaping the bunker and invading Red army with the indicative help of another ('found') family who adopted her as 'Helga', the Schmidts. The novel ends on a hopeful note as she emigrates to Australia, whereupon we learn that Anna, the novel's storyteller, may be Helga's granddaughter. It emerges by the novel's end that Anna has told this story not simply to work through a catastrophic historical legacy and argue for the importance of empathy for people who seem different, but because she is also sensitive to xenophobia and anti-immigrant sentiment in her small rural Australian town which, unlike post-war Germany, has no political consensus about its historical mistreatment of Aboriginal people and migrants and whose settler majority has often proved highly resistant to any meaningful *Vergangenheits Bewältigung*, reparative attempts to cope with a violent past.

Activating the reader

Anna's story is interspersed with the quest narrative of her friend and fascinated auditor Mark, who is uneasily aware of his obligations as an addressee of a fiction that is not didactic but rather ethically suggestive as a problematic narrative with contemporary resonances. He has been listening keenly to Anna and starts to interrogate his teachers and parents, attempting, as Hsu-Ming Teo argues, to raise disturbing ethical questions that relate the Holocaust to 'contemporary Australian concerns' (Teo 2015, 10). Mark begins to ask searching questions of his mother and father. He is worried by Hitler's successful infantilization of the German people, afraid that children inherit the sins of their parents, and inspired by Heidi's courageous assumption of ethical responsibility for the plight of others. Moreover the novel's interest in ordinary Germans such as Frau Gelber the housekeeper, and Frau Mundt the cook who at first supported Hitler but also suffered themselves during the war, has made the events of the Second World War less temporally distant and clearly understood as a comfortable contrast between good and evil.

Mark becomes a questing figure who asks his father a question germane to a settler-colonial context: how did great-great-grandpa acquire the family farm; did he steal it from "the Aborigines?" (French 1999, 85). In response Mark's father then replicates the tendency to shut down the conversation, already encountered by Heidi in the responses of Frau Mundt and Fraulein Gelber, to some of her questions when he angrily replies that it wasn't like that in those days, 'no one thought of it as stealing' (85). His father who has become threateningly peremptory, evasive, and intolerant in a manner that collapses the absolute temporal demarcation between past and present seemingly established by a ludically motivated story designed to pass the time, reveals that he's thin-skinned on questions of family and national history. Mark's (unnamed) father then embarks on a paroxysm of denial and obfuscation: "'the things they teach kids nowadays,' said Dad, attacking his sausages savagely. "It'd make more sense if they taught everyone to mind their own business. Do-gooders poking their nose in where it doesn't concern them'" (85).

At this juncture Mark is shocked to learn that parental authority can be an incubator of conformity and repressive silence, that certain ethical values including honesty and justice to the claims of others are easier to proclaim than materially enact, and that dominant masculinity forecloses on honest communication and expansive human relationships. The revelation that parents often wish to silence their children on matters pertaining to their own interests only compounds Mark's worry, in keeping with the Eichmann problematic, that what you think might be the right course of action can be very wrong indeed. Anna's story gets Mark thinking that the problem of Nazism and evil in general is the powerful and incrementally corrupting attraction of normative behaviour and attendant emotional practices and the very real challenges in protesting those norms that shape everyday behaviours. If everyone thinks something is right but you think it is wrong, what do you do then? The problem is not just the active commission of evil but the people who went along with it, until it was too late. It's entirely possible, as 'the Hitler stuff showed', that a whole country could be in the wrong (76). A lot of people just didn't think about things, and shied away from difficult questions, like his mum who, more wearily but no less determinedly than his father, quickly loses patience and asks him to leave off his inquiries (89).

Just like his parents who are now closing down conversation about their responsibility to acknowledge and amend historical crimes, people are all too willing to entrust their consciences to the blandishments of authorities and the repressive mechanisms of social conventions. Mark's journey towards understanding the importance of a critical sensibility is then accelerated by engaging with and in some respects reappraising the argumentative opinions of his straight-talking, civically active and inquisitive feminist teacher (and bus driver) Mrs Latter. She is perceived as something of an interfering do-gooder in the town but now represents to Mark an aspirational horizon of knowledge and critical inquiry that rejects parochialism and unthinking dogma. Mrs Latter wants Mark to question and be sceptical, to seek out the truth of the matter rather than relying on the confining discourses of an insular and self-authorizing community. In pondering Mrs Latter's exemplary critical spirit and rationalist proclivity for evidenced-based assertions and acknowledging that her stubborn independence of mind is precisely what makes her seem like an agitator to his small town, Mark recognizes the social ubiquity of anti-intellectualism past and present and opens himself, as other *Bildungshelden* we have encountered have done, to ethical illumination by people considered marginal and eccentric. Mark's uneasy but dedicated questioning, redolent of the protagonists we have discussed, mirrors Heidi's attention to the quotidian observations and generous humanity of her working-class carers, which educated her towards larger sympathies. Mark realizes that imitation is no longer a guide to correct behaviour as 'doing what everyone else did was no help either' (76).

Mark, in the tradition of a *Bildungsroman* that points towards an unofficial education which requires active inquiry rather than passive learning, is now distracted by the tedium of his school lessons and fails to find answers to his questions about morality in the school curriculum. Instead, beginning to discover a critical vocation, he is irrevocably 'pestered' by thinking (76) on ethical problems. Mark's restless awareness that his hometown is no longer satisfying his intellectual curiosity is indicative that *Hitler's Daughter* also broaches the question of one's future vocation. *Hitler's Daughter* subtly morphs Mark's perplexity into the story of his critical and creative development. Following the contours of Anna's story of wandering and migration, Mark is training himself to leave a secure conception of 'home' and become a journalist, writer and storyteller, educator, or perhaps artist, in order to imaginatively engage with larger problems that have been thrown into local relief.

We now turn to another narrative that less markedly but with greater consequence, enables its boy protagonist to develop his own calling, that of exploration, in the face of even the most aggressive systems of social control.

The Boy in the Striped Pyjamas

Let us turn our attention to John Boyne's 2006 novel *The Boy in the Striped Pyjamas* (hereafter *TBSP*). A global phenomenon, it has sold at least nine million copies, has been translated into fifty languages, and has been widely, if controversially, taught in schools in the United States, and the United Kingdom. In 2008 it was made into a Miramax film directed by Mark Herman with a stage version adapted by Angus Jackson developed in 2015. Many historians and adult readers loathe its story of a nine-year-old German boy named Bruno, the son of a Nazi commandant at Auschwitz, who befriends a young boy called Shmuel on the other side of Auschwitz's perimeter. Bruno has outraged some readers as an impossible contradiction, the German son of a Nazi commandant who is unerringly obtuse and naive: he mishears Auschwitz as 'Outwith', thinks that Hitler is called 'The Fury', and doesn't seem to know what the term 'Jew' means. Shmuel is a Jewish boy of the same age (tellingly they share a birthday which foretells the fraternal fate they will also share) who is a prisoner of the camp. Some readers, sensitive to 'Holocaust anxieties' such as those enumerated by Dirk Moses which include 'distorting the Holocaust in popular culture', 'the effects of Holocaust kitsch' and 'dismissing the victimization of the Jews to advance the victimization of others' (Moses 2016, 333), and wary of the novel's effect on children if taught in schools as a substitute for historical knowledge, have argued this novel is truly pernicious, a grotesque falsification of the horrors of the Holocaust. The eminent scholar Robert Eaglestone was appalled by *TBSP*s anodyne representation of the hideous reality of Auschwitz where the vast majority of young children were killed on arrival, suggesting that the book is as 'damaging to the memory of the Holocaust as the false memoir of Binjamin Wilkomirski/Bruno Grosjean. This children's book, with pretensions to an adult readership, turns the Holocaust into a childish fable, and makes Auschwitz as unreal as Camelot or Hogwarts School' (Eaglestone 2007). The orthodox Rabbi and scholar Benjamin Blech described the book *The Boy in the Striped Pyjamas* as 'not just a lie and not just a fairytale, but a profanation' since the notion that one could live in the vicinity of Auschwitz and 'simply not know' what was occurring there is a defence used by the Germans themselves to deny their complicity with genocide (Blech 2008). Debbie Pinfold argues that both novel and film make the 'innocent Bruno the "real" victim of the story' and by extension exculpates and extends the sympathy that accompanies this innocence to his parents (Pinfold 2015, 259).

The Neuberger Holocaust Education Centre in Toronto Canada made a similar point in 2013 when asked why they omitted the book from their educational resources:

> We were recently asked why we don't include the bewilderingly popular 'Boy in the Striped Pyjamas' in our recommended education resources . . . David Cesarani's Lit Review here does a fantastic job explaining the myriad problems with the book and film adaptation: Despite the book's intentions, he argues, the plot is highly improbable and gives credence to the defence that people did not, and could not, know what was happening within the death camps. Students who read it, he warns, may believe the camps 'weren't

that bad' if a boy could conduct a clandestine friendship with a Jewish captive of the same age, unaware of 'the constant presence of death'. (Neuberger Facebook post, 2013)

Many of these reviews echo the historian David Cesarani's highly critical assessment of *TBSP* as 'implausible', 'fiction in the worst sense of the word', and a dangerous 'distortion of history' since most Jewish children were gassed on arrival, and the fences were electrified. Cesarani muses that Bruno's accidental death in the gas chambers of Auschwitz transforms the Holocaust into a 'bizarre health and safety incident'. Cesarani was convinced that the novel's claims to be a 'fable' could not go unchallenged given the number of people at large who deny that the systematic mass murder of the Jews ever occurred and the book's subtext, that many Germans knew nothing or heartily disapproved of what was going on (Cesarani 2008, 3).³

Yet to state the obvious, the book is aimed at a child reader who prefers a young, underdetermined protagonist they can sympathetically engage with; the indoctrinated Hitler Youth demanded by some scholars and educators would have been a non-starter in genre terms. Moreover, that protagonist would not become the mobile focalizer of a variety of more desirable ethical traits important in contemporary contexts. If we peruse online reader feedback on popular sites such as Goodreads and Amazon books, we find that children around the target age of 9–13 as well their educators are deeply attached to the book and strongly identify with Bruno's and Shmuel's tragically fated friendship. These younger readers tend to be cognizant that the book is a self-styled 'fable' with allegorical resonances and that it has an intertextual relationship with an abiding feature of the genre of children's literature in which a child is led from safety to danger and from innocence to experience. These readers are perhaps more sympathetic to the story's literary strategy of deploying a naïve child narrator in the manner of *To Kill a Mockingbird* or *Catcher in the Rye* so that adult and institutional authority can be mocked and relativized. As Claudia Moscovici argues, 'the novel doesn't propose to offer a realistic historical account of the Holocaust' (Moscovici 2019, loc. 1477). Its evergreen literary technique, as Moscovici suggests, is one of defamiliarization in which Bruno's innocent perspective achieves a world upside down, exposing the 'assumptions of the grownups he deals with' (Moscovici 2019, loc. 1499). The subject positions exposed include his apolitical mother who is a sometimes reluctant but mostly acquiescent beneficiary of the Nazi system, and his conformist sister Gretel, who despite her cynical posturing lacks the initiative and courage to question adult prejudices. I also agree with Moscovici that *TBSP* is interested in the link between social conditioning at home and the normalization of class and racial hierarchies (Moscovici 2019, loc. 1504) and in that respect the novel is less sentimental kitsch than a successful 'thought experiment', inviting readers to reflect on a culture, not entirely alien to our own, that has invited young people to learn prejudice and racism from a very young age (Moscovici 2019, loc.

1510). As the following online reader responses to the novel also indicate, many readers find themselves deeply moved by a suspenseful and ultimately tragic story about a doomed but uplifting friendship between children. These readers are often mindful that the novel traces the developmental journey of a child who has many admirable if unformed moral qualities. They feel that the novel, in the tradition of historical fiction, engages the formative period of childhood in order to engage rather than alienate a younger reader and to impact a more hard-bitten adult reader tempted to regard the Holocaust as an already-known that is therefore ill-suited for fictional treatment.

> In my opinion, the global phenomenon that became this novel is well deserved. Despite its simple literature and its short length, the boy with the striped pajamas is a book filled with an incredible emotional charge, with a shaking and bright ending that will touch even the hardest reader. (https://www.goodreads.com/review/show/1420827939, accessed December 27th 2019)

> The author used a technique which was brilliant, taking readers into the mind and thoughts of a child whose father work [sic] for the 'Fury' (the Fuhrer) and who is sent to live in Out-With (Auschwitz), on the safe side of the fence, in an actual home. . . . The novel is labeled 'a fable' and I think this was a wise choice by both author and publisher. After all, no one knows exactly how a 9 year old son of a German officer would think, and young Bruno seems remarkably naive sometimes. But just as light sets off shadows more vividly, I think his exaggerated innocence allows readers to experience the horrors of Auschwitz that much more. For that reason, I don't think the accuracy of Bruno's character is all that important. The effect on the reader (THIS reader, anyway) is profound and deep. (http://www.seedlings.org/details.php?id=1194&cat=1 accessed December 19th 2019)

Other comments highlight an indicative dimension of the novel, an affirmation of explorative instincts and an illustration of the profound importance of friendship for growing minds.

> [Bruno's] innocence and curiosity are nicely contrasted with his sister's feigned sophistication. He begins exploring to learn more about where he is and to try to find a friend.(https://www.goodreads.com/book/show/39999.The_Boy_in_the_Striped_Pajamas) accessed December 19th 2019)

> In this fantastic book, my favourite character is Bruno because he is a nice, caring person and is not afraid to take risks. For example, he brings food to Shmuel, knowing that if he was caught he would be is [sic] serious trouble. Additionally, Bruno is an extremely clever person. Due to his love for exploring, he is not afraid to face danger, which he does at the end of the book. He is a great role model for any young boy. https://www.theguardian

.com/childrens-books-site/2015/sep/17/the-boy-in-striped-pyjamas-john-boyne-review (accessed December 19, 2019)

I decided to write this because I was disappointed by the comments of a couple of the other reviewers who were upset that the book did not include historical accuracy. I never thought I was purchasing a history book, and therefore did not expect to receive a history lesson. To me the message of the story is broader than the era it is set in. This is the tale of an unlikely friendship between two 9 yr old boys. That friendship is allowed to grow because of their innocence, and because they do not judge one another by their stations in life. It's a very powerful, moving fable. I loved it for exactly what it is. (http://vprb.blogspot.com/2015/03/the-boy-with-striped-pajamas.htmlI), accessed December 27th, 2019

It is clear that readers who enjoy and are moved by *TBSP* are not looking for conformity to a received historical narrative but are happy to read a fictional text that urges us to suspend disbelief and allows the reader to form an attachment to a character and their journey of discovery. Yet the text is not judged as historically trivial by those same readers. As we saw in *Hitler's Daughter*, the child protagonist can figure the shared hermeneutic process of understanding the relationship between private and public spheres, in which an ossified and repressive family structure is isomorphic with a national imaginary predicated on ignorance, fantasy, and conformism. Some readers' enthusiasm for the much-derided Bruno, the protagonist of *The Boy in the Striped Pyjamas*, suggests that the novel can be read as an indicative *Bildungsroman* of growing self-expression in which the principal character begins to manifest a variety of admirable traits including explorative curiosity, unalloyed and courageous commitment to friendship, and an intuitive grasp of debased or elevated moral qualities regardless of that person's apparent social standing. The enthusiasm for the fable-like dimension of the narrative perhaps indicates the pleasures of active readership involving inferences of emotional growth as Bruno becomes something of an inquiring detective figure in the manner of Aue and Stevens. Bruno's psychological development is not always explicitly manifest given the protagonist's immaturity and difficulties with processing enormities, yet can nevertheless be inferred from his outspokenness, explorative curiosity, problem-solving capacities, and courageous responses to authority figures such as his father.

At the beginning of the novel the reader is introduced to what seems to be a typical upper-middle-class household in Berlin in 1942. Bruno looks up to his father who has just been 'promoted' to commandant of Auschwitz but is becoming someone unrecognisable in the pursuit of career success, in his 'determination to get ahead' (Boyne 2008, 40) as his mother complains. The family's impending move to Auschwitz in occupied Poland prompts a fracture in his parents' relationship as does the chilling disclosure that the *paterfamilias* ultimately rules by force alone if persuasion proves ineffective. Early in the novel Bruno is dismayed to hear his mother bitterly complaining that Bruno's father makes 'all the decisions for us' (Boyne 2008, 14).

After moving to 'Outwith' Bruno is confronted with the shock of temporal cleavage, between a 'then' of domestic comforts in a bustling cosmopolitan city like Berlin in which he plays with friends and frequents markets and cafes, and the reality of cheerless occupied Poland. Upon protesting his situation more forcefully, his father's hypocrisy becomes increasingly evident, continually interrupting Bruno because 'none of the rules of normal family life ever applied to him' (Boyne 2008, 51). Lonely and subject to the seemingly arbitrary diktat of his father, Bruno seeks out the perspective of Maria, cursorily dismissed by his father as an 'overpaid' maid (17). He recognizes, despite Maria's polite attempts to distance herself, that she too is 'part of the family' and insists on a commonality that ignores rank and status; since both of them have been brought to Poland against their will, 'if you ask me, we're all in the same boat. And it's leaking' (58). His sister Gretel who he mostly disdains as a 'hopeless case', by contrast, idealizes their father, rejects Bruno's more fluid conception of family, and is profoundly obsequious towards authority figures in smart uniforms, always speaking of their father as if he could do no wrong. Tellingly, she perpetuates her family's exclusionary biases and dismisses Maria as a functionary at their disposal. Gretel, Bruno laments, 'never stopped to think that Maria was a person with feelings just like hers' (64). It is precisely Bruno's sympathy for working people, redolent of Heidi's attentions to the practical wisdom of her carers in *Hitler's Daughter* and of the demotic encounters critical to reorienting Stevens and Aue's journeys, together with his more elastic conception of 'family', that helps him appreciate that his sister is vain, materialistic, conformist, and preoccupied by surface appearances, soon besotted with a man in uniform, a sadistic, ambitious young Nazi officer named Lieutenant Kotler.

The cruel young officer Kotler, who begins an adulterous affair with Bruno's mother, is revealed to Bruno in the first instance as cruelly sneering towards those who are vulnerable or different (he disturbs Bruno and even Gretel by making fun of an overweight corporal) even before he shows sadistic anti-Semitic cruelty towards Pavel and Shmuel, the two primary Jewish characters in the novel. Although Gretel at twelve going on thirteen considers herself superior to her naïve younger brother, her obtuse conformism to social expectations renders her inattentive to her environment, with Bruno picking up early on that Auschwitz and its surroundings is not in fact a farm or rural retreat, and that their sojourn there is not a holiday. Inoculated to the empathetic theory of mind by her father's strict enforcement of hierarchical relationships between masters and servants, 'Germans' and 'Jews', Gretel cheerfully accepts racist ideology, attempting to persuade Bruno that the people on the other side of the fence are unworthy of interest or sympathy, 'never having had a bath in their lives' (37). When she turns thirteen the contemptuous Gretel puts away her dolls and the relational play they encourage and begins charting a distorted version of the war on a map of Europe given to her by her father. An isolated figure, probably emblematic of the withdrawal of German civilians into private life and delusional fantasy during the war, Gretel puts little pins onto the map and then congratulates herself that unlike Bruno, she can no longer afford to 'act like a child even if you can' (159). Gretel's foreswearing of innocence repeats her father's fatal act of submission to the superego, which he earlier related to Bruno. At Bruno's age the now rigidly careerist and conformist bourgeois *paterfamilias*, probably modelled on Rudolf Höss, disavowed the playful creativity and imaginative whimsy of childhood. Do you think I would have made such a success of my life, Bruno's father asks his rebellious son, if 'I hadn't learned when to argue and when to keep my mouth shut and follow orders?' (49).

As the novel progresses, Bruno's abandonment by his careerist father, now commandant at the genocidal concentration camp of Auschwitz, becomes more apparent. In a pivotal episode later in the eleventh chapter of the novel, Bruno in a moment of purposeful *kairotic* recollection, recalls how 'the Fury' along with his consort Eva Braun visited his obsequious father and awe-inspired family for dinner. 'The Fury' did not open the door for his companion, was brusque, and ignored conversational proprieties including paying sympathetic attention to the children, thus provoking fear and moral revulsion. Bruno realizes that Hitler is a 'horrible man' (124) and so shares an incipient moral taste with Heidi in *Hitler's Daughter*, the spontaneous but increasingly reflective capacity to affirm human basic human virtues such as warmth, kindness, and friendship, regardless of exclusionary classifications such as race or class.

Bruno's increasing self-reliance and willingness to 'explore' his environs and by extension his desires, rather than remain confined, brings him into contact with Pavel, seemingly a lowly kitchen hand, in reality a skilled Jewish doctor from Czechoslovakia who expertly bandages Bruno after he falls off a makeshift tyre swing that the resourceful boy had improvised for recreation. His curiosity about the stigmatized but nebulous social Other now piqued, Bruno begins making inquiries about the people dressed in pyjamas on the other side of the fence but is reminded once more that he has nothing in common with the Jews and should accept the privileged situation in which he finds himself. With exploration of his environment moving from a play phase to a rebellious posture, Bruno explicitly refuses comfort and expediency. The many incidents of unfairness, of moral coarseness, of adult hypocrisy, predispose him, the reader can infer, towards leaving the corrupted environs of the bourgeois family and seeking more authentic human relationships, a departure from a home now recognized as carceral and incapable of helping him solve pressing existential problems. As a would-be explorer ironically fulfilling his mother's once insincere promise that the trip to Outwith would be an 'adventure' (3), and as an avid reader of the coming-of-age classic *Treasure Island*, Bruno seeks out meaningful relationships with those excluded from the bourgeois family proper. He initially gets to know servants and helpers such as Maria and Pavel, which prepares him to meet his designated Other but in fact kindred spirit Shmuel at the perimeter fence of the camp.

As we have discussed, the *Bildungsroman* is a genre of palimpsests that often reflects critically, if not mournfully, on the 'broader sweep of history from matriarchal to patriarchal domination' (Abel et al. 1983, 164), offering radical subtexts and metaphors of buried cultural strata. It is notable that in his self-imposed exile Bruno, in another act of urgent recollection, remains fiercely loyal to the memory of his now absent grandmother, an urbane stage actress, fiercely anti-fascist who has encouraged him to perform and adopt different personae. She wanted him to remain agile, curious, playful, and questioning. His grandmother, perhaps signifying Weimar era cosmopolitanism, 'always found a way' to say what she wished, 'no matter how unpopular it might prove to be' (Boyne 2008, 91). Bruno's attachment to the memory of his grandmother who nurtured his performative creativity throughout childhood is juxtaposed to his Nazi father's ideological claptrap, focused on a bitter, revanchist conception of the nation's fallen glory, its destiny to reclaim national pride after the wrongs done to it by the Jews and assorted enemies. Bruno remembers how his grandmother sternly rebuked his mother for being impressed by his father's handsome new appearance as a commandant in uniform, a pattern of subordination repeating itself with Gretel and an implicit critique of the aesthetic appeal of 'fascinating fascism'. As Linda Herman writes in a 2009 US teacher's guide for the novel, whereas Gretel and Bruno's unnamed mother become self-absorbed and emotionally isolated, and thereby indifferent to wider human suffering, 'Bruno's desire to explore his world . . . pushes the plot forward' (Herman 2009, 22).

Bruno's love of exploration also helps him counter utilitarian and positivist approaches to education when his new tutor Herr Liszt tries to inculcate history and geography lessons rather than his own humanist preferences for 'reading and art' (Boyne 2008, 97). This is, of course, redolent of Dickens' *Hard Times* and its anti-utilitarian defence of 'fancy' as Bruno defiantly insists on the importance of fantasy and imaginative play, which helps him resist interpellation by coercive ideologies that refuse to accept the human need for free symbolic expression and emotional succour, and self-extension through role-playing. Bruno is not interested in learning a stifling nationalist story breeding *ressentiment* about the oppression of the Fatherland, but maintains a quixotic love of romantic adventure, and of picaresque stories about errant knights. As Paul Mendes-Flohr reminds us, as a humanistic ideal favouring the nurturing of one's inner life and development, *Bildung* prefers a plastic and dynamic conception of culture and learning to the idea of a fixed canon (Mendes-Flohr 1998, 229–30). With a fluid sense of his identity and its matriarchal crucible, and a theatrical love of role-playing as challenging the boundaries of selfhood, Bruno, a kind of wise fool, is brought to a moment of heightened perception that doubles as absolute naïveté. He cannot see the difference between those who wear decorated uniforms and the prisoners in pyjamas (Boyne 2008, 100). He wants to understand, in an implicit comprehension of contingency masquerading as necessity, 'who decided which people wore the striped pyjamas and which people wore the uniforms?' (Boyne 2008, 100). Finally offered a return to Berlin by his distressed mother who, Bovary-like, has resorted to the intoxicating escapism of a sexual affair with Kotler, Bruno, continuing on his independent path, is now ambivalent about returning to Berlin given his friendship with Shmuel. He utters the word but 'wasn't sure where "home" was anymore' (196), a confession of a now liminal identity in which, as we saw in *Hitler's Daughter*, elective affinities for 'found families' count for as much as one's biological origins. Bruno's uncertainly about where home lies also signifies to a discerning reader, and here we think of the reflective trajectory of Stevens, Aue, and Daniel Stein, an unwillingness to retreat back into the complacent ignorance of metropolitan domesticity or to neglect the significant social attachments he has formed, a reversal of the decision of many non-Jewish Germans and Europeans to forego inconvenient friendships with Jews and the politically ostracized.

Bruno's tragic decision not merely to sojourn at the perimeter fence of Auschwitz but to irreversibly commit himself to his friend Bruno by crossing over to the other side of the fence is Bruno's last great adventure. It is readable as a leap of faith into the unknown, in which imaginative freedom and unconditional friendship is both celebrated and finally extinguished by the cruel reality of a historical process that can no longer be deferred by the counterfactual possibilities of fiction. In putting on the 'striped pyjamas' of the Jewish inmates at Auschwitz Bruno is not, as some readers would have it, simply demonstrating an egregious naivety but fulfilling the lessons of his matriarchal genealogy, since it was his grandmother who always wore the right outfit and strongly encouraged him to 'feel like the person you're pretending to be' (205). Perhaps Bruno shares the resilience of Lucy from E.M. Forster's *A Room With a View*, someone who, as Gregory Castle observes, takes command of her own aesthetic education with limited opportunities to further it, and remains open to 'unconventional mentors'. (Castle 2019, 154). Bruno's declaration of everlasting friendship for Shmuel, which has already been affectively prepared for by his journey beyond the family microcosm, is a telling repudiation of his father's betrayal of his relationships with his own family, and by extension the Nazis' betrayal of Germany.

As was the case with *Hitler's Daughter*, the emphasis placed on a questing child protagonist who models an inquisitive reader alert to the dangers of social conditioning and sensitive to injustices in their own day and age forewarns us against assuming that these narratives exist on a single temporal plane, and are subordinate to the imperative to preserve an accurate account of the past. Instead, just as Mark helped the reader focus on problems that arise in interpreting the Nazi past when applied to an Australian colonial context, both child and adult readers allying themselves with Bruno might become more sensitive to the fact that in *TBSP* the ghettoization, segregation, and relentless dehumanization of Jews is uncannily familiar. If they think about post-war history or follow the news then, as Linda Herman suggests, the novel encourages them to 'look for such fences in real life' (Herman 2009, 23). Other instances of segregation including Jim Crow, South African apartheid, the so-called 'protection' era in Australia's historical mistreatment of Aboriginal people, refugee detention camps on Nauru and Manus Island, Trump's obsession with building a wall to keep out Mexicans and other Hispanics and his incarceration of children, the separation barrier in the West Bank and the isolation of Gaza, may come into view. The reader of *TSBP*, a fable, needs to take heed of Bruno's inquisitive and sceptical posture towards barriers that have supposedly been established for the sake of their own security or would appear to maintain a spatial separation between people of different kinds. As Susan Hirsch reminds us, the society of the *Bildungsroman* can have universal and symbolic import as an experiential field, thus implicating the reader in the experiences and education of the growing individual (Hirsch 1979, 303).

A reader might be impressed enough by Bruno's insistence on the right to explore boundaries and interact with those designated foreign and alien, that as Linda Herman also suggests, they might come to think about what they are reading in more indicative and allegorical terns, pondering that there is no such thing as a fool-proof fence, that fences can generate movements of human solidarity such that the erected fence 'ends up doing the opposite of what it was meant to do' (Herman 2009, 23). Shmuel and Bruno's friendship at the perimeter or boundary allegorizes that fear, hatred, and an increasing reliance on the security state is not inevitable, as suggested by the emergence of sanctuary cities in the United States during the Trump presidency. Finally, the bored and listless Shmuel might strike an explorative reader not simply as a malnourished inmate of a Nazi concentration camp but as also figuring the denied 'rights of the child' in a range of contexts including refugee camps. According to Article 31 of the UN Declaration on the Rights of the Child, a reader might come to realize through further research encouraged in pedagogical contexts, that children have the right to 'rest and leisure, to engage in play and recreational activities'.

Having begun identifying with a German child protagonist who struggles to free himself from interpolative nationalistic and family ideologies ('father knows best'), and who only incrementally challenges a system which offers him privileges and rewards, the reader of Bruno and Shmuel's intertwined narratives might also make greater efforts at understanding their position within an altered or heterodox cognitive map. As Ann Rider has suggested, a truly ethical Holocaust pedagogy is much more likely to be successful by not only developing empathic capacity for victims of abuse but also through recognition of the 'banal ideologies and institutions occupied by the perpetrators' (Rider 2013, 65). As Rider argues, helping students realize 'that ordinary people can become bystanders, and even perpetrators, is in fact essential if they are to recognise injustice in their own environment'

(Rider 2013, 65). I hope to have shown that as an agile literary form congenial to the varied requirements of historical fiction, select historical *Bildungsromane* for children, which insist on a life of inquiry and discovery and reject any premature conception of human destiny, are well placed to assist hermeneutic reflection on the past.

Chapter 5

THE COUNTERFEITERS AS BILDUNGSFILM
ALLEGORIZING JEWISH HISTORY

'Art takes the sting out of suffering... Any attempt to transform the Holocaust into art demeans the Holocaust and must result in poor art' – Michael Wyschogrod.[1]

In this chapter I will suggest that appraisals of Holocaust-themed cinema may benefit from greater attention to a conversation that has been going on within literary studies, historiography, and film studies for some time now as to whether it is precisely as *fiction* that historical cinema can articulate a sincere and ethically engaged relationship with the past. I will take as my chief example *The Counterfeiters* (*Die Fälscher* 2007), written and directed by Stefan Ruzowitzky, a film that unashamedly fictionalizes history by creating characters and scenarios that are not documented in its source text but does help to intensify audience interest in the ethical dilemmas with which they are confronted. *The Counterfeiters* is a noteworthy historical film as it has been largely well received, even by highly invested audiences, for the supple historical significations and ethical ambiguities of its *Bildungsheld* Sally Sorowitsch.

When a version of the literary *Bildungsheld* is transposed to historical film as a heroic protagonist it is perhaps unsurprising that there can be a suspicious response to the satisfying emplotment and narrative closure afforded by retracing the actions and moral growth of an individual against a historical background that is understood not for its own sake, but as facilitating the adventure-time of that hero's quest for understanding, redemption, and personal salvation. I would submit that a reaction against the *Bildungsfilm*, historical films that use a *Bildungsheld* to reanimate the past, motivates the critique of many commercially successful films that claim historical authenticity. I then go on to suggest that the critical rejection of the *Bildungsheld* as a cinematic trope is in some respects structured by a now well-established critique of the literary form of the *Bildungsroman* or at least the perceived *ideology* of that literary form as discussed in the introduction.

I would like to query a prominent assumption in critiques of historical film, mirroring the embarrassment many critics feel about the *Bildingsroman* in its 'classical' form, that the device of the *Bildungsheld* is a facile distraction that encourages the audience's empathetic identification with an individual, thereby foreshortening exploration of historical context, and discouraging an ethical spectatorship that is willing to forego aesthetic pleasure and engage with the horrifying dimensions of the Holocaust and other genocides. By contrast, analysing *The Counterfeiters* as a case study that discloses some of the potentialities of the genre of historical film to enhance the audience's own edifying trajectory, I will argue that its *Bildungsheld* Sally Sorowitch can be interpreted, like the protagonists we have analysed, as a productively conjunctural 'middle' character in the Lukacian sense. A German-speaking Russian-Jew, pragmatic criminal and sensitive artist, insider and outsider, Sally can encompass a spectrum of conflicting character traits and potential trajectories from criminality and perpetrator complicity to selfless heroism and civil courage. More importantly, like many of the characters we have studied, he assists the reader/viewer in revisiting and reappraising significant historical events.

In the case of Sally I will go on to suggest that he indexes a variety of significations about the past, present, and future of diasporic Judaism, constituting a node around whom various historical narratives and systems of valuation can freely circulate, just as *The Kindly Ones* wished to preserve a sense of Jewish alterity and *Daniel Stein* questioned Zionist conceptions of Jewish identity. It is precisely as a spur to historical and critical reflection on the historiography of the Holocaust, the contested legacy of diasporic Judaism, and the social and institutional dynamics of evil that *The Counterfeiters*, I hope to suggest, constitutes a major aesthetic achievement. That achievement cannot be interpreted without a prismatic critical optic that includes the phenomenology of film reception, historiographical awareness, and the kind of functional and indicative, rather than essentialist, interpretation of literary genre that we have deployed in this study.

Art after testimony

As applied to the events of the Second World War the periodizing designation 'art after testimony' recognizes that an era without living witnesses to the Holocaust is rapidly approaching. The inevitability that imaginative fiction will play a pivotal role in reconstituting the memory of the Holocaust has been the subject of speculation since as early as 1983, when Yosef Hayim Yerushalmi observed in *Zakhor: Jewish History and Jewish Memory* that despite the immense efforts of historical researchers, the image of the Holocaust was being shaped 'not at the historian's anvil, but in the novelist's crucible'. (Yerushalmi 1996, 98). The increasing 'remediation' of Holocaust memory by imaginative literature and popular culture is no small matter. Even amongst scholars, discussion of the constitutive role of fiction and cinematic representation in engendering historical consciousness of the Holocaust is beset by anxieties that tend to polarize discussion around *parti pris* positions. A lingering wariness of the function of the creative arts in representing historical catastrophe is hardly surprising given the profound investment in the preservation of the truth of the Holocaust and the sanctity of testimony, all the more so in the face of creeping denialism and the resurgence of nationalism and anti-Semitism in former bastions of liberal democracy. We should also bear in mind the considerable dismay at the exploitative and inaccurate forms Holocaust representation takes when produced for entertainment or translated for cultural consumption.[2]

I would submit that attempts to work out criteria for the historical, ethical, and aesthetic evaluation of literary and cinematic representations of the Holocaust also founder because of a profound disagreement over whether creative representations of traumatic historical events need to respect: (1) a reconstructive protocol that aims to respect and augment witness testimony and remain faithful to the historical record as a bulwark against motivated denialism or attempts at collective self-exculpation; (2) the irrepressible reality that historical fictions are shaped by artistic requirements including the need to condense historical detail, and are keenly attuned to the needs of contemporary audiences, such that they cannot simply be mimetic of the past.[3] In the view of adherents of precept (2), which I will call the 'communicative imperative', a Holocaust-themed fictional text should embrace imaginative and rhetorical devices congenial to its genre or form, including metaphor and symbolism. It might do so, for example, in order to explore ethical problematics that resonate beyond a particular historical context. In the phlegmatic words of Sue Vice, who has helped to inaugurate a post-testimonial approach to imaginative representations of the Holocaust, Holocaust fiction is 'simply a different genre from Holocaust testimony' (Vice 2000, 10), more dissonant and polyphonic, less interested in moral certainties.

The point is that there is no simple way to resolve the tension between curatorial and communicative imperatives as regards the pedagogical or social function of Holocaust-themed texts. This dilemma is, at least at first blush, somewhat surprising, as we may think that we can simply turn to the wishes of survivors and witnesses themselves. However, and I may be being just a touch too schematic, if we examine the public utterances of two very influential Holocaust survivors, we can remark a tension between Elie Wiesel's somewhat bombastic and sacralizing emphasis on the inaccessibility of the Holocaust to those who weren't primary witnesses – 'a *novel* about *Treblinka* is either *not a novel or not about Treblinka*' (Wiesel 1996, 7) – and the rational musings and interlocutory desires of Primo Levi. Whereas, as Matthew Boswell points out, Wiesel 'positions the Holocaust as a kind of sacred text that is ... undecipherable to the uninitiated' (Boswell 2012, 7), the paramount necessity for Levi was to communicate and explain his experiences after his release from Auschwitz. Unlike Wiesel he was less interested in the singularity ('uniqueness') of the Holocaust and instead warned in classic works such as *The Drowned and the*

Saved of a recrudescence of Nazism and the camp system as an ever-present possibility of Western politics. As Michael Rothberg has aptly commented, testimonial studies tend to be divided between two poles, emphasizing either the 'politically interventionist aspect of the testimonial articulation (*testimonio*, subaltern studies, human rights discourse) or the aporetic unrepresentability of traumatic experience (Holocaust studies and the psychoanalytic dimension of trauma studies)' (Rothberg 2016, 360). The contrasting attitudes of Wiesel and Levi have taken on an even greater representative significance as emotional vocabularies, markers of an appropriate attitude towards traumatic histories. On the one hand the curatorial imperative recommends 'Holocaust piety' as a solemn and reverential disposition towards a sacralized past that risks profanation by trivializing and appropriative representations. Against this injunction the communicative imperative recommends a kind of *kairotic* 'logophilia', a timely response to a historical legacy that threatens to be domesticated by routinized modes of commemoration. This imperative embraces performative discourse and a sometimes chaotic play of perspective as the appropriate means of working through a burdensome historical legacy that has unsettling contemporary implications.[4]

Another position which might assist our orientation in formulating principles for the interpretation of creative texts about the Holocaust and other genocidal atrocities is the paratextual discourse of culture producers, and the commentary of authors and directors about their creative practice. Yet difficulties quickly arise. For example, it is not unusual for the author of a historical novel or the director of a film that is based on the events of the Holocaust to simultaneously defend the meticulous research they have conducted and the historical authenticity of their novel or screenplay, while almost in the same breath arguing strenuously for its fictional structure and its capacity to resonate with younger audiences who did not live through the events in question. Let us take the controversial German film *Downfall* (*Der Untergang*, 2005) directed by Oliver Hirschbiegel as a notable example of a discourse that seeks to elide the heterogeneity of two seemingly incompatible imperatives, that of historical fidelity and creative interpretation. In interviews for *Downfall* Oliver Hirschbiegel airily dismissed some viewers' wariness of Bruno Ganz's charismatic and humanizing portrayal of Hitler which refuses the post-Chaplain tradition of Hollywood caricature. Hirschbiegel replied deadpan to anxieties about humanizing Hitler as an object of fascination or pity: 'we are not inventing anything. I don't show anything that he didn't do . . . everything is historically documented. Everything is absolutely authentic' ('Interview with Oliver Hirschbiegel interview', cited in Bathrick and Magshamrain 2007, 8). Asked whether the film had any kind of attitude towards its cast of inner-circle Nazis, the producer Berndt Eichinger weighed into similar effect: 'There is no moral [. . .] What we are trying to do is – as much as we possibly can – to present the facts, to tell history. And not to interpret history' (cited in Haase 2004, 52).

Eichinger's Rankean sentiments didn't last, however, since in a more revealing interview with *Frankfurter Allgemeine Zeitung* he disclosed that he gleaned the idea for the film from the source material he was reading, which offered him the possibility of portraying an allegorically pregnant microcosm: 'I read the galleys of Joachim Fest's *Der Untergang*, which deals with Hitler's final sixteen days . . . And there I found my dramatic starting point: *to portray in this concentrated period of time all that had happened in the past twelve years*, to revisit all the mechanisms, the entire structure, the way of thinking and the belief system, the attitude of compliance' (cited in Bathrick and Magshamrain 2007, 5, my emphasis). As Matthew Boswell explains in a scathing critique of the film, *Der Untergang* is a historical *interpretation* of the final days of Hitler's regime, because it 'incorporates a wide cast of characters from all echelons of Nazi Germany and aspires to anatomise a nation' and explain its political demise and ethical collapse, 'signposting the socio-political dimensions of the title through the tagline, "a nation awaits its . . . DOWNFALL"' (Boswell 2013, 149).

Of course, one could maintain that the ambivalence of witnesses and culture producers about the status of representations of the Holocaust, that is, the desire to embrace both epistemological responsibility and the metaphorically suggestive, is a healthy and productive state of affairs as the meaning of the past is constantly being reproduced, contested, and transformed through a variety of media and symbolic artefacts. We could submit that any evaluation of a novel or film dealing with a violent past should be able to sustain a multifaceted analysis which explores that novel or film's desire to say something new, interesting, or surprising while maintaining a vigilant focus on its capacity to do justice to the history it purports to evoke. But again, while that kind of representational agility is conceivable in theory, those acquainted with scholarship on Holocaust-themed imaginative fictions and recalling the very strong critical reactions to novels such as *The Kindly Ones* and *The Boy in the Striped Pyjamas* will recognize that textual analysis still struggles to give the communicative imperative of historical fiction its due, because it is ever mindful of the sometimes bullish and implicitly proprietorial demands of historical authenticity posited by invested audiences, commentators, and professional historians. Indeed, as I will seek to demonstrate, the constraints on discussing an imaginative cinematic representation of the Holocaust using an immanent evaluative vocabulary focused on form, genre, narrative mode, and reader or audience reception is even more prohibitive, because influenced by a structuring suspicion of the *Bildungfilm*, than is often recognized by observers wary of the heavily policed protocols of Holocaust representation.[5]

The *Bildungsheld* as violating ethical spectatorship

It is not often explicitly noted that conversations around Holocaust representation often work to consolidate the onerous insistence that an imaginative representation of the Holocaust *should not focus on the lives of individuals*. Critics sympathetic to the curatorial imperative not to flatten or smooth over violent histories such as the Holocaust tend to feel that given the history of collective suffering, a redemptive storyline of an individual surviving in the face of adversity is at best otiose and falsely optimistic and at worst traduces the reality of mass murder. In her introduction to *A Thousand Darknesses: Lies and Truth in Holocaust Fiction* (2011), Ruth Franklin sheds some light on this insistence on fidelity to a collective past when she remarks that in the background of many evaluations of Holocaust or Second World War-themed imaginative fictions we can locate a profound desire to recapture a historical totality, a desire that interrupts recognition of that texts' specific narrative achievement. Franklin names this yearning the 'holy grail of Holocaust literature: that forever desired and never-to-be-attained text that will provide us with a direct channel to the Holocaust' (Franklin 2011, 7). As a sop to audience identification, the represented individual is held to vitiate an unspoken and perhaps liturgically motivated desire to commemorate vanished communities and to remember the fallen.[6]

If we turn our attention to the burgeoning, yet still barely respectable genre of historical feature film, the suspicion generated by its preoccupation with legendary or notable individuals extends well beyond the still limited canon of Holocaust-themed cinema. Take, for example, a forensic critique of the much-lauded historical film *Hotel Rwanda* (2004) by the historian and genocide scholar Mohamed Adhikari. He takes issue with the film's sentimental focus on its *Bildungsheld*, Paul Rusesabagina, who becomes increasingly more humane, politicized, and resourceful in a desperate situation. The problems with focusing on Rusesabagina are manifold according to Adhikari. His principal complaint is that the film's focus on Rusesabagina as a heroic saviour of besieged Tutsis in the Hotel Colline divorces the events portrayed from their complex context. A ghastly set of events in which 80 per cent of the Tutsi population succumbed to genocidal violence is substituted with a palatable narrative of one man's deeds of rescue and self-sacrifice (Adhikari 2008, 176). The costs of this approach include an exaggeration of Rusesabagina's feats in saving refugees, a serious diminution of the film's ability to explain the causes and legacy of the Rwandan genocide, and the reproduction of racist tropes in which the Westernized Paul affirms his humanity against a background of tribalist savagery. The survival of Rusesabagina, his wife, and adopted nieces who promise the reconstitution of the family unit and the return of civilian normality in the future ultimately minimizes, according to Adhikari, the traumatic violence of genocide.

In her excellent recent study of atrocity cinema, Shohini Chaudhuri is almost as scathing about the film as an ersatz history, describing *Hotel Rwanda* as a kind of 'African *Schindler's List*', which 'focuses on the tale of one exceptional man while purporting to be a document of what really happened' (Chaudhuri 2014, 67). Given that 'what really happened' does not exclude individual agency, we have to wonder whether Chaudhuri feels the focus on the deeds of an individual is not merely historically problematic but fails the more confronting demands of ethical spectatorship. She laments that moralistic historical dramas that foster 'identification with heroic "good men"' ... relieve viewers of their own responsibility while reassuring them about their moral place in the world' (50). Lawrence Baron intones to similar effect when he argues that 'biographical films about the exceptions to the rule of complicity in or passivity towards genocide can easily degenerate into hagiographic accounts of saintly individuals whose exploits eclipse the abominations they opposed' (Baron 2010, 4). In prefatory remarks to a recent interview with *Son of Saul* director László Nemes, Megan Ratner shares Chaudhuri's desire for reader or audience discomfort rather than the pleasures of empathetic involvement when she insists that in a conventional Holocaust film, even a harrowing panorama 'verges on reassurance' as it offers the reprieve of distance. Ratner by contrast celebrates Nemes' immersive point of view which asks the audience to 'respond but not to identify', to instead view the world of the camp as 'counter-human, nonsensical yet lethal' (Ratner 2016, 58).

While not always recognizing that the genre it is dealing with is often that venerable chestnut, the *Bildungsroman*, commentary on Holocaust-themed texts safeguard themselves from charges of aestheticism by celebrating a modernist programme of sensory derealization and reproducing a discourse of intense suspicion towards a potentially redemptive narrative trajectory of increasing moral maturity. Reproducing Fraiman's critique of the genre's individualistic bias as applied to the compromised cognitive labour of many commercially successful historical films, Chaudhuri suggests that when 'the *Bildungsroman* is adapted to films about distant conflicts, the protagonist's moral growth is situated against an oppressed people's struggle, dividing the plot into foreground and background material'. The conversion of a character like Oskar Schindler to the good side, Chaudhuri argues, can only serve to 'purify the past of its ambiguities' as a 'celebratory narrative of salvation turns survivors into "winners", triumphing over adversity' (Chaudhiri 2014, 53, 73).

The response to *The Counterfeiters* is an example of a historical film that has received high praise but is still considered to narrate the cathartic journey of its *Bildungsheld*, who survives against enormous odds, at the expense of historical complexity. Consider Mary Wauchope's excellent review of the film in the journal *Shofar*, which is mostly praising, nuanced and appreciative of its ethical ambiguities. Yet in her conclusion, Wauchope once more becomes mindful that she is appraising a commercially successful historical feature film that takes full advantage of genre tropes including a heist narrative and a noir anti-hero in Sally. She then summarizes that in *The Counterfeiters* attachment to character leaves the moral issues entertained in *The Counterfeiters* at the end of the film not only 'unresolved, but unaddressed' (Wauchope 2010, 71). The last phrase gave me pause as the claim that the film leaves moral issues unaddressed is odd given Wauchope's subtle exploration of the film's interest in the 'grey zone' of judging moral complicity catalysed by the actions of privileged prisoners, as famously analysed by Primo Levi in *The Drowned and the Saved* (1987). Wauchope's principal objection is now familiar to us. While the film does use shifting relationships to highlight 'complex ethical debates', our attachment to the character of Sally and the 'will he, won't he succeed in forging the US dollar' heist narrative, means that the 'film's plot is ultimately driven by the traditional suspense mechanisms of a thriller' in which good triumphs over evil, success over failure, survival over death (Wauchope 2010, 71).

The film scholar Brad Prager agrees with Wauchope's anxiety about the insidious ability of the *Bildungsfilm* to foreground an optimistic narrative in even starker terms when he suggests rather dogmatically in an analysis of *The Counterfeiters* that 'popular modes of coming to terms with the Holocaust . . . presuppose that there can be some understanding between victims and contemporary observers'. Prager judges an implicit contract between culture producers and their audience as a false currency predicated primarily on 'purchasing reconciliation and papering over collective wounds'. (Prager 2011, 91). What strikes me here is that Prager assumes that historical feature films, even when skillfully done, by dint of their very need to communicate to an addressee, represent a turning away from the horrors of an unresolved history which he frames as *a priori* unrepresentable. I think in the name of certain critical piety that Prager is avoiding a point made by Robert Rosenstone, an influential theorist of historical film and a representative of the communicative imperative in approaching historical texts, who suggests that the history film enacts 'a mode of historical thinking, one with its own rules of engagement with the past' (Rosenstone 2013, 86). The question I will pursue for the remainder of this chapter is whether *The Counterfeiters*' attentive representation of an individual who 'weathers plot' corrupts its capacity to interpret a multivalent history as so many critics we have cited seem to believe. Along with the film critic Alison Landsberg I will suggest in my interpretation that we need to be more attuned to the 'specific power of film to bring distant events near, to produce affect, to physically and psychologically engage audiences', producing a form of political engagement that has an 'affective component' (Landsberg 2013, 11). In addressing Sally's engaging qualities, we can draw on Franco Moretti's recognition that however middling their abilities, the protagonist of a *Bildungsroman* assists the reader in meeting the moment of trial and ordeal like no other character in the text because her or his character really only exists in process, in those years of apprenticeship in which they are prolonging the discovery of vocation, discovering the new and transformative, and dilating the moment of decision and closure.

The Bildungsheld of The Counterfeiters as a mediating character

An interesting dimension of the reception of *The Counterfeiters* is that it has garnered an Academy Award (an Oscar for best foreign language film in 2008)

5. The Counterfeiters *as* Bildungsfilm

and has largely escaped censure despite being made by a non-Jewish Austrian (Director Stefan Ruzowitsky) with a largely non-Jewish cast in the key roles (such as *Inspector Rex's* Karl Markovics as Sally Sorowitsch). The film also took plenty of dramatic licence with the source material on which it was based. The film quarries but does not replicate its source text, Auschwitz survivor Adolf Burger's *The Devil's Workshop: a Memoir of a Nazi Counterfeiting Operation*, which was first published in 1983 with a number of subsequent editions including an English translation in 2009. *The Counterfeiters* is partially based on Adolf Burger's memoir of his participation in the Third Reich's Operation Bernhard (1942–5), a currency counterfeiting operation authorized by Heinrich Himmler and supervised by its namesake, Sturmbannführer Bernhard Krüger. The operation sought to undermine the Allied economies and finance Third Reich operations, including intelligence gathering, by counterfeiting the British pound sterling and later the US dollar. The currency counterfeiting operation was one of the largest the world has ever seen and led to the post-war reissue of the British pound sterling. At the Sachsenhausen concentration camp near Berlin, 144 Jewish prisoners of thirteen different nationalities were forced to work on producing counterfeit pounds and dollar notes worth billions. They included professional printers, graphic artists, typographists, and bankers. The inmates were to be killed when the project ended, and they knew it. They forged around 133 million pounds, which would be worth around $6 billion in today's money. Most of it never reached Britain as the war-wracked Luftwaffe lacked the planes to drop it. Burger is one of only two prisoner characters in the film that has an authentic historical name and is not a synthesis of several real-life prisoners involved in Operation Bernhard (the other is the opera singer, Isaak Plappler, who was still living when the film was made – see the director's commentary on the DVD, *The Counterfeiters*, 2007). Here we have a notable strategy of the *Bildungsroman* as an historical fiction with hybrid or mediating protagonists who are able to explore various social stratifications, in which 'the assembled team of inmates represents a microcosm of society, with members from all walks of life and social statuses' (Burt 2011, 309). The various social strata depicted not only confounds the homogenizing discourse of anti-Semitism but, in the self-interest that the characters then manifest under conditions of extreme duress, points towards the collapse of respectable society that Arendt diagnoses as one of the truly horrifying legacies of totalitarianism.

Adolf Burger (1917–2016) was closely involved with the film's production and with checking the screenplay for authenticity. He was a Jewish Slovak typographer, memoir writer, and Holocaust survivor involved in Operation Bernhard. During the Second World War Burger began to print false baptismal certificates for Jews scheduled for deportation, which stated that they had been Roman Catholic from birth or baptized so before the Second World War. Slovaks with such documents were not deported. Burger's activity was discovered. He was arrested on 11 August 1942 and assigned to work at the new arrivals' selection ramps at Auschwitz-Birkenau. After eighteen months at Auschwitz-Birkenau Burger was transferred to the Sachsenhausen concentration camp in April 1944, and eventually to the Ebensee site of the Mauthausen camp network where he was liberated by the US Army on 6 May 1945. The character Adolf Burger barely resembles his actual namesake, a genial and self-effacing man. In the film the character of Adolf Burger is a communist agitator, idealistic but also dogmatic and intransigent, heedless of self-preservation and interpreting every impulse by other prisoners towards personal survival and hedonistic enjoyment as complicit with the Nazis. He wants to sabotage the Nazi war effort at all costs, but somewhat more ambiguously has himself been assigned to the 'Kanada' warehouse where he can ransack the property of those newly arrived on deportation trains. His wife has been detained and is later killed in the women's section of Auschwitz, an event which consolidates Burger's decision to sabotage the counterfeiting operation.

The film's centre of gravity, its *Bildungsheld*, is the character Sally Sorowitch, who is based on the Russian Salomon Smolianoff, a significant but relatively minor personage in Burger's memoir. As Burger records, Smolianoff, formerly an art student and painter and an émigré from the Bolshevik revolution, was the only professional money forger of the 144 political prisoners in the forger unit commanded by Krüger (Burger 2009, 158). In Ruzowitzky's film he is the lead protagonist and in every scene, the camera often looks over his shoulder as he enters one morally challenging or disorienting scenario after another. The real Smolianoff was sent to the Mauthausen concentration camp and made himself useful to the SS guards as a portraitist. He was selected for Operation Bernhard, transferred to the Sachsenhausen concentration camp in 1944, and eventually to the Ebensee site of the Mauthausen camp network, where he was liberated by the US Army on 6 May 1945, soon afterwards disappearing into obscurity in South America. Smolianoff died in Argentina in 1960.[7] It is Sally's journey inwards, his sensitization to memory, that will differ from the responses of other characters and help him to improvise a personal ethic gleaned from a variety of urgent memories and experiences.

The other significant character in this film is Friedrich Herzog, who was based on the historical figure Bernhard Krüger, an SS officer in the German Security Main Office, or RHSA. Not wanting to go to the Eastern Front himself, and perhaps mindful of the fate of the Jewish concentration camp prisoners in his employ if his factory were closed, Krüger succeeded in establishing a new operation to forge American dollar notes from September 1944. Instructing his workers to work as slowly as possible, he managed to stall the operation until the war ended, permitting the prisoners to be liberated after they were transferred to camps in Austria in May 1945. His historical role in both exploiting, killing, and perhaps also prolonging the life of Jewish prisoners is so ambiguous that Ruzowitzky notes that Isaak Plappler and the real Adolf Burger actually argued about him on the set of the film. It is clear, however, that this is not another German film that is intent, like *Downfall*, on creating 'good Germans' who have a skerrick of decency and demur at Hitler's fanaticism and instability even if they are pillars of the Nazi inner sanctum. The unctuous yet vicious, self-serving Herzog is constantly depicted in the film as threatening Sally and his men with death if the operation doesn't succeed. Nevertheless, Herzog does provide the film with quite a few moments of low comedy as he seriously believes himself to be a respectable *paterfamilias* and aspiring middle-manager, and, as Burt points out, his obsession with producing 'the dollar!' provides ironic commentary, in the manner of *The Kindly Ones*' trope of ironic inversion, on the Nazi stereotype that the Jews are obsessed with money (Burt 2011, 316).

What we know is that throughout the actual Operation Bernhard Capt. Krüger and his team of SS guards spared their Jewish prisoners the degradations they had known previously in Nazi camps.[8] The inmates had decent food, civilian clothes, cigarettes, books, and board games. They even received parcels from outside. They were allowed to grow their hair and listen to the radio. They worked eight-hour days. Adolf Burger played ping-pong with the SS which is transposed to a viscerally disturbing scene in the film in which Burger and Sally trade insults and then blows while playing table tennis as inmates are shot just beyond the sectioning fence. The privileged prisoners' suspension from the brutality of camp life is represented in the film by its diegetically significant musical score, with operetta music constantly playing in the background of the workshops, and the occasional staging of cabarets. If anything the film also heightens the violence and chaos that were a quotidian backdrop to their activities through the constant menacing presence and occasional sadism of a typically 'brutal' Nazi in Hauptscharführer Holst, who kills the tuberculosis-suffering Kolya in a climactic scene in the proximity of the prisoners. The real Burger when interviewed in 2009 about the veracity of the film script, that he himself worked on, denied its veracity.

> No, it was a movie. You have to read the book and then you will know the truth. The SS officers never screamed at us as they did in the movie. They never shot anyone in front of us as they did in the film. Six prisoners who fell ill were murdered, but never in front of us. ('Interview: Adolf Burger', 2009)

The Counterfeiters is not a collective story of survival as represented in *The Devil's Workshop*, where the writer Burger constantly uses the pronoun 'we' when describing mutual decisions made by the group: 'So we decided to prolong the production of dollar bills so that they could not be used by the secret service' (Burger 2009, 163). Indeed the actual Adolf Burger calmly denied that he performed any heroic deeds of defiance or was prepared to sacrifice his own survival for the greater good.

> In real life, I was not such a revolutionary as I was made out in the movie. The actor [August Diehl] who played me came to see me before the film was made, but I didn't recognise myself in his performance. ('Interview: Adolf Burger', 2009)

When confronted with imminent death at gunpoint the choice, as he records, was not particularly difficult in itself. This is how the actual Adolf Burger explains his actions in an interview with *The Jewish Chronicle*:

> Of course it [the forgery] helped them. It was a lot of money and they were able to purchase weapons and food with it. They took our notes around the world and exchanged them for local currencies and then bought what they needed... We did not think about that. In a camp your objective is to survive. And if someone is standing over you with a gun, you do whatever they ask you to do. ('Interview: Adolf Burger', 2009)

Arguably Ruzowitzky's employment of more vividly realized dramatis personae does not turn its back on this story of collective endurance but it does seek to heighten audience interest by accentuating the very difficult choices faced by prisoners who wished to survive the concentration camps, deploying a *mise en scene* of claustrophobic psychological warfare in the tradition of *Twelve Angry Men*. The main argument, on which the plot and survival of the characters hinge, is whether Sally will support or ultimately denounce the character Adolf Burger's (hereafter referred to as 'Burger') ideologically driven desire to sabotage the counterfeiting operation which puts the lives of the 'privileged prisoners' at risk. Sally shares grave concerns with other prisoners about the danger of this course of action which may lead to their deaths, but he ultimately covers for and enables Burger's activities long enough for them to survive the fleeing Nazis, despite the wheedling but also threatening entreaties of Herzog. This suspenseful storyline, which for Wauchope casts a pall over the film's historical purchase, has little to do with the account in the real Adolf Burger's memoir which identifies a former Dutch officer called Abraham Jacobson as possessing the 'moral courage' to sabotage the counterfeiting work so it would no longer be used by the German secret service (Burger 2009, 163).

Rather than observing the rather contingent vacillations of audacity and conformity one would expect in such a situation, Ruzowitzky has instead crafted a philosophically motivated *Bildungsfilm* with an invented *Bildungsheld* who is uneasily poised between moral alternatives: is he a Kapo or comrade? Will a political exile with an implied history of suffering at the hands of a collectivist ideology in Bolshevik Russia continue to abide by his cynical credo articulated in the film's opening scenes: 'Our people? I'm me and the others are the others?' Will his traumatic history at the hands of the Russians and then Nazis foreclose his ability to recognize principled resistance? In the tradition of the *Bildungsroman* we are dealing with a film with realist elements but symbolically overdetermined in that the characters encountered by the *Bildungsheld* are, as Swales has suggested, 'relatable to the hero's potentiality' (Swales 2012, 30). For example as a parvenu wishing to survive and focused on the main chance, Sally Sorowitsch understands Herzog intimately: 'Herzog's a crook. I know how to handle him.' Yet he is also repelled by the hypocrisy of Herzog's cultured cynicism and utilitarian individualism. Herzog, a former communist, is prepared to forego any principle or allegiance to gain an advantage, already preparing himself for post-war life in the West as a managerial technocrat.

The film's motif of *confronting one's doppelgänger* reminds us of Dostoevksy's great Menippean satire, *Crime and Punishment*, where Raskolnikov, having committed a supposedly pure 'utilitarian' murder to escape penury and to redistribute wealth in a corrupted society, is almost comically appalled by his acquisitive future brother-in-law Luzhin's defence of bourgeois materialism and self-interest on the same rationalist-utilitarian grounds with which he, Raskolnikov, has justified his murder of the pawn broker. Sally's choices are further complicated by his ambivalence towards Burger's principled idealism, a stance that risks jettisoning the lives of those who are now closest to the two men. Yet his prisoner's code of always defending one's brethren and the increasingly risky actions he takes to care for the innocent Kolya who comes to resemble a son or younger brother to him, indicate the possibility of wider solidarities as his care for someone reminding him of his younger self reconstitutes the possibility of an elective family.

The key dialogue between the characters of Sally and Burger illuminates the dilemma they face:

Sally: 'No one's prepared to die for a principle'
Burger: 'That's why the Nazi system works'
Sally: 'We're alive. That's worth a hell of a lot'
Burger: 'Exactly. Isn't it about more than your own shitty little life?'
Sally: 'Our shitty life is the only thing we have ... We'll have to pay for it if we don't deliver. All of us will pay'
Burger: 'Yes'

In an interview Ruzowitzky robustly defends creating scenarios in a 'dramatic, existential framework' ('The Counterfeiters media release' 2010, 10) that provoke thought about the proportionality of 'idealism and pragmatism' in moral judgement while, as Wauchope argues, allowing the 'audience to identify with both positions' (Wauchope 2010, 63).

Yet it is Sally and not Burger who the audience is encouraged to identify with throughout the film, the viewer often looking just over his shoulder in handheld point-of-view shots, and this is in part because Sally is the most worried about the immediate consequences of the sabotage. Sally gets increasingly close to some other prisoners, in particular, as we have discussed, a young Russian man called Kolya, an art student, with whom he shares his soup and discusses art-historical topics. This is a crucial scene in the film because it represents Sally's reawakening artistic interests and his moving away from pure self-interest, all the while being offered another model of human solidarity that is not predicated on theoretical constructs such as the people or the greater good. Sally's gesture in sharing the soup has been described as similar to what Primo

Levi described as 'us-ism' in which you might show generosity to another person with whom you have fledgling solidarity in your immediate circle on an ad hoc basis without any general altruistic principles that cannot assist survival in such a brutal environment. Sally ends up protecting Burger from retribution by other inmates as a matter of basic humanity but his increasingly fond memories of his artistic past refigure the work of memory which was once predicated on the rejection of human loyalty and the hatred of any version of collectivism, enabling Sally to push back against aspects of Burger's idealistic posturing which seem to be a mask for misanthropy and a cover for projects of vengeance and domination.

A Bildungsroman 'about many things' The Counterfeiters as a historical interpretation of Jewish experience

In this final section of this chapter I want to suggest that it is precisely as a *Bildungsfilm* that *The Counterfeiters* has proved to be a particularly satisfying and stimulating experience for a variety of cinemagoers who desire to understand the linkages between past and present. As Jane Lydon puts it, 'we need histories which don't close off the past, but rather link it to the present, showing us how we got to where we are' (Lydon 2004, 148). I would suggest that this is because the film does enact a 'mode of historical thought' that contributes to historical understanding. It does so by entertaining and affecting the viewer in myriad ways using cinematic techniques such as thematic condensation (the question of privileged prisoners), metaphorical devices (the table tennis scene symbolizing leisured privilege in a world of dead and dying), suspense (will the heist be successful and will the prisoners escape with their lives?), and the sharpening of philosophical differences (arguments for pragmatism, idealism, utilitarianism) between characters in pursuit of dramatic effect and contemporary relevance.

I would also suggest that the character of Sally Sorowitsch is dramatically effective and intellectually stimulating because, as a *Bildungsheld* with deep roots in a heterogeneous, picaresque literary tradition, he maps certain contradictions and complexities in the historical experience of the Jewish diaspora. Lacking a fixed point of view, by no means identifying himself with other Jews, particularly in the film's early phases, Sally is something of a liminal 'middle character', like Daniel Stein neither pure victim nor perpetrator. Drawing on Dalley's *The Postcolonial Historical Novel*, which defends select historical novels as responsibly contributing to historical consciousness, I would argue that we can read *The Counterfeiters* as using a variety of narrative techniques to confirm and enlarge the extant historical record by establishing meaningful connections between inventive representations and our historical understanding. I would particularly like to draw on Dalley's conception of 'indexical' representations whereby particular events, characters, and deliberative situations condense or gesture towards the *Nachträglichket* of traumatic collective histories, counterfactual possibilities, and lingering problems in judging the past.

To begin with a discussion of Sally as focalizing the viewer's attention in the film. In interviews Ruzowitzky has suggested that Sally is a much-loved character by audiences, much preferred to Burger for the most part, even though there is a late and climactic scene in which the camp's emaciated inmates stare in bewilderment at the well-fed privileged prisoners they encounter and instead demonstrate a touching affection for Burger because he is the only one trying to destroy the Nazi war effort without compromise. In our cinematic response to Sally it is questionable whether we are responding to a historical personage who we celebrate or condemn for their deeds. Rather there are intertextual resonances, and a cinematic phenomenology that heightens our responsiveness. As Stefanie Rauch argues, the impact of Holocaust films on individuals as realist texts is sometimes overstated because 'genre needs to be considered as a part of viewers' preconceptions' (Rauch 2018, 176).[9] In Sally we enjoy a flawed noir anti-hero as discussed by Wauchope: damaged, haunted, resilient, desperately trying not to be seduced by chthonic forces from his past. Overlaid with this noir heritage we have a fluid *Bildungsheld* who, like Oskar Schindler or Paul Rusesabagina, becomes politicized and outgrows mere commercial pragmatism and concern for immediate kin (Rusesabagina adopts his nieces, Sally thinks of Kolya as a kind of adopted son) and so assumes a position of responsible communal leadership while engaging in belated reflection on his complicity in the horrors that now confront him. Sally's *kairotic* sensitivity to the needs of his fellow prisoners does not congeal into an ideology but is succoured by friendship and a dawning sense of hope in his own rehabilitation and reabsorption into community. He is an example of the picaresque hero of historical fiction as discussed by Bakhtin, someone whose individual fate finds manifold points of connection with a social totality and with a possible historical future (Bakhtin 2010, 23).

Between past and future

If we look at Sally as evoking certain thorny aspects of Jewish diasporic history, then in some respects he's the accursed wandering cosmopolitan Jew expelled from one home after another, a perceptive 'stranger' in the parlance of Georg Simmel who is unencumbered by traditional patterns of thought and behaviour. In his privileged relationship with Herzog based on reciprocal favours, we sense a reprisal of the so-called court Jew, the grasping social parvenu who has little interest in the overall emancipation of the Jewish people, who looks down at other Jews because unlike him, they refuse to 'adapt' to a hierarchical and anti-Semitic society. But of course as Sally comes to identify with his fellow Jews and endure violent anti-Semitism we glimpse the tenets of secular or Herzlian Zionism in which ethnic solidarity and effective political mobilization seeking to ensure the survival of one's people, despite very significant cultural and class differences, becomes necessary in the face of violence, betrayal, and the caprice of the powerful. If adaptation once signalled an assimilationist desire to forget who one is, in a context in which many of the prisoners stubbornly cling to their former social roles or seek to avoid painful memories through nostalgia and hedonism, then the pathetic spectacle in one of the final scenes in Sachsenhausen where Sally ignores Atze's advice to 'forget about' the recently suicided Loszek, as he seeks to bury him respectfully amongst a world of dead and dying, illustrates just how far Sally's more attentive and less generalized relationship to the past has assisted his personal growth.

The film has other indexical stratagems. It recognizes that many of the survivors were 'privileged prisoners' with all of the shame and guilt consequent upon what Lawrence Langer has called 'choiceless choices', that that has entailed. An early scene in which Sally enters prisoners' barracks at Auschwitz-Birkenau only to be threatened by a Jewish Kapo reminds us of Primo Levi's account of the disorienting arrival in the concentrationary universe:

> the arrival in the Lager was a shock because of the surprise it entailed. The world into which one was precipitated was terrible, yes, but also indecipherable: it did not conform to any model, the enemy was all around but also inside, the 'we' lost its limits ... One entered hoping at least for the solidarity of one's companions in misfortune, but the hoped-for allies, except in special cases, were not there ... [this] became manifest from the very first hours of imprisonment, often in the instant form of a concentric aggression on the part of those in whom one hoped to find future allies ... The privileged prisoners were a minority within the Lager population, but they represent a potent majority among survivors. (Levi 1988, 23–4, 26)

Yet the film doesn't go as far as Langer in suggesting that moral choice as we know it was superfluous, and that inmates were left with the 'futile task of redefining decency in an atmosphere that could not support it' (Lawrence 1980, 226). Sally's sharing of soup or rediscovery with Kolya of his love of art reminds us of Levian strategies of minor resistance in which sharing food with other inmates or quoting Dante as a rebuke to the automatism of one's situation are on a continuum with major acts of resistance such as the uprising of the Warsaw Ghetto or the uprising of SonderKommando in 1944.

An analysis of Burger as both a nemesis and tempter of Sally necessitates comment on his interesting historical genealogy. He is a vivid reminder of the role played by the Jewish left intelligentsia, including communists, in resistance to fascism and anti-Semitism and the search for utopian alternatives to the majority/minority politics of the nation-state. Yet like many an idealist become authoritarian leader he forfeits existing solidarities in the present for abstract notions of human welfare; as he becomes isolated from his peers Burger eschews the politics of persuasion and entreaty and instead instinctively justifies the secretive imposition of authoritarian solutions in the name of the greater good. His increasingly abstract interest in the welfare of those beyond the camps, with hints of the altruistic mania of Dickens' Mrs Jellyby of *Bleak House*, is shadowed by a will-to-power for which individuals are mere cyphers, means but not ends in themselves. Yet his powerful discourse about the importance of principles for which we must be willing to sacrifice ourselves reminds us of the Lutheran pastor Martin Niemöller's famous 'First they came for the Socialists' speech. An emaciated prisoner's tender embrace of Burger also reminds us that we have a mild case of Stockholm syndrome by the end of our viewing experience, that the film has cunningly manipulated our sympathies so that we care more for its characters than the faceless many beyond the fence.

In the tradition of the *Bildungsroman*, Burger has pedagogical value as a personality and possible mentor. As with Settembrini in *The Magic Mountain* he trains Sally's judgement as both an ethical purist who refuses to succumb to an atavistic situation, and a one-sided ideologue unsympathetic to human frailty and irrational desire. It is because of the unwavering Burger, both principled and unconsciously mimetic of his context, that Sally doesn't become a Kapo. Who became a Kapo? asks Primo Levi. Sometimes it was Jews who saw in the particle of authority that was being offered to them the only possibility of escaping the 'final solution' – the sadistic, the frustrated, but also 'the many among the oppressed who were contaminated by the oppressors and unconsciously strove to identify with them' (Levi 1988, 32). Rejecting Burger's contaminated death-drive, and Herzog's odious arriviste mentality typical of a corporate middle-manager, a reflective Sally can affirm the lives of others as a necessary response to the exigencies of his situation. In the tradition of the female-authored *Bildungsroman* we can see that the journey inwards prompted by events has encouraged relationality rather than an unsustainable autonomy, and a return to the question of his vocation that is now open to reflection on his social responsibilities.

Finally, the character of Herzog helps to open up a field of enquiry as to the 'banality of evil' and the relationship between the Holocaust and bureaucratic modernity. Herzog knows exactly 'what he is doing' which contradicts Arendt's assertions about Adolf Eichmann's inability to conceive of the enormity of his deeds in her report on his Jerusalem trial *Eichmann in Jerusalem* (1963). On the other hand Herzog's dedication to self-advancement is reminiscent of Arendt's study of Eichmann as a careerist bureaucrat. Herzog's desire to forge a Swiss passport reminds us of the many technically gifted Nazis who fled to the United States and Australia; his appeals to Sally that they are of a similar pragmatic ilk does partially remind us that we need to be trained to see the 'ordinariness' of evil and not simply its more spectacular or diabolical manifestations as absolute alterity. The inclusion of Herzog and his oily self-interest is not only far more interesting dramatically than the reproduction of the Nazi as atavistic barbarian, it is also keeping pace with Holocaust historiography. As historian Dan Stone has argued:

> Recent research has brought us back to the postwar notion of the Third Reich as a gangster regime ... the appeal of Nazism was the promise of an entrée into politics for arrivistes with no sense of commitment to the political process [who] looted and stole as much as they could.... The Nazis were not only the most notorious murderers in history but also the greatest thieves. (Stone 2010, 55)

To conclude, we need to reflect on an unusual situation in which a survivor, who collaborated on the screenplay, is pleased with a film that bears only passing resemblance to his own experiences. It is at this juncture that we need to consider the film's historical work in slightly more expansive terms as Rosenstone has suggested and as a less restrictive conception of the *Bildungsfilm* as focused on relatable identification and narrative closure would indicate. What the film does achieve, according to the real Adolf Burger, who checked and approved the screenplay and described the film's release as a 'high point' of his life, is a representation of a larger and more banal truth in keeping with the historiographical élan of *The Kindly Ones*, that the Nazis, metaphysical pretensions aside, were counterfeiters of virtue, mere 'common criminals'. 'The Nazis murdered millions for ideological reasons, but they were also ordinary criminals', he said.

> In my opinion it's a good film. And the reason I agreed to it, without conditions, when the producers approached me was because the English barred any investigation into the whole affair at the Nuremberg Trials. To this day people don't know that they counterfeited so much money. Now when this film comes out everybody will learn that the Nazis weren't just murderers – they were ordinary counterfeiters. That's what I wanted to achieve, and that's what I have achieved. ('Interview with Adolf Burger', 2007)

Of course we need to remember that in a 1958 interview the real Bernhard Krüger, who Burger despised, claimed without irony that 'Smolianoff' was the 'only real criminal' involved in Operation Bernhard. So Burger understands the film *The Counterfeiters* as a potent rebuke to any veneer of respectability put on the actions of lower-ranking Nazis and military officials.

Burger doesn't say much about it in interviews, but in his own attempts as a survivor to reach younger audiences, he seems to have no problem with the film's provocative dialogism, its desire to highlight a core moral dilemma in any age, the tension between pragmatism and idealism, the moral duty to observe an intrinsic moral code and the weighing up of options and priorities demanded by attention to consequences. Ruzowitzky feels that on an abstract level a younger audience can engage with the dilemmas arising from privilege, akin to the nagging unease felt by affluent Westerners today: 'Is it possible to enjoy our rich, sheltered lives in the face of all the suffering in the world?' (cited in Wauchope 2010, 68). Ruzowitsky is thus not at all squeamish about the rhetorically adroit communicative imperative we have spoken of:

> For a present-day audience, an angry 'That's how it was!' is no longer enough. We have to talk about the Holocaust and so have a moral obligation to do so in a way that reaches as many viewers as possible. So, yes, a film about the Holocaust should be exciting as well as entertaining, in the best sense of the word. ('The Counterfeiters media release', 11)

In conclusion I hope to have suggested in a multilayered analysis of *The Counterfeiters* that Robert Rosenstone is correct in saying that productive criticism of historical feature films means eschewing a reductive historicist analysis and embracing what we might call the 'thought-work' that has helped to shape that film's creative decisions. As this chapter and the next indicate, we require a combination of genre and stylistic criticism with an awareness that the fictional structure of a text or film, by virtue of genre strategies, has its own means of enacting a mode of historical thought. In the case of the historical *Bildungsfilm*, a precipitous assumption about its bias towards a pleasingly redemptive narrative has obscured discussion of its intellectual curiosity and historiographical positioning, in other words the long-standing proclivity of the genre of the *Bildungsroman* itself towards thought experiment.

Chapter 6

A PROTAGONIST FOR DARK TIMES

REPURPOSING MEMORY AND THE FUTURE OF CIVIL COURAGE IN MARGARETHE VON TROTTA'S BIOPIC *HANNAH ARENDT*

> 'If I refuse to remember, I am actually ready to do anything' – Hannah Arendt. ('Some Questions of Moral Philosophy', 94)

This chapter is an extended meditation on Hannah Arendt's dictum, in part referring to her groundbreaking conception of Adolf Eichmann, that a person who doesn't remember is ready to do anything, to take any action and betray any solidarity. Arendt's suggestive observation suggests that a person who refuses to remember will avoid the kind of heterodox reflection on their personal memories that our protagonists often grew into in previous chapters. Such a person will not honour singularities of experience and moments of interpersonal connection with their sustained attention and will therefore lack controls around their future conduct. They will fail to make lasting promises to themselves about the kind of person they wish to be and the ethical commitments that they should make to others.[1]

My interpretation, drawing on a conception of the genre's *kairotic* urgency and psychological turn, focuses on the German director Margarethe von Trotta's 2012 biopic *Hannah Arendt* as a depiction of a fictionalized protagonist who experiences a mature ethical awakening in a moment of profound existential and analytical crisis as she confronts traumatic wounds reopened by her attendance of the trial of Adolf Eichmann in Jerusalem in 1961. I suggest the film is interested in the way that this high-profile trial itself turned into a trial of Arendt's character and loyalties upon the publication of her highly controversial 'reports' on the Eichmann trial in *The New Yorker* in 1963. In this interpretation I suggest that the character 'Hannah Arendt' is subtly depicted as the questing protagonist of a *Bildungsroman* whose character is tested by various ordeals including a potentially shattering confrontation with her own unresolved past, in which she must reconcile and repurpose memories of imprisonment, despair, personal betrayal, and statelessness.

Ellen McWilliams has pointed out that female-authored fictions have often described a late awakening or blossoming of female creativity and desire (McWilliams 2009, 38). I will suggest that the character Hannah Arendt's struggles to reconcile herself to her past and speak meaningfully to the present can also be described in similar terms, as her response to the arrest of Eichmann and attendance at his Jerusalem trial becomes an 'occasion for introspection as well as education once more that [. . .] awakens her soul to "sensitivity and memory"' (Abels, Hirsch, Langland 1983, 29). It is a journey in keeping with the pluralism of the female *Bildungsoman* as described by Susan Fraiman, involving a re-entry into social connection and relationality rather than an individualistic focus on separation, discontinuity, autonomy (Abels, Hirsch, Langland 1983, 37). An indicative aspect of the film is the chronotopic complexity of the protagonist who, like many of our protagonists including Sally Sorowitsch, comes to honour her passionate inquisitiveness as a younger person, and develops her vocation as a public-facing intellectual, finding various ways to revive the Socratic heritage and insert herself vigorously into the marketplace of ideas.

In conversation with other critics of the film, but also in keeping with my emphasis in this book on the fluidity of *Bildung* as its protagonists willingly undertake an extra-mural process of self-formation at critical biographical and socio-historical junctures, I discuss the character of Hannah Arendt as precariously situated, in her own parlance, 'between past and future'. Diamond and Jurist point out that for the philosopher Hannah Arendt thinking is an 'uncertain, creative exercise' suspended in a fragile yet fertile temporal interval in which I can 'anticipate the future, think of it as though it were already present, and I can remember the past as though it had not disappeared' (*The Life of the Mind*, cited in Diamond and Jurist, 110). It is in this gap in time in which human beings can make 'a stand against past and future' (Arendt 2006, 10), breaking up the flow of 'indifferent time', aware that they exist in a precarious yet fruitful interval equally determined by the no longer and the not yet, a moment that may in itself 'contain the moment of truth' (Arendt 2006, 9).

The character of Hannah Arendt in this film is herself plagued by the rise of totalitarianism and her searing experience of its political and personal depredations, while attempting to confront its far-reaching epistemological and ethical challenges with novel and creative modes of thinking that are not derivative of outworn and ineffective moral and religious paradigms. Arendt as represented in this film will draw indicative attention to the *kairotic* dimensions of her thinking as practised and enacted in worldly spaces. A seeking protagonist, living in the question of how the unimaginable has come to pass, Arendt is figured as articulating her thought according to the needs of *Kairos*, as shaping her discourse to speak opportunely, to respond to a historical moment with urgency and with an awareness of the affective needs of her spectators. I will suggest that in the film Arendt's ability to engage in *Selbstdenken*, a mode of thinking that never forgets its relationship to the world, culminates in her public address, defending her ethos, to fascinated students at The New School. These receptive students, proxies in some respects for the viewing audience, are deeply troubled by the recent past but, poised between past and future, also wish to understand the contemporary implications of overwhelmingly painful historical events.

Viewers can participate in the indicative hermeneutics of *Hannah Arendt* as a *Bildungsfilm*, as they watch Arendt travel beyond the comfortable precincts of her émigré salon, fashion an entirely new perspective on events she had once subsumed in more theological terms as a form of 'radical evil', and work through insurgent memories which acknowledge that she herself may have been seduced by the charm of metaphysical ideas and proved insufficiently courageous when drawn into an affair with Martin Heidegger. The film engages a reflective audience as it carefully includes surrogates for interested spectatorship including, most prominently, young and still impressionable characters such as Arendt's assistant Lotte Köhler and other students of Arendt at The New School. My contention is that the oft-highlighted presence of younger spectators to Arendt's passionate thinking in *Hannah Arendt* suggests that we need not subscribe wholly to her key concept of the banality of evil but can nevertheless appreciate and valorize Arendt's exemplary civil courage as a mature protagonist. In an agonistic context, Arendt publicly defends her startling and destabilizing characterization of Adolf Eichmann, one of the principal architects of the Nazi genocide of European Jews, as a banal and mediocre functionary who should not be confused with a diabolical monster or even a wilful criminal. Like other protagonists we have discussed whose explorative curiosity has indicative significance, the quest for understanding and journey of memory undertaken by Arendt assists younger onlookers, including Lotte, to appreciate independent thought that speaks truth to power, and to recognize manifestations of the banality of evil in their own social context.

I will suggest that in a similar fashion to Stevens, Aue, Daniel Stein, and Sally Sorowitsch, the film presents a narrative of tentative awakening and ethical growth after a tumultuous period of personal crisis. Yet how do we understand this growth given that many of Arendt's hostile interlocutors in the film, and her subsequent legion of critics, feel that with her utterances on the 'word and thought defying banality of evil' Arendt demonstrated that she was in fact merely demonstrating a 'perverse' or self-regarding concern with her own philosophical brilliance? What sort of maturity and attention to character formation can we discern when characters in the film wonder whether she is in danger of being retraumatized by the Eichmann trial and ponder that her infamously sarcastic tone in her book *Eichmann in Jerusalem*, and her seeming obliviousness to the outrage her views may generate, is indicative of a self-protective attitude towards her suppressed pain?

The stakes are heightened when the context for judgement and deliberation in this film is the Eichmann problematic of which we have been speaking. In this film we cannot speak precipitously of the Eichmann problematic as an inherited trope for historical, sociological, and philosophical inquiry but as the diegetic crucible shaping Arendt's fraught confrontation with the man himself. As Joel Rosenberg discusses in reference to this unsettling but well-recognized problematic, Arendt's 'report' on the Eichmann trial 'polemically turned Eichmann into the emblem of a broader social malady from which no nation is wholly immune', addressing the 'lack of empathy, critical awareness, and self-understanding on the part of many, which enabled a profound historical evil to take root in the wider world' (Rosenberg 2014, 203). In *Hannah Arendt*, these ubiquitous moral deficiencies are not yet a well-recognized philosophical topos but a volatile context for her developing thinking and emergence as an independent thinker. Arendt's attendance at the trial and gradual realization that Eichmann was more insipid than infernal, her dawning awareness of Eichmann's refusal to 'think' or actively remember the true scope of his atrocious deeds, must be thrashed out in the volatile context of sceptical or antagonistic interlocutors who are incredulous at her attempts to overturn received wisdom. In the background of Arendt's thinking on Eichmann is that thoughtless conduct and betrayal inheres in the men who have been closest to her, including the perfidious Martin Heidegger, who seduced her as an eighteen-year-old and then joined the Nazis, but also her current husband, the supportive but slippery Heinrich Blücher, who is revealed in one of the opening scenes as regularly engaging in extra-marital affairs. In this context of male perfidy, the question of how human beings become habituated to thoughtless conduct and insensitive to the impact of their choices on other people is an intrinsic dimension of the film's layered chronotope.

Drawing on flashbacks of encounters with Heidegger at the University of Freiburg and on her return to Germany in 1950, and foregrounding Arendt's experiences as a detainee at Gurs concentration camp in Southern France, the film suggests that Arendt's developing thinking and assumption of responsibility for understanding the past is intrinsically related to the creative repurposing of her memories in a manner that bears comparison with the improvising protagonists that we have already discussed. In *Hannah Arendt*, memory, 'one of the most important [...] modes of thought' (Arendt 2006, 4), is integral to the developing animus of her character; for Arendt thinking is spurred by continual reflection on lived experience, and by an attunement to exemplary instances of virtuous character that one has witnessed, or important experiences of activity in the public realm that one has participated in. Thus the 'anti-doctrinal character of thinking' described by Hyvönen and Möller is largely a function of energetic remembrance for Arendt (Hyvönen and Möller 2017, 146). As Arendt puts it in *The Life of the Mind*, 'Remembrance has a natural affinity to thought; all thoughts [...] are after-thoughts. Thought trains rise naturally, almost automatically, out of re-membering, without any break' (Arendt 1978, *Willing*, 37).

As Hyvönen and Möller point out, Arendt did not think of memory as passive but as mediated by imaginative representation; it was precisely the function of a memory-enriched thought process to disrupt linear conceptions of time in order to unearth that which is 'rich and strange', suppressed traditions of political thought or activity that might be reactivated in the present, in the gap between an unresolved past and a dangerously uncertain future (Hyvönen and Möller 2017, 150). My point is to suggest that alongside the historical texts that we have studied, *Hannah Arendt* foregrounds a complex, non-sovereign, associative and irreverent version of memory that tends to exceed the protagonist's own ego defences and initial frame of reference. If the *Bildungsroman* is a genre increasingly amenable to the unconscious and to the heterogeneous impulses of an unreliable narrator, then a variety of conscious and unconscious forces can be integrated in order to point to the layered temporality that informs thought and action. I would suggest that *Hannah Arendt* is a self-aware version of a genre in which, as Franco Moretti points out, there is a tendency to build up the self and make it the 'centre of its own structure' rather than decompose it in the manner of classical psychoanalysis (Moretti 2000, 11).

In particular I would like to suggest that the film highlights the various character traits that inform Arendt's signature and non-privative conception of *Selbstdenken*, thinking for oneself, without ideological crutches, on behalf of a world that requires constant provocations to critical reflection. As Diamond and Jurist suggest, when, in the person of Eichmann, Arendt comes 'face to face with her own unconscious terrors and longings' (Diamond and Jurist 2018, 87), she does not retreat from the complexity of phenomena but instead we see her 'defying simple answers or facile explanation' as her thinking, poised between past and future, grows out of her own experience, dwells on matters and events at hand, and refuses to engage in the repetition of 'complacent repetition of "truths" which have become trivial and empty' (*The Last Interview*, cited in Diamond and Jurist 2018, 87). As Diamond and Jurist point out, and here we touch on an indicative dimension of the film in which the subject is implicated in a trial by ordeal that risks comfort, privilege and a stable conception of one's 'home', Arendt's conception of thinking from the standpoint of other perspectives engages her multiple experiences as German philosophy student, internment camp inmate, stateless person, émigré, theorist of the American polity, public intellectual and salonnière, lover, and faithful friend. In that respect we can see her work on Eichmann, which respects no conventional position or ethical tradition, as the 'crescendo of her tolerance for multiplicity, in others as well as in herself, rendering her ultimately a doyenne of diversity' (Diamond and Jurist 2018, 114). As Diamond and Jurist suggest, *Hannah Arendt* enables us to appreciate Arendt's capacity to 'tolerate, embrace, and reflect on her multiple selves' in all their contradictions and inconsistencies' as the very spark of the 'extraordinary originality of her thinking' (Diamond and Jurist 2018, 114).

Diamond and Jurist's interpretation points to Arendt's multiplicity as sustaining her internal resources when her perspective is challenged and sometimes angrily confronted. It suggests we need to consider in detail aspects of her biography and elements of her post-war thinking that Arendt is reactivating during the Eichmann trial, as she thinks aloud in the precarious interval between past and future. We will need to bear in mind Arendt's sense of responsibility as an educator, her reprise of Socrates as a public intellectual intent on provoking intellectual complacency, her increasing fears for the health of democracy in Cold War America, her suspicion of all forms of instrumentalism, and her need to continue a life's journey away from constricting circumstances. With all of these features of her thought and activity in mind, I want to draw attention to the film's interest in Arendt's epiphanic moments and narrative *peripeteia*, in which, recalling the inchoate emancipative desires of Stevens, Arendt needs to remove herself for a time from the preening, showy and cloistered atmosphere in her New York apartment which threatens to devolve into a theatre for grandstanding by middle-aged male intellectuals with historical axes to grind, as is the case with Hans Jonas. It is noteworthy that during her stay in Israel, she will, in the manner of *Daniel Stein, Interpreter*, experience an idiosyncratic, *kairotic* version of the Jerusalem syndrome as a swerve away from ethnocentric belonging and towards the planetary consciousness required by future generations.

One aspect of her journey beyond the privative and ethnocentric towards an intensifying *Selbstdenken*, a mode of thought that retains a partisanship for the world, its plurality and future prospects, is for Arendt to affirm a more expansive conception of her family and nearest associates that will include the incorporation of her friend and assistant Lotte Köhler into her conception of nearest family. Although Arendt's father died when she was young, *Hannah Arendt* accentuates her character's lack of family structure as her mother is not mentioned and the cherished quasi-paternal figure, great friend, mentor, and former teacher Karl Jaspers does not figure in the film. Friendship remains, which will have geopolitical significance as Arendt the cinematic character explicitly denounces an unreflective ethnocentric love of the Jewish people that does not involve the only meaningful love she is capable of, the love of 'persons'. As Lotte herself puts it, 'God gave us family, but thank God we can choose our friends' (47 minutes). In examining the tentative growth of Arendt's character we will need to discuss the importance of her friendship with Lotte in prompting Arendt's admission to the pain she has caused, as she begins to respond to letters individually, answering for her own thinking publicly in the manner in which the philosopher Hannah Arendt had praised her mentor Karl Jaspers.[2] Arendt's movement away from the privilege of philosophical speculation enjoyed by the clubby, chummy atmosphere of her mostly male New School colleagues, is mimetic of her own reflections on Socrates as the public philosopher par excellence. It will also suggest that Arendt gains strength from the support of her students who appreciate her willingness to display her own personality in an atmosphere poisoned by groupthink and outright misogyny. In order to understand the evolution of Arendt's journey as a thinker in this film, we need

Arendt and the reconstruction of ethics

If we are to interpret Arendt's journey towards understanding a different dimension of evil and re-asserting her position as an independent public intellectual in this film then we must spend some time on her return to pondering ethical questions after the Second World War. Arendt became convinced that the Second World War, the rise of totalitarianism and the events of the Holocaust, was a far-reaching moral catastrophe that had permanently sundered our faith that existing ethical traditions and value systems were sufficient to protect civilizations 'when the chips were down'. So-called morality had collapsed into a set of 'mores', customary behaviours and conventions that could be changed at will according to the requirements of power (Arendt 2003, 54). In response to a shattered Judeo-Christian Western tradition, Arendt helped revive the agentive focus of neo-Aristotelian virtue ethics, which encourages the habitual cultivation of context-sensitive ethical dispositions supported by the deliberations of practical rationality and acute emotional intelligence (see Nussbaum 1999, 163). In her post-war thinking Arendt affirmed the civic importance of ethical autonomy, urging related virtues such as healthy scepticism, judgement informed by 'taste' and imaginative reflection, and the courage required for civil disobedience. These virtues enacted a partiality for the world as a pluralistic public-political space hospitable to varied phenomena, opinions, and interests.

In the manner of the philosophical novel that tests the applicability and consequences of ideas, Von Trotta's film will bring Arendt's agentive focus into a confrontation with the emotional climate that followed the Second World War in which the need to 'think without banisters' can struggle to find footing in a world divided into ideological camps, and in which an original understanding of the past was deemed subservient to an ethic of bearing witness to victims of the Nazis and to maintain a focus on the horrific results of millennia of anti-Semitism.

Von Trotta's film explores this challenge and chooses to focus on a pivotal and still resonating episode in Arendt's life and career. It depicts her decision to travel to Jerusalem and cover the sensational trial of the Nazi SS officer and architect of the Holocaust Adolf Eichmann, who had been captured by Mossad agents in Buenos Aires in May 1960. The film ends with Arendt's attempts to rebut *ad feminam* criticisms of her paradigm-shattering conception of 'the banality of evil' in her book *Eichmann in Jerusalem: A Report on the Banality of Evil*, which appeared in April 1963. The book was initially published as a series of four reports on the trial appearing in *The New Yorker* in February and March of 1963. Von Trotta's film ends in late 1963 with a kind of fictionalized Socratic apologia, in which Arendt, in front of a packed auditorium of enthralled tertiary students and doubtful or hostile colleagues, gives a spirited defence of her infamous portrait of Eichmann as a functionary, someone who had renounced all personal qualities in his careerist ambition to contribute to what he understood to be a world-historical movement.

Referred to in German simply as 'Die Kontroverse', Arendt's report on the Eichmann trial unleashed a storm of controversy that has never entirely died down.[3] The ferocious criticism over Arendt's supposedly exonerating portrait of Eichmann quickly turned into a less edifying trial of Arendt's character and judgement, as ruefully noted in the film by *The New Yorker* editor William Shawn, who commissioned Arendt's report on the trial. Arendt was famously accused by a long-term friend and correspondent, the German-Jewish émigré intellectual Gershom Scholem, of having insufficient 'Ahavat Israel' or love of the Jewish people, a damning indictment which, in *Hannah Arendt*, is transposed to the dying Kurt Blumenfeld but is also intimated by former friends who excoriate her as a German intellectual who 'looks down on us Jews'. As Roger Berkowitz writes in his commentary on the DVD version of the film, Arendt astounded and appalled much of her readership, particularly the American Jewish community, in arguing that Eichmann was not a sadistic anti-Semite but rather a mediocre 'joiner' with a bureaucratic mentality. Arendt recast Eichmann as an obedient servant whose loyalty to the Nazi movement gave him a sense of importance while dulling spontaneous moral reflexes. Notoriously, Arendt claimed that Eichmann, owing to his solipsistic dependence on cliché and sanitized bureaucratic euphemisms, lacked criminal intent or obvious self-interest. Rather he was unable to 'think'; to see the world imaginatively and empathically from the standpoint of others, and thus 'did not know what he was doing' in organizing and ordering the deaths of millions of Jews. Adi Ophir observes that we are still living in the aftermath of Arendt's 'emptying of the Nazi subject', no longer something reassuringly atavistic and barbaric as was the assumption at Nuremberg, but a floating signifier: ordinary, insidious, opaque in motivation, more readily defined by privation of the good, perhaps inseparable from the depersonalizing processes of modernity itself (Ophir 2015, 116).

The interest of von Trotta's film is precisely, as many have recognized, that it is a multifaceted articulation of the *mise en scène* of Arendt's developing thinking on the Eichmann affair. The question of interpretation has revolved around whether we interpret the film as hagiography or as complicating Arendt's conception of thought as a deliberative *internal* conversation that forges the subject as, at the very least, a conscientious objector who refrains from wrongdoing. Arendt's presumption was that active conscience would have prophylactic effects when it came to wrongdoing. A thinking person in Arendt's sense of the term will keep themselves company and is therefore unable to live with a murderer, that is, themselves: 'my conduct towards others will depend on my conduct towards myself' (Arendt 2003, 96)

After the Second World War Arendt was attentive to the habitus of thinking as a contemplative activity that foreswore public engagement and, as we have discussed, spoke of the need to 'philosophize without banisters' – without the canonical support of existing traditions of metaphysical and epistemological inquiry. What this meant in practice was a sustained critique of the authoritarian proclivities of the 'professional thinker' in the Platonic tradition who despises the chaotic volatility of democratic opinion and seeks to support and legitimize tyrants and, in Heidegger's case, the Führer himself. Arendt made it clear on numerous occasions that she no longer sought the mantle of a 'philosopher' or of a 'professional thinker' (Arendt 1978, 3).[4] Thinking, she argues in *The Life of the Mind*, is a matter that can 'no longer be left to "specialists" as though thinking [...] were the monopoly of a specialized discipline' (Arendt 1978, 13).

In a venerable yet marginalized conception of thinking embodied in Socrates' dialogical praxis and revived in Kant, who felt that reason required 'publicity' if it was to benefit humanity, Arendt was deeply disturbed by the position that thinking should be the prerogative of a few (Arendt 1978, 13). For Arendt, thinking is no longer to be identified with metaphysical profundity and the authenticity of an inner essence, but, in passages imbued with the ethic of *Bildung*, with communicative desire and performative enjoyment, the 'urge to display' oneself as a thinking and speaking being: 'thinking beings have an urge to speak, speaking beings have an urge to think' (Arendt 1978 *Thinking*, 99). Thinking is no longer primarily a cognitive activity but a ceaseless task of self-relation and self-scrutiny that requires an exuberant internal conversation. In arguing for thought as a controlled exercise in self-interrogation, Arendt draws on the Third Earl of Shaftesbury's enthusiasm for the Socratic dialogue as a model of 'self-study'. Shaftesbury had in mind a dramatic contrivance in which thinking divides itself into two characters (say appetitive and rational, enthusiastic and sceptical) that engage in a robust process of 'inward converse'. This is an interrogative process of question and response by which, Shaftesbury hoped, one becomes reflectively resolute rather than inertly egotistical, confident that in one's firmest opinions one is 'the same person today as yesterday and tomorrow as today' (Shaftesbury, 84). As Arendt puts it in *The Life of the Mind*, 'thinking always involves remembrance' (Arendt 1978, 78), a process of 'striking roots' in which a once ethically vacillating subject can thereby 'stabilize themselves' (Arendt 2003, 95).

It is more than likely that Arendt had in mind Heidegger's treacherous conduct after the Nazi rise to power when she mused that 'absence of thought is not stupidity; it can be found in highly intelligent people' (Arendt 1978, 13). For Arendt thinking is embedded in a world of appearances; it is allied to intersubjective judgement, tact, acculturated taste, and reconciles us to the world rather than encouraging us to pass over into a Platonic universe of intelligible forms. It is the labour of thinking amongst tangible phenomena that helps prepare us for the 'timely' faculty of nuanced judgement in which we make important, context-sensitive decisions. Where the professional philosopher despises surface impressions, brackets reality and personifies concepts rather than answering to her, his or their own experiences, there is a vital activity of demotic thinking that is always looking for a concrete historical or textual exemplar available to the senses, for a model or ideal type of representative significance. Arendt placed great store in Socrates as the paragon of the thinker who unites 'apparently contradictory passions, for thinking and acting [. . .] who did not shun the marketplace, who was a citizen among citizens, doing nothing, claiming nothing except what in his opinion every citizen should be and have a right to' (Arendt 1978 *Thinking*, 167).

Returning to *Hannah Arendt* as it draws on these various Arendtian conceptions of publicly engaged thinking and deliberation, some prominent critics assume that the film's portrayal of Arendt's presence at the Eichmann trial, which she feels has been corrupted by the crude political aims of Israel's prime minister David Ben Gurion, betrays a debt to classic legal films like *To Kill a Mockingbird* (Robert Mulligan, 1962) and *Twelve Angry Men* (Sidney Lumet, 1957). In liberal dramas like these, a disinterested, self-sacrificing advocate for truth is subject to the hostile partiality of mob opinion. The apparent lionization of Arendt the 'thinker', granted the prerogative to disdain the obstinate mythologies of the multitude, has proved a provocation. In a review in *The New Republic* tellingly entitled 'Hannah and Her Admirers', David Rieff argues that the film is little more than a hagiography of Arendt the great thinker or difficult genius, in which opposition to her daring new conception of evil is caricatured as prejudiced vilification. Rieff gives the example of careerist Thomas Miller, a faculty colleague at the New School in New York, who sneers what could be called the reductive 'campaign' line against Arendt: that she was malicious, had a German-Jewish or 'Yekke' disdain towards the Jewish people, and lacked heart: 'that's Hannah Arendt: all cleverness and no feeling' (1.21). Rieff suggests that Arendt's staunch defence of her convictions is strengthened by the diminution of every other available position on the Eichmann trial. With the exception of her friend and fellow philosopher Hans Jonas, other challenges to her position, whether from New York intellectuals such as Lionel Abel and Norman Podhoretz, university administrators, sinister Israeli functionaries such as Siegfried Moses, or the anonymous hate mail Arendt receives, is presented either as 'grotesque (Abel and Podhoretz), splenetic (the administrators), pathetic (Blumenfeld) or crazed (the neighbor)'. In a review of the film the prominent critic Ruth Franklin agrees, arguing that the film deliberately focuses on dramatic night scenes and dark interiors in order to make the 'implication clear: illumination will come from her' (Franklin 2013, 27).

Rieff comments archly that the students in the New School audience greet her final words with what in the old Soviet Union used to be called 'stormy applause'. He assumes a didactic positioning of the audience, which is clearly meant to react the same way as her adoring students, embracing her vanquishment of error, superstition, and bigotry. Rieff judges von Trotta's film as an artistic failure combining an intellectual ambition to 'make Arendt's ideas comprehensible to a new generation' and an 'antiquarian refusal of any dialectical or critical relation to these ideas'. It is a 'film about ideas that remains intellectually detached from them' (Rieff 2013).

Of course the film's supposed idealization of Arendt is running into a prevailing headwind: many feel that Arendt was fooled by Eichmann's performance at the trial and that a recent study, Bettina Stangneth's *Eichmann Before Jerusalem*, detailing Eichmann's Argentina period in the 1950s, is conclusive evidence that he was indeed a fanatical anti-Semite who lamented his inability to complete his 'work', the genocide of the Jewish people.[5] Rieff's and Ruth Franklin's reviews amongst others are emboldened by this turn of events which seems to have legitimized the initially outraged reaction to Arendt's controversial thesis and the 'malicious' tone in which she wrote. In 2014, the president of the American Historical Association, Jan Goldstein, acerbically described Arendt's *Eichmann in Jerusalem* as a 'colossal rhetorical failure and maybe a moral failure as well. She has ignored her audience and its personal stake in her subject matter' (cited in King 2015, 307).

However, if we turn to some of the scholarship on the film, it tends to position *Hannah Arendt* as a subtle interrogation of the 'psychogenesis' of her analysis of Eichmann that cuts against the grain of her own philosophical and phenomenological postulates about the nature of thinking, ethics, and judgement. For some critics sympathetic to Arendt but unconvinced by her portrait of Eichmann, the film addresses a lacuna in Arendt's scholarship. The film's complex reimagining of Arendt's thinking as an activity that takes place under emotional strain, in public and quasi-public spaces, and in the midst of agonistic conflicts, may reveal its protagonist as unreliable in accounting for her motivations and serve to complicate her philosophy of thinking as an essentially private activity of recuperative withdrawal that should not be conflated with consequential 'action'. Long-time scholars of Arendt, used to debating the contemporary implications of her sometimes idiosyncratic theoretical lexicon, feel that the film only deepens the mystery over her core philosophical thesis of the 'banality of evil'. As Richard King argues in *Arendt in America* (2015) Arendt, in 'calling her book "a report", foreswore extended philosophical or ethical reflection altogether'. Thus as King points out, the 'philosophical foundations for her judgments or the sources of her ruminations are often hard to pinpoint' (King 2015, 304). For critics of the film who are more sympathetic to Arendt's philosophy, the intensity of the rancour surrounding her observations has obscured both the critical presuppositions of her paradigm-changing idea (such as her earlier interest in mass society and its correlatives in alienation, corrosive cynicism, and atomized 'worldlessness' as a precondition of totalitarianism) and its possible affective genesis in a traumatic past. They feel that in von Trotta's film Arendt is not simply depicted as a heroic representative of disinterested thought in the face of hostile opposition but what she described in *The Human Condition* as a political 'actor' in the public arena, someone who 'discloses [him]self without ever either knowing himself or being able to calculate beforehand whom he reveals' (cited in Azoulay 2015, 126). In the remainder of this chapter we will need to consider what sort of political actor and public personality Arendt will reveal herself to be under the duress of a public trial of almost limitless hostility towards her.

The film's screenwriter Pamela Katz's contribution to a special issue of the feminist cultural studies journal *dossier* makes it clear that her screenplay is intended to help us understand Arendt as a vulnerable human being who may lack self-awareness; with von Trotta she was 'committed to shining a light on [Arendt's] character and emotions' (Katz 2015, 89). To understand the character of Arendt it was important to realize that the Eichmann period revealed, more than any other, 'the life of Hannah Arendt as one defined and derailed by exile' (Katz 2015, 87, 89). Although facing the Nazi Eichmann in all his shocking banality must have been a deeply troubling personal experience, Katz's screenplay explores the consequences of Arendt's refusal to acknowledge that her emotions might have influenced her subsequent observations. While the idea of the 'banality of evil' is undeniably the product of her unique genius, the pain of her past certainly 'burst through the tone in which she wrote'. Arendt's insistence that she was relating 'facts' was 'weakened by the ironic undertow of her writing'. It was this mordant tone, and 'not her groundbreaking theory – that unwittingly revealed the pain she hid from everyone. A film focusing on the Eichmann years offered the opportunity to expose the woman behind that tone and the personal turmoil buried beneath her genius' (Katz 2015, 89–90).

Katz's argument is that Arendt's interpretation of Eichmann's elective 'inability to think' was startlingly original on an intellectual level. However, it revealed an aspect of personality that was more psychically revealing than she realized. Having suffered personal betrayal Arendt was invested in the humanist notion, as we have seen, that a vigorous process of lay reflection can help people abstain from evil doing, or even 'condition them against it' (Arendt, *Life of the Mind*, cited in Katz, 90). Despite Arendt's painful realization that intelligence was no barrier to inhuman behaviour, she still 'placed her hopes in the world of thought'. (Katz 2015, 90). This despite the fact that the very man who had taught her how to 'think' (deliciously referred to by Mary McCarthy in parodic faux German accent as Arendt's 'King of Thinking') had joined the Nazi Party. Projecting a *passionate thinking* that is the prerogative of all and that countermands a profound desire to 'function' rather than assume responsibility for others, Arendt 'sought protection. . . . She needed to believe that a new understanding of evil could protect her, an understanding as emotional as it was intellectual' (Katz 2015, 91).

The important point Katz makes is that in constructing Eichmann and his ilk as the negative image of 'thinking', Arendt was demonstrating her vulnerability to traumatic recollection, not showing off her intelligence as suggested by Norman Podhoretz in an infamous review of *Eichmann in Jerusalem*, 'The Perversity of Brilliance', which sets off a bitter dispute in the film between Arendt's detractors and supporters. Through the transferential association of Eichmann with the vacuity of 'thoughtlessness' rather than genocidal hatred and personal sadism, Arendt sought 'protection from the kind of murderous betrayal that destroyed her country and sent her into exile' (Katz 2015, 91).[6] Making a point that can refer us to the relational interests of the female-authored *Bildungsroman*, Katz indicates that her poignant screenplay is interested in Arendt's (in)capacity to care for herself or reconstitute her fragile psyche through the medium of critical thought alone. The spectator is acutely aware of the tension between her stoic commitment to critical reflection at personal cost and her obtuse 'deafness to the provocative tone of her work' which hints at repressed pain and vulnerability – traumatic wounds that will be sorely tested by the potential onset of a 'third exile' incurred by her observations on the Eichmann trial, an exile at its most damaging when it culminates in the loss of lifelong friendships (Katz 2015, 91).

In a fine analysis of the film, 'Arendt on the Couch', Bonnie Honig suggests the film illuminates a libidinous repetition compulsion in which Arendt must again and again experience the threat of exile and expulsion, suffer betrayal and the severe testing of friendship, as the very condition of her thinking (Honig 2015, 95). Arendtian thinking, Honig submits, is interwoven with *eros* and provokes and invokes a threshold experience of betrayal and suffering that is part of the 'life-world' of thinking (Honig, 95). Honig's interpretation of Arendt's eroticized repetition compulsion is tantalizing as it does point us towards her desire for agonism and her need to sharpen differences with others, but aspects of the film emphasizing Arendt's very real vulnerabilities including a possible relapse into despair and her profound distress and shock when viewing the testimony of witnesses at the trial, point us, I would suggest, towards Arendt's public and private discourse as guided by a response, both principled and timely, to the needs of her various audiences as they grapple with the new and unprecedented threat of recrudescent totalitarianism.

Arendt's spectators

For the remainder of this chapter I ponder whether the film offers a conception of Arendt's thinking that is urgent and audience aware, as neither the manifestation of an heroic individual immune to normative pressures nor the self-protective manifestations of a somewhat naïve rationalism as suggested by Katz. With Ariella Azoulay I query whether Arendt's thinking, which is almost always depicted in and amongst spectators, particularly young people such as her secretary and confidante Lotte Köhler, may rather possess the 'revelatory quality of action and speech' which is 'carried out in a networked form by whoever participates in it' (Azoulay 2015, 122). I follow Azoulay's point that in making the film von Trotta and Katz had to begin by disregarding Arendt's conception of thinking as a distinct form of human activity that 'does not manifest itself outwardly' and has a 'very restricted impulse to communicate to others' (Arendt, 'Responsibility and Judgment', cited in Azoulay 2015, 123). Arendt's model of thinking as harmonizing and stabilizing the self through introspection, offering respite from the urgent need to disperse oneself as various personae in the public sphere, is perhaps, as Azoulay points out, already complicated by the cinematic medium itself, which focuses on Arendt's thought processes in a bustling *mise en scène*, that is, in the midst of agonistic disputations, disruptive encounters, and conflicting emotional and political exigencies.

I would argue that in an indicative manner, Arendt is depicted in the film as standing up for herself and for anyone 'who insists on asserting her right to express her opinions publicly'. In its *kairotic* adumbration of the future awaiting the young people Arendt addresses, the film is thus less about thinking as a privative process that helps a gifted genius to gestate an epochal idea and more a representation of Arendt's conception of politics: 'speaking and acting before others about matters having to do with the public realm' (King 2015, 303). As King argues, this is a film that 'places the argument for the expression of ideas in public at its center' (King 2015, 303). I would add that the film has a particular interest in the spectatorship of young people as witnesses to history. They are present at, watch, and contribute to Arendt's maturing deliberations on the banality of evil throughout the film. In the early 1960s, with the United States soon to enter the Vietnam war and with a very young Israeli nation soon needing to decide whether it will be a democratic polity or an expansionist colonial power, the film continually draws attention to the presence of youthful spectators. Children and young people are present in many of the scenes in which Arendt thinks about, converses on, and struggles to articulate an emerging philosophical idea that will prove of immense value to scholars, writers, artists, historians, sociologists, psychologists, philosophers, and film-makers, as they attempt to make sense of the ubiquity of malfeasance in their own societies. Where Rieff assumed that the students simply support Arendt's philosophical arguments, their applause might convey a more profound, prospective appreciation of the applicability of the 'banality of evil' to a variety of ever-present human behaviours from apathy, ambition and conformism to cowardice and self-delusion. These unreflective modes of relating to self and other support the machinations of the powerful and discourage concerted political resistance.

Arendt's *Men in Dark Times* is a book of biographical portraits often tacitly referenced in the film, as when Arendt's husband Heinrich Blücher wonders whether Arendt's attendance at the Eichmann trial will return her to the 'dark times'. Arendt's implicit response is to demonstrate the value of *Selbstdenken*, thinking for oneself, in public and political terms, a concept of thinking that she associates with one of her intellectual heroes, Gotthold Ephraim Lessing. In *Men in Dark Times* Arendt praised the Enlightenment-era dramatist, philosopher and aesthetician as an exemplar of *Selbstdenken* as a mode of thinking without 'ideological crutches' which, in its need to communicate with a projected audience, displays a constant reference to the world. *Selbstdenken* is not, Arendt argues, a form of thinking that is a 'manifestation of a self' or implies a Stoic 'retreat' into a sovereign subject independent of external vicissitudes. It manifests worldly judgement and the need for tactical intervention. Individuals, created for 'action, not ratiocination', elect such a manner of thinking because they wish to move 'in the world in freedom' (Arendt 1983, 9). Thus Lessing, in his self-fashioning, was less preoccupied with the 'results' of his thinking in the form of conclusions or solutions to problems than with stimulating 'others to independent thought' (Arendt 1983, 10). Anticipating dialogue, Lessing was 'concerned with the effect [of action and speech] upon the spectator, who as it were represents the world' (Arendt 1983, 7).

If we turn to the film's illumination of Arendt's *Selbstdenken* as it takes shape in the midst of increasing tensions and excitement about her provisional observations upon Eichmann's mediocrity, we can now understand her emerging thinking on Eichmann as invested in its worldly effects, particularly in preserving freedom of thought in an increasingly close-minded post-war world that threatens to limit her choices to being either a friend or enemy of Israel and the Jewish people. On more than one occasion Hans Jonas and later Kurt Blumenfeld attempt to co-opt Arendt's report on the Eichmann trial by impressing upon her the importance of 'one of us' that is, Jews, reporting on it. Presumably Arendt is tasked by her paternalistic interlocutors with not only demonstrating the horrors of the Holocaust but its significance as the culmination of transhistorical gentile anti-Semitism. Arendt's resistance to blandishments of this kind, which are simultaneously threats to subordinate her intellectual freedom to ethnocentric imperatives, manifests in fierce displays of *Selbstdenken* in which she replies strongly but also jokes, parries, deflects, and queries. Arendt's robust *Selbstdenken* seems indicatively concerned with the exemplary effects of her comportment on younger spectators as they negotiate an era in which the Holocaust has demonstrated that older religious and philosophical traditions have proven powerless to prevent the moral 'collapse of respectable society'.

Arendt enacts her emerging thinking on Eichmann and the nature of evil in public spaces, from classrooms at the New School to cafes in Jerusalem and soirées in her apartment, spaces in which inquisitive younger spectators are ubiquitous. Her highly disputatious but also witty and inclusive public display of disagreement with would-be male lovers and guardians is likely a response to a key scene in the film in which Arendt, at around eighteen years of age, was seduced by the thirty-five-year-old, married Heidegger in his office. In a critical scene Heidegger, in order to forge intimacy and complicity, insists that thinking is a 'lonely business' for kindred souls, its worldly consequences none of their concern. It is no accident that when Arendt ruefully recalls one of the judges saying to Eichmann that 'if there had been more civil courage then things would have turned out differently', the film immediately segues to Heidegger's first private meeting with an awestruck younger Arendt. Young women, assumed in that era to be modest and decorous in public, will need an exemplar of spirited independence, without deference, if they are to refuse co-optation and betrayal by the men in their lives.

Like the subject of her habilitation, Rahel Varnhagen, Arendt is a Jewish female *salonnière* in von Trotta's film; her New York apartment is not a private residence but a convivial space for intense conversation between émigré intellectuals who heatedly discuss issues of concern in their native German tongue. In most of the scenes in the apartment Arendt's conversation and musings are in the presence of her young secretary Lotte Köhler, played by Julia Jentsch, an actor whose earlier incarnation as the great figure of conscientious resistance to the Nazis in *Sophie Scholl: The Final Days* (2005) inscribes with greater significance her wry expression and appreciation for Arendt's independence of mind. When the cinematic character Arendt comments that Eichmann was not demonic, but 'unable to think', Lotte is enthusiastic. She 'loves' the much-stigmatized phrase because, I would hazard, she appreciates that Arendt's conclusions will renew understanding and transgenerational inquiry into the Holocaust, always in danger of combative ethnocentric appropriation by conservatively minded, self-appointed representatives of its uniqueness. Arendt refuses to work in Blücher's office so that she can remain in the busy living area of the apartment, working closely with Lotte, her disciple, friend, protector, and later trustee and literary executor. Where Arendt seeks out Lotte's opinion in quasi-public spaces, Heinrich sees her as an intermediary that can help him conduct discrete affairs. This she pointedly refuses to do. In Arendt's apartment, Lotte is sitting directly behind Hans Jonas, carefully captured in shot, as he boasts of his military service and intones with aggressive self-satisfaction that 'one of us' will be present to report on this 'great trial', a fundamental breach of the salon's appreciation of diverse opinion and its cultivation of the individual. Indeed it might be argued that Arendt is unconsciously absorbing the reality, even before she sets off for the Jerusalem trial, that the democratizing and meritocratic ethos of her émigré salon may soon bow to nationalistic pressures as occurred at the turn of the nineteenth century in Germany after the Napoleonic invasions as described in her study *Rahel Varnhagen*. Part of the context for Arendt's musings on evil may be the latent recognition that freedom of thought must be preserved against private agendas; we are often reminded in the film that Hans Jonas wishes to quash Arendt's complex connection to her German past, and that Arendt's scepticism about the aims of the Jerusalem trial flies in the face of powerful contemporary currents such as the need to uphold Israel's legitimacy.

Examples of young people as 'witnesses to history' abound in the film. When, early in the film, Arendt, herself a dedicated educator who has an excellent rapport with her students, and her ailing friend Kurt Blumenfeld are discussing in the streets of Jerusalem whether Eichmann is the 'predator' Blumenfeld depicts or a stunning mediocrity, a 'ghost' with a cold, the camera lingers in close-up on two very young female Israeli soldiers leaning against a wall as they walk past. The soldiers then walk up the steps behind them as the conversation progresses. Only minutes earlier in the film Arendt had been reminded that the trial is important for Israel's youth who have to know what the Nazis did. Sadly Israel's youth are wont to presume the concentration camp survivors are either cowards who failed to resist or 'criminals' and 'whores', that is, so-called privileged survivors. A wary Arendt asks Blumenfeld whether the bombastic prosecutor Gideon Hausner is best placed to help Israel's young understand what their parents suffered. Here we have an indication that Arendt may later offer her reflections on the meaning of the Jerusalem trial and the ethics of remembrance by writing against a nationalist narrative predicated on a binary of perpetrator and victims, a narrative that encourages younger Jews to see themselves as real or potential victims of anti-Semitism regardless of geopolitical context.

In her final apologia in the New School auditorium, the camera frequently cuts to an unnamed young woman who had first appeared as a student in her German seminar, identified as 'Elizabeth' in the credits, who is in raptures at Arendt's proud, defiant defence of her analysis of Eichmann. Arguably Elizabeth is less preoccupied with Arendt's philosophical thesis, than her insistence on the dreadful moral consequences of being a nobody, of refusing to be a thinking 'person' who makes calibrated choices about how they will appear in the world. Arendt argues resoundingly that given the totality of moral collapse in Europe amongst both persecutors and victims, which includes the behaviour of some Jewish councils, it is 'profoundly important to ask these questions' of ethical behaviour in 'dark times' when morals so easily reveal themselves as 'mores'. Understanding, Arendt argues, is 'not the same as forgiveness'. It is the responsibility of anyone who wants to put pen to paper on the subject. The camera pans to Elizabeth, who is fascinated but also intrigued as to why Arendt discussed the Holocaust as a 'crime against humanity', perhaps presaging the dedication of her own generation to ensuring genocide is judged within the framework of international law.

Now talking prospectively, in front of a young audience who will soon contribute to the libertarian and anarchist strains of the New Left as it challenged pseudo-scientific Marxist dogma, Arendt argues that the manifestation of the wind of thought is not knowledge but the ability to discern right from wrong, 'beautiful from ugly'. We are reminded here that her judgement of Eichmann was necessarily an exercise in moral taste that will resonate with communities of readers to come. To perform thinking in public, the viewer might glean from this emphasis on taste and tact, is not in a simple sense to express one's interiority but to evince discernment as required by a conversational context. Arendt impresses on her overwhelmingly youthful audience that 'thinking gives people the strength to prevent catastrophes in those rare moments when the chips are down', notably getting the wording of 'chips' right having learned the art of idiomatic speech in English from Mary McCarthy. The eager and sustained applause that follows focuses on the enraptured Elizabeth, who looks to those beside her, beaming and desirous of confirmation of her own elated feelings. The film itself has already amply demonstrated the perfidy of Arendt's New School colleagues who abandon her at the first pretext, while a scene subsequent to her public address will show her eating alone at the staff cafeteria. I think King is right that the support by young people for Arendt in the film is a 'worldly' response, indeed itself a manifestation of *Selbstdenken*, to Arendt's historically pregnant betrayal by friends and colleagues. They admire her *kairotic* willingness to assume responsibility for free inquiry and to enact civil courage in the aftermath of McCarthyism. Her willingness to assume that responsibility begins in the presence of Lotte herself, who has borne the burden of reading Arendt's hate-filled correspondence and shielding her from them. When, as mentioned, Arendt decides for herself that she must respond to those to whom she has inadvertently caused so much pain, we see that supportive friends such as Mary McCarthy and Lotte have guided her movement away from 'lonely thinking' and defensive egoism, and towards *Selbstdenken* as a mode of caring for the world.

In celebrating a public speech that clearly evinces Arendt's pain at the offence she has caused and the calumny she has endured, Elizabeth and Lotte stand ready to uphold Arendt's chosen role as provocateur in the Socratic manner. As Arendt argued, 'to make a decision is not to react to whatever qualities are given me, but to make a deliberate choice among the various potentialities of conduct with which the world has presented me' (Arendt 1978 *Thinking*, 37). While I can certainly agree with viewers of *Hannah Arendt* that it complicates Arendt's sanguine conception of thinking as a function of lucid self-consciousness, it nevertheless 'thinks with' her, illuminating thought as an activity that is sceptical of convention, courageous and agile in its response to the historical moment, capable of rethinking and redescribing an unresolved past that demands a continual reckoning.

CONCLUSION

The Bildungsroman in a Genocidal Age is itself an indicative study. I have attempted to defer or suspend premature psychological, moral, and historicist judgements and demonstrate the edifying power and intellectual and ethical pleasures of closely reading select historical *Bildungsromane*. In the interpretations I have pursued I have sought to cultivate and exemplify dispositions including avid curiosity, intellectual freedom and interpretive tact, in order to influence future readers of the genre. I would hope those readings are understood as emerging from eager conversation with the increasing diversification and sophistication of genre studies of the *Bildungsroman* in recent decades. This is to say that reading the contemporary *Bildungsroman* has something to do with the receptive ethos of *Bildung* itself as we converse with other interpretations and willingly inhabit the prolonged, picaresque adventure-time and chronotopic complexity of the text, enjoying its novelty, variety, and defiance of canonical expectations. This study, then, can be considered a contribution to a self-aware and curatorial discourse in literary studies that since the turn of the century, has worried about what might be lost in sustaining a permanently suspicious, paranoid, or phobic attitude towards literary texts. *The Bildungsroman in a Genocidal Age* is loosely allied to neo-formalisms that do not wish to see textual significance atrophied by a premature recourse to context while its emphasis on the historical motivations of the *Bildungsroman* has also suggested that texts do indeed point us towards urgent problems of historical understanding.

In exploring polyfunctional protagonists that intimate the possibility of growth and insight only to remind us of our own capacity for blindness and complicity, we are moving, as Susan Fraiman hoped, beyond the notion that the novel of development is 'invested, by definition, in notions of linear progress and coherent identity' (Fraiman, 4). The *Bildungsroman* has long been a mixed type and a texture of contradictions, combining philosophical and realist elements, narrative impetus and indefinite excursus, the historically particular and symbolically suggestive, the capacity for growth and a fascination with arrested development, all combined with the tantalizing possibilities of the not yet. Within its folds there is the capacity for local and separable responses where, as a reader, we can feel deeply affected by a protagonist's longing for mobility and socialization, anxiety about the cultural and psychical damage wrought by narratives of development that expunge whimsy, play, and care, and a willingness to reflect on our own educational trajectory.

In an essay that I continue to find profoundly helpful as a theoretical resource, 'Paranoid and Reparative Reading', Eve Kosofsky Sedgwick has welcomed an ecology of literary interpretation that entwines weak and strong theories, in which 'imaginative close reading' using 'local theories and nonce taxonomies' (Sedgwick 2003, 145) still has value, and where the task of criticism is in part developing an 'experimental vocabulary' and a 'wide affective range' (145) that does justice to the reading experience. In *Falling Short* (2020) Aleksandar Stević reminds us of the fungibility of a genre that cannot be easily teleologically historicized as moving from the stable or traditional form to the more interesting or self-revising variant. I hope my study, which does not have an evolutionary logic in mind and pays close attention to children's literature, bears out his point that the genre continues to probe the 'changing demands of modern socialization' (Stević 2020, 184). It does so by recognizing that the Eichmann problematic, the burden of freedom and the attractions of normativity and conformism, has been explicitly recognized, redescribed, and challenged by a genre engaged in a quest for understanding, florid in its wealth of subject matter, and dedicated to an ethics of candid remembrance.

The novels and films I have chosen to analyse do ask pertinent questions, I hope, about our socialization in an age in which human connection, dialogical experiences, and critical reflection on our shared world continue to diminish. It is by no means jejune or mistaken to wonder how we might *kairotically* revise our sense of the past or redescribe ourselves and our priorities. We can and should continue to cultivate certain intellectual and social virtues and develop our inner resources as we are tested by manifold experiences. The associative ethic of *Bildung* continues to resonate in contemporary thought as in Hannah Arendt's well-known conceit of *amor mundi* or love of the world, in which we cultivate and exemplify our care for pluralistic public spaces, for a world of phenomenal differences. Arendt captured a non-sovereign ethos aligned to this ethic of care in the notion of *Selbstdenken*, in which we do not seek to be, as Susan Fraiman terms it, a 'masterful individual' who is dominant, knowing, and self-righteous, but acknowledge that development cannot be expedient or transactional, it is not 'one clear thing, but many, unsure, contested and changing things' (Fraiman 1993, 138). Schiller himself surely appreciated the interlocutory potential of the genre for the reader in these terms as it continues to facilitate an exchange of views and stimulate the interrogation of cherished ideas.

As Jed Esty reminds us, the structural and stylistic possibilities of the genre have continued to widen, meaning that the influence of *Bildungsromane* on representations of the Holocaust and the Second World War is deserving of sustained attention. We are now, he suggests, well positioned to examine the genre's capacity to 'direct meaning to the future' (Esty 2012, 213). That future, if we are thinking of how to develop a vocabulary and affective range appropriate to complex imaginative representations of the Holocaust, might begin to explore how readers are often assisted by the versatility of the *Bildungsroman* to engage a variety of their intellectual and emotional dispositions in the unfinished project of historically aware character formation.

NOTES

Introduction

1. This study is indebted to the illuminating analyses of Jenni Adams and Sue Vice eds., *Representing Perpetrators in Holocaust Literature and Film* (2013), and attempts to take note of Jenni Adams' point that critics' need to 'retain an openness to the variety and range of functions which representations of Holocaust perpetrators might serve', 3–4.
2. For a comprehensive introduction to national and thematic studies of the *Bildungsroman* see Sarah Graham's edited collection *A History of the Bildungsroman* (2019). For a noteworthy discussion of the survival of the ethos of *Bildung* in literary modernism see Gregory Castle (2006). Jed Esty (2012) has made a significant contribution to discussions of the intersection between modernist and postcolonial studies of the genre and for the importance of the coming of age narrative to the America literary imaginary see Kenneth Millard (2007). Sarah Lyons (2018) offers an excellent survey of recent approaches to the genre in Victorian studies.
3. I'm borrowing this term from the energetic introduction to Jesper Gulddal, Stewart King, and Alistair Rolls eds., *Criminal Moves: Towards a Theory of Crime Fiction Mobility* 2019, 1–24).
4. Jeffrey Sammons' much discussed article (1981, 229–246) is a good example of this anxiety.
5. It's important to note that this not an isolated instance, nevertheless Derek Lee's article on Neil Gaiman affirms Gaiman's undermining of the 'rules' of the *Bildungsroman*, his critical re-enchantment of a disillusioned narrative form. In a fairly routine manoeuvre Lee's article creates a foil in which the classic narrative trajectory of the *Bildungsroman*, awaiting subversion, deconstruction and so on is 'always a progression from the quixotic idealism of youth towards the systematized logic of adulthood' (2016, 555–6).
6. See Reinhart Koselleck's critique of socio-historical criticisms of *Bildung*, criticisms which tend to obscure its emphasis on dynamic sociability and anti-canonical animus (2002, 174–6).
7. I draw here on Franco Moretti's discussion of Frédéric Moreau in Flaubert's *L'Éducation Sentimentale* as an example of an increasingly prominent tendency in the *Bildungsroman* to hold back plot rather than accelerate it, postponing definitive choices that involve decision, separation, and exclusion (2000, 175), and so, according to Moretti, preserving as long as possible a 'state of *psychosocial indetermination*' (177). It needs no particular emphasis to suggest that the protagonist who defers concrete instantiation is particularly congenial to the explorative and counterfactual energies of the postcolonial historical novel. See, for example, Tony Hughes D'Aeth's discussion of the character of Bobby Wabalanginy

in Kim Scott's historical novel *That Deadman Dance*, a cultural intermediary dedicated to an ethics of coexistence, who helps the novel stave off a moment of 'primal defeat', the end of amicable relations between settlers and Indigenous people and the beginning of racial exclusion and spatial segregation (2016, 26).

8 For a discussion of this liminal temporal register as a catalyst for political thought, see Hannah Arendt's preface to *Between Past and Future: Eight Exercises in Political Thought* (2006, 3–15).

9 See Jerome Kohn's introduction to *Thinking without a Banister* for a discussion of Arendt's critique of the utility of preconceived categories in judging totalitarian movements and the modern condition (in Arendt 2018, ix-xxix); for a brief description of the importance of this metaphor to Arendt as a way of capturing a certain kind of groundless thinking, see her reference to her penchant for the term in the same volume (Arendt 2018, 473).

10 The discussion is too voluminous to summarize but for recent perspectives see for example Richard J. Golsan and Sarah Misemer (2017).

11 The increasing critical interest in perpetrator representations associated with critics such as Sue Vice, Jenni Adams, Matthew Boswell, Erin McGlothlin, and Debarati Sanyal, and the hugely influential conception of multidirectional memory articulated by Michael Rothberg, are indebted to the problematic Arendt inaugurated, of how our understanding of the Holocaust and other genocides can puncture complacency and generate understanding of psychological and structural conditions for complicity and injustice in our own societies as well as opening up vistas for comparative analyses. For a discussion of Arendt's concept and its influence on aesthetic representations see R. Clifton Spargo (2006, 161–72).

12 See, for example, Patricia Owens (2008, 105–21).

13 David Miles' suggestion that in the nineteenth century the *Bildungsroman* shifts its focus from the 'world without to the world within', turning towards the psychological time of memory, in which the picaro is transformed into the confessor, are important insights relevant to the texts we will be analysing (1974, 989). Elizabeth Abel, Marianne Hirsch, and Elizabeth Langland eds. germinal study *The Voyage In: Fictions of Female Development* makes a similar point in analysing female fictions of development in which awakening and growth may take place in maturity and its 'time span may only exist in memory' (1983, 14).

14 As Astrid Erll and Ann Rigney suggest, '"remembering" is better seen as an active engagement with the past, as performative rather than as reproductive. It is as much a matter of acting out a relationship to the past from a particular point in the present as it is a matter of preserving and retrieving earlier stories' (2009a, 2).

15 See Abel, Hirsch, and Langland's introduction to *The Voyage In: Fictions of Female Development* (1983, 3–19).

Chapter 1

1 Noteworthy and valuable narratological analyses of the novel include Kathleen Wall (1994), James Phelan and Mary Patricia Martin (1999), and Elke D'hoker and Gunther Martens (2008). For an important discussion of the implied narrator as constructive agent see Ansgar F. Nünning (2005).

2. These readings include Renata Salecl, who describes Stevens as a 'functionary who tries by all available means to avoid his desire' (2000, 185); Lilian Furst, who suggests that Stevens 'obviously puts his obligations as butler over any personal feelings he may have' (2007, 540); Peter Euben, who compares Stevens to Adolf Eichmann and argues that Stevens 'cedes his own moral agency and judgment for his new "master" even as the latter is drawn into the quagmire of pro-Nazi sympathies' (2008, 105); John McGowan, who argues that Stevens' conception of dignity 'illustrates the human cost of a rigid sense of professional requirements' (2008, 236); Monika Gehlawat, who argues that the 'denial of the human in Stevens' is his 'primary act of self-cultivation' (2013, 495); and Michel Terestchenko, who suggests that Stevens, alienated from his own freedom, is an example of Sartrean bad faith and 'destructive obedience', helping us to advance Stanley Milgram's analysis of ordinary human beings who become 'executors of monstrous orders' (2007, 78). Some of these readings may follow in the wake of Gillian Rose's argument for *The Remains of the Day* as radicalizing the genre, offering us a Nazi *Bildungroman* that can assist us in recognizing 'our ineluctable grounding in the norms of the emotional and political culture represented' (1996, 54). Such readings struggle themselves not to dehumanize Stevens, reading his dedicated professionalism narrowly as an allegory of complicity and obedience rather than as a simultaneous attempt to lend dignity to his life and transcend the conditions of servitude.
3. See Reinhart Koselleck (2002).
4. In claiming, as mentioned earlier, that Stevens 'obviously puts his obligations as butler over any personal feelings he may have' towards his father, Lilian Furst ignores very real demands on Stevens' time and labour and the enormous pressure put on him by Lord Darlington, who had already removed his beloved father from his duties; accounts such as these, while bothered by Stevens' claims the event was a professional 'triumph', paper over Stevens' continual preoccupation with the fate of his father and whether Stevens' narrative suggests an invidious contrast between Miss Kentons' sympathetic treatment of his father compared to Lord Darlington's oblivious disregard of his welfare (2007, 530–53).

Chapter 3

1. Daniel manifests divided loyalties in a manner not atypical of retentive *Bildungshelden*, between an aspiration for post-traumatic renewal and secure foundations as a Jewish subject in the land of Zionistic fantasy and the force of memory as it draws on manifold post-traumatic experiences of alterity, dialogue, and adaptation.
2. For an excellent short history of the life of Oswald Rufeisen see Shalom Goldman (2011). For a biography see Nechama Tec (1990).
3. I am indebted to the entry on the 'tzaddik' in Louis Jacobs (1995). I am grateful to John Docker for drawing my attention to Daniel as a *tzaddik* figure of justice.
4. See Hamish Dalley's *The Postcolonial Historical Novel* (2014) for this point.
5. For a discussion of how *Daniel Stein, Interpreter* raised the ire of nationalist critics in Russia for its multi-ethnic focus and depictions of Russian Orthodoxy see Sutcliffe (2009, 498).

6 Nadia Kalman's ambivalent review in *The Jewish Review of Books* (2011) is more positive but worries that the novel was awarded the Russian National Literary Prize because its theme of conversion expresses the hope that in Russia, where anti-Semitism is resurgent, 'Jews might finally melt into the mainstream'.
7 The *locus classicus* of a Zionist-influenced genre of critical polemic critiquing Jewish assimilation in Western European societies from the late eighteenth century as a disastrous abandonment of Jewish identity and communal solidarity is Gershom Scholem (1976 [1964]). For a critique of the reification of strategies of adaptation as assimilationist, as it affects our understanding of German-Jewish intellectual history, see Ned Curthoys, *The Legacy of Liberal Judaism: Ernst Cassirer and Hannah Arendt's Hidden Conversation* (2013b).
8 Affirmative theorizations of the interpretive and ethical legacy of the Jewish diaspora include Daniel Boyarin and Jonathan Boyarin, (1993) and Ella Shohat (2006).
9 Ulitskaya's brilliant depiction of Daniel's paradoxical renewal of his Jewishness through his conversion to Christianity is felicitously summed up by Butler's description of her sometimes utopian post-Zionist meditations in *Parting Ways* as 'tarrying with the impossible' (2012, 1).
10 'Haskalah' is the Jewish Enlightenment, beginning around the middle of the eighteenth century in German-speaking lands and associated with the promotion of Jewish secular learning, the revival of biblical scholarship in Hebrew, and the critique of rabbinical authority over Jewish communities.
11 See also Yovel (1989).

Chapter 4

1 My thanks to Ika Willis, who alerted me to this concept which she sourced in part from Mattilda Bernstein Sycamore's collection *Dangerous Families: Queer Writing on Surviving* (2011).
2 *Downfall* is also partially structured as a *Bildungsroman* in which the younger German viewer is engaged by the surrogate Traudl Junge (played as astoundingly ingenuous by Alexandra Maria Lara), who is gradually released from the thrall of Hitler's paternal charisma.
3 The controversy continues to this day with recent research rekindling concern over the widespread teaching of the novel to British children. See https://www.theguardian.com/world/2022/jan/27/the-boy-in-the-striped-pyjamas-fuels-dangerous-holocaust-fallacies.

Chapter 5

1 Cited in Ruth Franklin (2011, 6).
2 For a notable warning about the incremental effects of assimilating the Holocaust to the optimistic needs of the American cultural imaginary see Alvin H. Rosenfeld (1995, 35–40).
3 As the influential scholar of historical film Robert Rosenstone puts it, 'the history film cannot be judged through the current canons of either written history or the

genre analysis of film studies, but by combining the two'. Robert A. Rosenstone (2013, 84).

4   Matthew Boswell's *Holocaust Impiety in Literature, Popular Music, and Film* (2012) influenced by Gillian Rose's critique of the sanctimonious strictures of the perceived gatekeepers (Claude Lanzmann, Elie Weisel and others) of Holocaust memorialization *Mourning Becomes the Law* (1996), has helped inaugurate a critical interest in the transgressive energy of Holocaust-themed texts that wish to provoke a moral crisis in the reader or viewer, shattering reconstructive protocols of representation that perhaps unwittingly maintain psychological distance from those events.

5   For a discussion of the precepts of a 'Holocaust etiquette' and their surprising lack of purchase on the field of children's literature see Hsu-Ming Teo, (2015, 1–21). For a discussion of the dynamics of 'Holocaust anxiety' as they affect historiographical and aesthetic debates over Holocaust representation see A. Dirk. Moses (2016, 332–54).

6   Speaking of the sacralizing imperative of Holocaust memorial institutions such as Yad Vashem and the United States Holocaust Memorial Museum, Avril Alba (2015, 7) argues that the memorial practices of these institutions 'more often than not find their starting points in the sacred symbols, rituals, archetypes and narratives of the Jewish tradition'.

7   See 'The Counterfeiters' media release by Mongrel Media, http://www.mongrelmedia.com/index.php/filmlink?id=c09c2fed-5686-4e63-9853-b0cc11afecee. Accessed May 26, 2023.

8   For a lively account of the forgery operation see Lawrence Malkin, *Krueger's Men: The Secret Nazi Counterfeit Plot of Block 19* (2006).

9   As Lawrence Baron points out, 'viewers do not enter theatres as a tabula rasa. Instead they bring with them a mental storehouse of all the movies they have seen' (2010, 3).

Chapter 6

1   For a discussion of how Arendt construes moral character in Kantian terms as the ability to make lasting commitments to oneself, see Ned Curthoys (2011, 58–78).

2   See Hannah Arendt, 'Karl Jaspers: a Laudatio' in *Men in Dark Times* (1983): 'to take it upon oneself to answer before mankind for every thought means to live in that luminosity in which oneself and everything one thinks is tested' (1983, 75).

3   For a meticulous account of the controversy see Anson Rabinbach (2004, 97–111).

4   On this point see '"What Remains? The Language Remains": A Conversation with Günter Gaus', in Hannah Arendt (2013, 1–38).

5   Bettina Stangneth (2014). For a review of Stangneth's book that assumes it has put paid to Arendt's interpretation of Eichmann see Richard Wolin (2014), and for a critique of Wolin see Seyla Benhabib (2014).

6   Joel Rosenberg puts it well in 'Into the Woods': 'is the paradoxical historical knot that bound the philosopher's stratospheric (albeit woodland) *Denken* with the Nazi bureaucrat's catastrophic thoughtlessness what filmmaker von Trotta was asking us all along to see?' (2014, 211).

BIBLIOGRAPHY

'Dershowtiz: Goldstone Is a Traitor to the Jewish People'. *Haaretz*, 31 January 2010. https://www.haaretz.com/2010-01-31/ty-article/dershowitz-goldstone-is-a-traitor-to-the-jewish-people/0000017f-f801-d2d5-a9ff-f88d9b790000 (accessed 19 May 2023).

'Interview: Adolf Burger'. *Jewish Chronicle*, 26 February 2009. https://www.thejc.com/lifestyle/interviews/interview-adolf-burger-1.7824 (accessed December 2018).

Abel, Elizabeth, Marianne Hirsch, and Elizabeth Langland. *The Voyage in: Fictions of Female Development*. Hanover: University Press of New England, 1983.

Adams, Jenni, and Sue Vice. *Representing Perpetrators in Holocaust Literature and Film*. London: Vallentine Mitchell, 2013.

Adhikari, Mohamed. '*Hotel Rwanda*-The Challenges of Historicising and Commercialising Genocide'. In *Revisiting the Heart of Darkness–Explorations into Genocide and Other Forms of Mass Violence*, edited by Henning Melby, and John Y. Jones, 173–95. Oxford: Routledge, 2008.

Ahmed, Sara. *The Cultural Politics of Emotions*. Edinburgh: Edinburgh University Press, 2014.

Alba, Avril. *The Holocaust Museum: Sacred Secular Space*. Basingstoke and New York: Palgrave Macmillan, 2015.

Apter, Emily. *The Translation Zone: A New Comparative Literature*. Princeton: Princeton University Press, 2006.

Arendt, Hannah. *The Life of the Mind*. London: Secker and Warburg, 1978.

Arendt, Hannah. 'On Humanity in Dark Times: Thoughts about Lessing'. In *Men in Dark Times*, 3–31. New York: Harvest Books, 1983.

Arendt, Hannah. *Eichmann in Jerusalem: A Report on the Banality of Evil*. New York: Penguin Books, 1994.

Arendt, Hannah. 'Some Questions of Moral Philosophy'. In *Responsibility and Judgment*, edited by Jerome Kohn, 149–6. New York: Schocken Books, 2003.

Arendt, Hannah. *Between Past and Future: Eight Exercises in Political Thought*. New York: Penguin, 2006.

Arendt, Hannah. *The Last Interview and other Conversations*. New York: Melville House Publishing, 2013.

Arendt, Hannah. *Thinking Without a Banister: Essays in Understanding, 1953–1975*. New York: Schocken, 2018.

Azoulay, Ariella. 'Arendt's Guidelines for a Fictionalized Cinematic Portrait'. *Differences* 26, no. 2 (2015): 121–31.

Baer, Brian James. 'Interpreting *Daniel Stein*; or, What Happens When Fictional Translators Get Translated'. In *Transfiction. Research into the Realities of Translation Fiction*, edited by Klaus Kaindl, and Karlheinz Spitzl, 157–75. Philadelphia: John Benjamins Publishing Company, 2014.

Bakhtin, Mikhail Mikhaïlovich. *Problems of Dostoevsky's Poetics*. Manchester: Manchester University Press, 1984.

Bakhtin, Mikhail Mikhaïlovich. *Speech Genres and Other Late Essays*. Austin: University of Texas Press, 2010.

Bathrick, David, and Rachel Leah Magshamrain. 'Whose Hi/story Is It? The U.S. Reception of "Downfall"'. *New German Critique* 34, no. 102 (Fall 2007): 1–16.

Baron, Lawrence. 'Introduction: Holocaust and Genocide Cinema: Crossing Disciplinary, Genre, and Geographical Borders'. *Shofar* 28, no. 4 (2010): 1–9.

Bathrick, David, and Rachel Leah Magshamrain. 'Whose Hi/Story Is It? The US Reception of "Downfall"'. *New German Critique* 102 (2007): 1–16.

Bauman, Zygmunt. *Modernity and the Holocaust*. Ithaca: Cornell University Press, 2000.

Bauman, Zygmunt, and Leonidas Donskis. *Moral Blindness: The Loss of Sensitivity in Liquid Modernity*. Cambridge: Polity Press, 2013.

Benhabib, Seyla. 'Who's on Trial? Eichmann or Arendt?' *The New York Times*, 14 September 2014. http://opinionator.blogs.nytimes.com/2014/09/21/whos-on-trial-eichmann-or-anrendt/?_r=0 (accessed 26 February 2023).

Benjamin, Walter. 'Theses on the Philosophy of History'. In *Illuminations*, edited by Hannah Arendt, 245–55. New York: Schocken Books, 1968.

Blech, Benjamin. 'Review of *The Boy in the Striped Pyjamas*'. *Aish.com*, 23 October 2008. https://www.aish.com/j/as/48965671.html (accessed 17 December 2019).

Boes, Tobias, and Karl Morgenstern. 'On the Nature of the "Bildungsroman"'. *PMLA* 124 (March 2009): 647–59.

Boswell, Matthew. *Holocaust Impiety in Literature, Popular Music, and Film*. Basingstoke: Palgrave Macmillan, 2012.

Boswell, Mathew. '*Downfall*: The Nazi Genocide as a Natural Disaster'. In *Representing Perpetrators in Holocaust Literature and Film*, edited by Jenni Adams, and Sue Vice, 147–64. Edgware: Vallentine Mitchell, 2013.

Boswell, Matthew. 'Holocaust Literature and the Taboo'. In *The Bloomsbury Companion to Holocaust Literature*, edited by Jenni Adams, 179–97. London: Bloomsbury, 2014.

Boyarin, Daniel, and Jonathan Boyarin. 'Diaspora: Generation: And the Ground of Jewish Identity'. *Critical Inquiry* 18, no. 4 (1993): 693–725.

Boyne, John. *The Boy in the Striped Pyjamas*. London: Random House, 2008.

Brister, Rose, and Belinda Walzer. 'Kairos and Comics: Reading Human Rights Intercontextually in Joe Sacco's Graphic Narratives'. *College Literature* 40, no. 3 (2013): 138–55.

Buckley, Jerome. *Season of Youth: The Bildungsroman from Dickens to Golding*. Cambridge: Harvard University Press, 1974.

Bukiet, Melvin Jules. '"Daniel Stein, Interpreter" Reviewed'. *Washington Post*, 7 May 2011. https://www.washingtonpost.com/entertainment/books/book-world-daniel-stein-interpreter-reviewed/2011/03/17/AFVSZtgG_story.html (accessed 16 May 2023).

Burger, Adolf. 2007 interview cited in https://www.radio.cz/en/section/panorama/ambitious-nazi-counterfeiting-plot-recalled-by-holocaust-survivor (accessed 3 December 2018).

Burger, Adolf. *The Devil's Workshop*. London: Frontline Books, 2009.

Burt, Raymond L. 'A Genuine Dilemma: Ruzowitzky's *The Counterfeiters* as Moral Experiment'. In *New Austrian Film*, edited by Robert von Dassanowsky, and Oliver C. Speck, 307–18. New York: Berghahn Books, 2011.

Butler, Judith. *Parting Ways: Jewishness and the Critique of Zionism*. New York: Columbia University Press, 2012.

Cassirer, Ernst. *An Essay on Man: An Introduction to a Philosophy of Human Culture*. Yale: Yale University Press, 1944.

Castle, Gregory. *Reading the Modernist Bildungsroman*. Gainesville: University Press of Florida, 2006.

Castle, Gregory. 'The Modernist Bildungsroman'. In *A History of the Bildungsroman*, edited by Sarah Graham, 143–73. Cambridge: Cambridge University Press, 2019.

Cesarani, David. 'Striped Pyjamas'. *The Literary Review*, no. 359 (October, 2008): 3.

Chatman, Seymour Benjamin. *Coming to Terms: The Rhetoric of Narrative in Fiction and Film*. Ithaca: Cornell University Press, 1990.

Chaudhuri, Shohini. *Cinema of the Dark Side: Atrocity and the Ethics of Film Spectatorship*. Edinburgh: Edinburgh University Press, 2014.

The Counterfeiters media release (Press) by Mongrel Media. http://www.mongrelmedia.com/index.php/filmlink?id=c09c2fed-5686-4e63-9853-b0cc11afecee (accessed 26 May 2023).

Cristoff, Peter. 'The Book That Changed Me: Hannah Arendt's *Eichmann in Jerusalem* and the Problem of Terrifying Moral Complacency'. *The Conversation*, 23 November 2022. https://theconversation.com/the-book-that-changed-me-hannah-arendts-eichmann-in-jerusalem-and-the-problem-of-terrifying-moral-complacency-187600 (accessed 8 May 2023).

Curthoys, Ned. 'Hannah Arendt: A Question of Character'. *New Formations* 71, no. 71 (2011): 58–78.

Curthoys, Ned. 'Redescribing the Enlightenment: The German-Jewish Adoption of Bildung as a Counter-Normative Ideal'. *Intellectual History Review* 23, no. 3 (2013a): 365–86.

Curthoys, Ned. *The Legacy of Liberal Judaism*. New York: Berghahn Books, 2013b.

Curthoys, Ned. 'Tarrying with the Impossible: *Daniel Stein, Interpreter* and the Politics of Translation'. *Australian Literary Studies* 28, no. 3 (October 2013c): 28–43.

Curthoys, Ned. 'Evaluating Risk in Perpetrator Narratives: Resituating Jonathan Littel's *The Kindly Ones* as Historical Fiction'. *Textual Practice* 31, no. 3 (May 2017): 457–75.

Curthoys, Ned. '*The Counterfeiters as Bildungsfilm*: A Genre Study'. *College Literature* 48, no. 4 (Fall 2021): 653–76.

Dalley, Hamish. *The Postcolonial Historical Novel: Realism, Allegory, and the Representation of Contested Pasts*. London: Palgrave Macmillan, 2014.

D'hoker, Elke, and Gunther Martens, eds. *Narrative Unreliability in the Twentieth-Century First-Person Novel*. Berlin: de Gruyter, 2008.

Diamond, Diana, and Elliot Jurist. 'Multiplicity, Dissociation, and Mentalization in *Hannah Arendt* by Pam Katz and Margarethe von Trotta'. In *Cinematic Reflections on the Legacy of the Holocaust: Psychoanalytic Perspectives*, edited by Diana Diamond, and Bruce Sklarew, 85–121. New York: Routledge, 2018.

Eaglestone, Robert. 'Boyne's Dangerous Tale'. *The Jewish Chronicle*, 23 March 2007. https://www.pressreader.com/uk/the-jewish-chronicle/20070323/283867273779095 (accessed 17 December 2019).

Erll, Astrid, and Ann Rigney. 'Introduction: Cultural Memory and Its Dynamics'. In *Mediation, remediation, and the dynamics of cultural memory*, edited by Astrid Erll, and Ann Rigney, 1–14. Berlin: de Gruyter, 2009a.

Erll, Astrid, and Ann Rigney, eds. *Mediation, Remediation, and the Dynamics of Cultural Memory*. Berlin: De Gruyter, 2009b.

Esty, Jed. *Unseasonable Youth: Modernism, Colonialism, and the Fiction of Development*. Oxford: Oxford University Press, 2012.

Euben, J. Peter. 'The Butler Did It'. In *Naming Evil, Judging Evil*, edited by Ruth W. Grant, 103–20. Chicago: Chicago University Press, 2008.

Evans, Rhiannon. 'Emotional Pedagogy and the Gendering of Social and Emotional Learning'. *British Journal of Sociology*, 38, no. 2 (2017): 184–202.

Fraiman, Susan. *Unbecoming Women: British Women Writers and the Novel of Development*. New York: Columbia University Press, 1993.

Franklin, Ruth. *A Thousand Darknesses: Lies and Truth in Holocaust Fiction*. Oxford: Oxford University Press, 2011.

Franklin, Ruth. 'Hannah Arendt'. *Salmagundi* 178/179 (2013): 25–32.

French, Jackie. *Hitler's Daughter*. Sydney: Harper Collins, 1999.

Furst, Lilian R. 'Memory's Fragile Power in Kazuo Ishiguro's "*Remains of the Day*" and WG Sebald's "Max Ferber"'. *Contemporary Literature* 48, no. 4 (2007): 530–53.

Gehlawat, Monika. 'Myth and Mimetic Failure in *The Remains of the Day*'. *Contemporary Literature* 54, no. 3 (2013): 491–519.

Gerber, Jane S. *The Jews of Spain: A History of the Sephardic Experience*. New York: Free Press, 1992.

Gjesdal, Kristin. 'Bildung'. In *The Oxford Handbook of German Philosophy in the Nineteenth Century*, edited by Michael N. Forster, and Kristin Gjesdal, 695–719. Oxford: Oxford University Press, 2015.

Golban, Petru. *A History of the Bildungsroman: From Ancient Beginnings to Romanticism*. Cambridge: Cambridge Scholars Publishing, 2018.

Goldman, Shalom. 'Meet Brother Daniel: A Jew-Converted-Christian-Turned-Monk'. *Haaretz*, 18 August 2011. https://www.haaretz.com/life/books/2011-08-18/ty-article/meet-brother-daniel-a-jew-converted-christian-turned-monk/0000017f-e9cb-d639-af7f-e9df3b6f0000 (accessed 25 May 2023).

Golsan, Richard J., and Sarah Misemer, eds. 2017. *The Trial That Never Ends: Hannah Arendt's Eichmann in Jerusalem in Retrospect*. Toronto: University of Toronto Press.

Graham, Sarah, ed. *A History of the Bildungsroman*. Cambridge: Cambridge University Press, 2019.

Graham, Sarah. 'The American Bildungsroman'. In *A History of the Bildungsroman*, edited by Sarah Graham, 117–42. Cambridge: Cambridge University Press, 2019.

Gray, Michael. '*The Boy in the Striped Pyjamas*: A Blessing or Curse for Holocaust Education?'. *Holocaust Studies* 20, no. 3 (2014): 109–36.

Gulddal, Jesper, Stewart King, and Alistair Rolls. 'Criminal Moves: Towards a Theory of Crime Fiction Mobility'. In *Criminal Moves: Modes of Mobility in Crime Fiction*, edited by Jesper Gulddal, Stewart King, and Alistair Rolls, 1–24. Liverpool: Liverpool University Press, 2019.

Haase, Christine. '*Downfall* (2004): Hitler in the New Millennium and the (ab)uses of History'. In *New Directions in German Cinema*, edited by Paul Cooke, and Chris Homewood, 39–56. London: I.B. Tauris, 2011.

Herman, Linda. *Novel Units, Teacher's Guide to The Boy in the Striped Pyjamas*. Bulverde: Novel Units Inc, 2009.

Hesse, Isabelle. *The Politics of Jewishness in Contemporary World Literature: The Holocaust, Zionism, and Colonialism*. London: Bloomsbury Publishing, 2016.

Hirsch, Marianne. 'The Novel of Formation as Genre: Between Great Expectations and Lost Illusions in Studies in the Novel'. *Genre* 12, no. 3 (1979): 293–311.

Hirsch, Marianne. 'Spiritual *Bildung*: The Beautiful Soul as Paradigm'. In *The Voyage in: Fictions of Female Development*, edited by Elizabeth Abel, Marianne Hirsh, and Elizabeth Langland, 23–48. Hanover: University Press of New England, 1983.

Honig, Bonnie. 'Arendt on the Couch'. *Differences* 26, no. 2 (2015): 93–105.

Hughes-d'Aeth, Tony. 'For a Long Time Nothing Happened: Settler Colonialism, Deferred Action and the Scene of Colonization in Kim Scott's *That Deadman Dance*'. *The Journal of Commonwealth Literature* 51, no. 1 (2016): 22–34.

Hyvönen, Ari-Elmeri, and Frank Möller. 'Visualising Political Thinking on the Screen: A Dialogue Between von Trotta's Hannah Arendt and Its Protagonist'. *Journal for Cultural Research* 21, no. 2 (2017): 140–56.

Ishiguro, Kazuo. *The Remains of the Day*. London: Faber, 2021.

Jacobs, Louis. *The Jewish Religion: A Companion*. Oxford: Oxford University Press, 1995.

James, David. 'Artifice and Absorption: The Modesty of the Remains of the Day'. In *Kazuo Ishiguro: Contemporary Critical Perspectives*, edited by Jean Mathews, and Sebastian Groes, 54–66. London: Bloomsbury, 2010.

James, Henry. 'Brooksmith'. In *Henry James: Complete Stories, Vol. 3 1884–1891*, edited by Edward Said, 759–75. New York: Library of America, 1999.

Jeffers, Thomas. *Apprenticeships: The Bildungsroman from Goethe to Santayana*. New York: Palgrave Macmillan, 2005.

Johnson, Patricia. 'Elizabeth Gaskell's *North and South*: A National *Bildungsroman*'. *The Victorian Newsletter* 85, (Spring 1994): 1–9.

Kalman, Nadia. 'Brother Daniel, Sister Ulitskaya'. Review of *Daniel Stein, Interpreter* by Ludmila Ulitskaya. *Jewish Review of Books* Summer 2011. https://jewishreviewofbooks.com/articles/85/brother-daniel-sister-ulitskaya/ (accessed 21 May 2023).

Katz, Pamela. 'But She's a Thinker'. *Differences* 26, no. 2 (2015): 86–92.

King, Richard H. *Arendt and America*. Chicago: University of Chicago Press, 2015.

Kinneavy, James L., and Catherine R. Eskin. 'Kairos in Aristotle's Rhetoric'. *Written Communication* 17, no. 3 (2000): 432–44.

Kokkola, Lydia. *Representing the Holocaust in Children's Literature*. New York: Routledge, 2013.

Koselleck, Reinhart. 'On the Anthropological and Semantic Structure of "*Bildung*"'. In *The Practice of Conceptual History: Timing History, Spacing Concepts*, translated by T.S. Pressenter et al., 174–6. Stanford: Stanford University Press, 2002.

Kristeva, Julia. 'A Propos des *Bienveillantes* (De l'abjection à la banalité du mal)'. *L'Infini* 99 (Summer 2007): 23–35.

LaCapra, Dominick. 'Historical and Literary Approaches to the "Final Solution": Saul Friedländer and Jonathan Littell'. *History and Theory* 50, no. 1 (2011): 71–97.

Landsberg, Alison. 'Politics and the Historical Film: Hotel Rwanda *and the Form of Engagement*'. In *A Companion to the Historical Film*, edited by Robert A. Rosenstone, and Constantin Parvulescu, 9–29. London: Wiley Blackwell, 2013.

Langer, Lawrence. 'The Dilemma of Choice in the Deathcamps'. *Centerpoint* 4, no. 1 (1980): 222–31.

Lanzmann, Claude. 'The Obscenity of Understanding: An Evening with Claude Lanzmann'. *American Imago* 48, no. 4 (1991): 473–95.

Laukötter, Anja, Benno Gammerl, Bettina Hitzer, Daniel Brückenhaus, Jan Plamper, Joachim C. Häberlen, Juliane Brauer, Magdalena Beljan, Magrit Pernau, Pascal Eitler, Stephanie Olson, Uffa Jensen, and Ute Frevert. *Learning How to Feel: Children's Literature and Emotional Socialization, 1870–1970*. Oxford: Oxford University Press, 2014.

Lee, Derek. 'The Politics of Fairyland: Neil Gaiman and the Enchantments of Anti-Bildungsroman'. *Critique: Studies in Contemporary Fiction* 57, no. 5 (2016): 552–64.

Levantovskaya, Margarita. 'The Russian-Speaking Jewish Diaspora in Translation: Liudmila Ulitskaia's Daniel Stein, Translator'. *Slavic Review* 71, no. 1 (2012): 91–107.

Levi, Primo. *The Drowned and the Saved*. London: Abacus, 1988.

Levi, Primo. *Survival in Auschwitz: The Nazi Assault on Humanity*. New York: Touchstone Books, 1996.

Lima, Maria Helena. *Decolonizing Genre: Caribbean Women Writers and the Bildungsroman*. Baltimore: University of Maryland, 1993.

Littell, Jonathan. *The Kindly Ones*. Translated by Charlotte Mandell. New York: Harper Collins, 2010.

Lodge, David. *The Art of Fiction: Illustrated from Classic and Modern Texts*. New York: Vintage, 2011.

Løvlie, Lars, Klaus P. Mortensen, and Sven Nordenbo, eds. *Educating Humanity: Bildung in Postmodernity*. Oxford: Blackwell, 2003.

Lukács, Georg. *The Theory of the Novel: A Historico-Philosophical Essay on the Forms of Great Epic Literature*. Translated by Anna Bostock. London: Merlin Press, 2006.

Lydon, Jane. 'A Strange Time Machine: *The Tracker, Black and White*, and *Rabbit-Proof Fence*'. *Australian Historical Studies* 35, no. 123 (2004): 137–48.

Lyons, Sara. 'Recent Work in Victorian Studies and the Bildungsroman'. *Literature Compass* 15, no. 4 (2018): 1–12.

M.M. Bakhtin. 'The *Bildungsroman*'. In *Speech Genres and Other Late Essays*, translated by Vern W. McGee, 10–59. Austin: University of Texas Press, 1987.

Malkin, Lawrence. *Krueger's Men: The Secret Nazi Counterfeit Plot of Block 19*. New York: Brown and Company, 2006.

Maynard, John R. 'The Bildungsroman'. In *A Companion to the Victorian Novel*, edited by Patrick Brantlinger, and William Thesing, 279–310. Malden: John Wiley, 2008.

McGlothlin, Erin. *The Mind of the Holocaust Perpetrator in Fiction and Nonfiction*. Detroit: Wayne State University Press, 2021.

McGowan, John. 'Sufficient Unto the Day: Reflections on Evil and Responsibility Prompted by Hannah Arendt and Kazuo Ishiguro'. *Soundings: An Interdisciplinary Journal* 91, no. 3/4 (2008): 229–54.

McMullin, Irene. 'The Amnesia of the Modern: Arendt on the Role of Memory in the Constitution of the Political'. *Philosophical Topics* 39, no. 2 (Fall 2011): 91–116.

McWilliams, Ellen. *Margaret Atwood and the Female Bildungsroman*. New York: Routledge, 2009.

Mendelsohn, Daniel. 'Transgression'. 18–21. *The New York Review of Books*, 26 March 2009, 56:5.

Mendes-Flohr, Paul. 'Cultural Zionism's Image of the Educated Jew: Reflections on Creating a Secular Jewish Culture'. *Modern Judaism* 18 (1998): 227–39.

Michaels, Walter Benn. 'Forgetting Auschwitz: Jonathan Littell and the Death of a Beautiful Woman'. *American Literary History* 25, no. 4 (2013): 915–30.

Miles, David H. 'The Picaro's Journey to the Confessional: The Changing Image of the Hero in the German Bildungsroman'. *PMLA* 89, no. 5 (October 1974): 980–92.

Millard, Kenneth. *Coming of Age in Contemporary American Fiction*. Edinburgh: Edinburgh University Press, 2007.

Moretti, Franco. *The Way of the World: The Bildungsroman in European Culture*. London: Verso, 2000.

Morgenstern, Karl, and Tobias Boes. 'On the Nature of the "Bildungsroman"'. *PMLA* 124, no. 2 (March 2009): 647–59.

Moscovici, Claudia. *Holocaust Memories: A Survey of Holocaust Memoirs, Histories, Novels, and Films*. London: Hamilton Books, 2019. Kindle Edition.

Moses, A. Dirk. 'Genocide and the Terror of History'. *Parallax* 17, no. 4 (2011): 90–108.

Moses, Anthony Dirk. 'Anxieties in Holocaust and Genocide Studies'. In *Probing the Ethics of Holocaust Culture*, edited by Claudio Fogu, Wulf Kansteiner, and Todd Presner, 332–54. Cambridge: Harvard University Press, 2016.

Moyn, Samuel. 'A Nazi Zelig: Jonathan Littell's *The Kindly Ones*'. *The Nation*, 4. 2009. https://www.thenation.com/article/archive/nazi-zelig-jonathan-littells-kindly-ones/ (accessed 28 May 2023).

Neuberger Holocaust Education Center, Facebook post of 6 August 2013. https://en-gb.facebook.com/HoloCentre/posts/we-were-recently-asked-why-we-dont-include-the-bewilderingly-popular-boy-in-the-/667320063297302/ (accessed 17 December, 2019).

Nünning, Ansgar F. 'Reconceptualizing Unreliable Narration: Synthesizing Cognitive and Rhetorical Approaches'. In *A Companion to Narrative Theory*, edited by J. Phelan, and P.J. Rabinowitz, 89–107. London: Blackwell Publishing, 2005.

Nussbaum, Martha. 'Virtue Ethics: A Misleading Category'. *The Journal of Ethics* 3, no. 3 (1999): 163–201.

O'Brien, Susie. 'Serving a New World Order: Postcolonial Politics in Kazuo Ishiguro's *The Remains of the Day*'. *MFS Modern Fiction Studies* 42, no. 4 (1996): 787–806.

Ophir, Adi. 'A Barely Visible Protagonist'. *Differences* 26, no. 2 (2015): 106–20.

Owens, Patricia. 'The Ethic of Reality in Hannah Arendt'. In *Political Thought and International Relations*, edited by D. Bell, 105–121. Oxford: Oxford University Press, 2008.

Oxford English Dictionary. Oxford: Oxford University Press. https://www.oed.com/view/Entry/94417?redirectedFrom=indication#eid

Phelan, James, and Mary Patricia Martin. 'The Lessons of "Weymouth": Homodiegesis, Unreliability, Ethics, and *The Remains of the Day*'. In *Narratologies: New Perspectives on Narrative Analysis*, edited by David Herman, 88–109. Columbus: Ohio State University Press, 1999.

Phelan, James. *Living to Tell About It: A Rhetoric and Ethics of Character Narration*. Ithaca: Cornell University Press, 2005.

Phelan, James. 'Estranging Unreliability, Bonding Unreliability, and the Ethics of *Lolita*'. In *Narrative Unreliability in the Twentieth-Century First-Person Novel*, edited by Elke D'hoker, and Gunther Martens, 7–28. Berlin: Walter de Gruyter, 2008.

Pinfold, Debbie. 'The Sins of the Fathers: Mark Hermans *The Boy in the Striped Pyjamas* (2008) and Cate Shortland's *Lore* (2012)'. *Oxford German Studies* 44, no. 3 (2015): 254–70.

Prager, Brad. 'Music After Mauthausen: Re-Presenting the Holocaust in Stefan Ruzowitzky's *The Counterfeiters* (2007)'. In *New Directions in German Cinema*, edited by Chris Homewood, and Paul Cooke, 77–93. London: I.B. Tauris, 2011.

Rabinbach, Anson. 'Eichmann in New York: The New York Intellectuals and the Hannah Arendt Controversy'. *October* 108 (Spring 2004): 97–111.

Ratner, Megan. 'Imagining the Unimaginable: Interview with László Nemes on *Son of Saul*. *Film Quarterly* 69, no. 3 (2016): 58–66.

Rauch, Stefanie. 'Understanding the Holocaust through Film: Audience Reception between Preconceptions and Media Effects'. *History and Memory* 30, no. 1 (Spring/Summer 2018): 151–88.

Rider, Ann N. 'The Perils of Empathy: Holocaust Narratives, Cognitive Studies and the Politics of Sentiment'. *Holocaust Studies: A Journal of Culture and History* 19, no. 3 (Winter 2013): 43–72.

Rieff, David. 'Hannah and Her Admirers'. *The Nation*, 19 December 2013. https://www.thenation.com/article/archive/hannah-and-her-admirers/ (accessed 28 May 2023).

Riggan, William. *Pícaros, Madmen, Naïfs, and Clowns: The Unreliable First-Person Narrator*. Norman: University of Oklahoma Press, 1981.

Rimmon-Kenan, Shlomith. *Narrative Fiction: Contemporary Poetics*. New York: Routledge, 2003.

Robbins, Bruce. *The Servant's Hand: English Fiction from Below*. New York: Columbia University Press, 1986.

Rose, Gillian. *Mourning Becomes the Law: Philosophy and Representation*. Cambridge: Cambridge University Press, 1996.

Rose, Jacqueline. *The Question of Zion*. Melbourne: Melbourne University Press, 2005.

Rosenberg, Joel. 'Into the Woods: Eichmann, Heidegger, and Margarethe von Trotta's Hannah Arendt'. *Jewish Film & New Media* 2, no. 2 (2014): 201–16.

Rosenfeld, Alvin H. 'The Americanization of the Holocaust'. *Commentary* 99, no. 6 (June 1995): 35–40.

Rosenstone, Robert A. 'The History Film as a Mode of Historical Thought'. In *A Companion to the Historical Film*, edited by Robert A. Rosenstone, and Constantin Parvulescu, 71–87. Malden: John Wiley and Sons, 2013.

Roth, Zoë. 'War of Images or Images of War? Visualizing History in Jonathan Littell's The Kindly Ones'. *Journal of Modern Literature* 41. no. 1 (Fall 2017): 81–99.

Rothberg, Michael. *Multidirectional Memory: Remembering the Holocaust in the Age of Decolonization*. Stanford: Stanford University Press, 2009.

Rothberg, Michael. 'The Witness as "World" Traveler: Multidirectional Memory and Holocaust Internationalism before Human Rights'. In *Probing the Ethics of Holocaust Culture*, edited by Claudio Fogu et al., 355–72. Cambridge: Harvard University Press, 2016.

Ruzowitsky, Stefan Dir. *The Counterfeiters*. Madman Entertainment, 2007.

Said, Edward. *Freud and the Non-European*. London: Verso, 2003.

Salecl, Renata. *(Per)versions of Love and Hate*. London: Verso, 2000.

Sammons, Jeffrey L. 'The Mystery of the Missing Bildungsroman, or What Happened to Wilhelm Meister's Legacy?'. *Genre* 14, no. 2 (1981): 229–46.

Sandberg, Eric. '"This Incomprehensible Thing": Jonathan Littell's *The Kindly Ones* and the Aesthetics of Excess'. *The Cambridge Quarterly* 43, no. 3 (2014): 231–55.

Sanyal, Debarati. *Memory and Complicity: Migrations of Holocaust Remembrance*. New York: Fordham University Press, 2015.

Scherzinger, Karen. 'The Butler in (the) Passage: The Liminal Narrative of Kazuo Ishiguro's *The Remains of the Day*'. *Literator: Journal of Literary Criticism, Comparative Linguistics and Literary Studies* 25, no. 1 (2004): 1–21.

Scholem, Gershom. 'Against the Myth of German-Jewish Dialogue'. In *On Jews and Judaism in Crisis: Selected Essays*, edited by Werner J. Dannhauser, 61–4. New York: Schocken, 1976.

Sedgwick, Eve Kosofksy. *Touching Feeling: Affect, Pedagogy, Performativity*. Durham: Duke University Press, 2003.

Sherwood, Harriet. 'The Boy in the Striped Pyjamas "May Fuel Dangerous Holocaust Fallacies"'. *The Guardian*, 27 January 2022. https://www.theguardian.com/world/2022/jan/27/the-boy-in-the-striped-pyjamas-fuels-dangerous-holocaust-fallacies (accessed 25 May 2023).

Shohat, Ella. *Taboo Memories, Diasporic Visions*. Durham: Duke University Press, 2006.

Short, Geoffrey. 'Learning from Genocide? A Study in the Failure of Holocaust Education'. *Intercultural Education* 16, no. 4 (2005): 367–80.

Slaughter, Joseph R. *Human Rights, Inc.: The World Novel, Narrative Form, and International Law*. New York: Fordham University Press, 2009.

Sorkin, David. 'Wilhelm Von Humboldt: The Theory and Practice of Self-Formation (Bildung), 1791–1810'. *Journal of the History of Ideas* 44, no. 1 (1983): 55–73.

Sorvari, Marja. '"To Tell the Truth as I Understand It": Lived Religion, Post-Secularism and Gender in Liudmila Ulitskaia's *Daniel Stein, Interpreter*'. *Slavonic and East European Review* 95, no. 2 (2017): 252–70.

Spargo, R. Clifton. '1961, Jerusalem: Eichmann and the Aesthetic of Complicity'. In *The Edinburgh Companion to Twentieth-Century Literatures*, edited by Brian McHale, and Randall Stevenson, 161–72. Edinburgh: Edinburgh University Press, 2006.

Stangneth, Bettina. *Eichmann Before Jerusalem: The Unexamined Life of a Mass Murderer*. New York: Random House, 2014.

Steinberg, Michael P. 'Seeing Hearing Thinking: Introducing the *Differences* Dossier on Margarethe von Trotta's *Hannah Arendt*'. *Differences* 26, no. 2 (2015): 61–9.

Stévic, Aleksandar. *Falling Short: The Bildungsroman and the Crisis of Self-Fashioning*. Charlottesville: University of Virginia Press, 2020.

Stock, Jennifer, ed. *Contemporary Literary Criticism*, Vol. 454. Farmington Hills: Gale, 2020.

Stone, Dan. *Histories of the Holocaust*. Oxford: Oxford University Press, 2010.

Stone, Dan. 'From Stockholm to Stockton: The Holocaust and/as Heritage in Britain'. In *Britain and the Holocaust: Remembering and Representing War and Genocide*, edited by Caroline Staples, and Olaf Jensen, 212–29. London: Palgrave Macmillan, 2013.

Suleiman, Susan Rubin. 'When the Perpetrator Becomes a Reliable Witness of the Holocaust: On Jonathan Littell's *Les Bienveillantes*'. *New German Critique* 36, no. 1 (2009): 1–19.

Sutcliffe, Benjamin. 'Liudmila Ulitskaia's Literature of Tolerance'. *Russian Review* 68, no. 3 (2009): 495–509.

Swales, Martin. *The German Bildungsroman from Wieland to Hesse*. Princeton: Princeton University Press, 1978.

Swales, Martin. 'Johann Wolfgang von Goethe (1749–1832): The German Bildungsroman" In *The Cambridge Companion to European Novelists*, edited by Michael Bell, 124–39. Cambridge: Cambridge University Press, 2012.

Sycamore, Mattilda Bernstein, ed. *Dangerous Families: Queer Writing on Surviving*. New York and Abingdon: Routledge, 2011.

Tec, Nechama. *In the Lion's Den: The Life of Oswald Rufeisen*. New York: Oxford University Press, 1990.

Teo, Hsu-Ming. 'History, the Holocaust, and Children's Historical Fiction'. *Text* Issue 28 (April 2015): 1–21.

Terestchenko, Michel. 'Servility and Destructiveness in Kazuo Ishiguro's the Remains of the Day'. *Partial Answers: Journal of Literature and the History of ideas* 5, no. 1 (2007): 77–89.

Thakkar, Sonali. 'Resurfacing Symptomatic Reading: Contrapuntal Memory and Postcolonial Method in *The Remains of the Day*'. *Cambridge Journal of Postcolonial Literary Inquiry* 4, no. 1 (2017): 89–108.

The Earl of Shaftesbury. 'Soliloquy, or Advice to an Author'. In *Characteristics of Men, Manners, Opinions, Times*, edited by Lawrence E. Klein, 110–202. Cambridge: Cambridge University Press, 1999 [1711].

Theweleit, Klaus. 'On the German Reaction to Jonathan Littell's *Les Bienveillantes*'. *New German Critique* 106, no. 1 (Winter 2009): 21–34.

Tripp, Valerie. 'Vitamins in Chocolate Cake: Why Use Historical Fiction in the Classroom?" 2011. https://teachinghistory.org/nhec-blog/24679 (accessed 17 December 2019).

Troupin, Orit Yushinsky. 'Carcizans: The Quest for Origin and the Assault on Alterity in Jonathan Littell's *The Kindly Ones*'. *Partial Answers: Journal of Literature and the History of Ideas* 18, no. 2 (2020): 315–34.

Ulitskaya, Ludmila. *Daniel Stein, Interpreter*. Translated by Arch Tait. Melbourne: Scribe, 2011.

Vice, Sue. *Holocaust Fiction*. New York: Routledge, 2000.

Wajnryb, Ruth. 'Cure for the Jewish Condition Lands Daniel in a Lion's Den. Review of *Daniel Stein, Interpreter* by Ludmila Ulitskaya'. *Sydney Morning Herald*, 5 September, 2011, p. 30. https://global.factiva.com/redir/default.aspx?P=sa&an =SMHH000020111104e7b50009x&drn=drn%3aarchive.newsarticle.SMHH000 020111104e7b50009x&cat=a&ep=ASE (accessed 21 May 2023).

Wall, Kathleen. '"The Remains of the Day" and Its Challenges to Theories of Unreliable Narration'. *The Journal of Narrative Technique* 24, no. 1 (1994): 18–42.

Wauchope, Mary. '*The Counterfeiters*: Seeking Moral Lessons from a Holocaust Thriller'. *Shofar: An Interdisciplinary Journal of Jewish studies* 28, no. 4 (2010): 57–71.

Wells, Susan. 'Benjamin's Rhetoric: Kairos, Time, and History'. *Philosophy & Rhetoric* 55, no. 3 (2022): 252–73.

Westerman, Molly. 'Is the Butler Home? Narrative and the Split Subject in *The Remains of the Day*'. *Mosaic: A Journal for the Interdisciplinary Study of Literature* 7, no. 3 (September 2004): 157–70.

Wiesel, Elie. 'The Holocaust as Literary Inspiration'. In *Dimensions of the Holocaust*, edited by Elie Wiesel, Lucy Dawidowicz, Dorothy Rabinowitz, and Robert McAfee Brown, 5–9. Evanston: Northwestern University Press, 1996.

Wolin, Richard. 'The Banality of Evil: The Demise of a Legend'. *Jewish Review of Books* 19, (Fall 2014): 28–32.

Wulf, Christoph. 'Perfecting the Individual: Wilhelm von Humboldt's Concept of Anthropology, Bildung and Mimesis'. *Educational Philosophy and Theory* 35, no. 2 (2003): 241–9.

Yerushalmi, Josef Hayim. *Zakhor: Jewish History and Jewish Memory*. Seattle: University of Washington Press, 1996.

Yovel, Yirmiyahu. *Spinoza and Other Heretics: The Marrano of Reason*. Princeton: Princeton University Press, 1989.

INDEX

Page numbers followed with "n" refer to endnotes.

Adams, Jenni 40, 43, 50, 51, 134 n.11
ad feminam 8, 59, 117
Adhikari, Mohamed 96
anti-Semitism 8, 33, 37, 40, 44, 46, 47, 51, 58, 61, 73, 74, 84, 93, 99, 106, 125, 127, 135 n.6
   Hitler 12, 50
   violence 60, 105
anti-Zionism 61
Apter, Emily 69
Arendt, Hannah 7–9, 18, 33, 46, 49, 99, 107, 111, 112, 116, 134 n.11
   banality of evil 8, 9, 13, 107, 113, 117, 121, 122, 124
   conception of conscience 33
   conception of thinking (*Selbstdenken*) 13, 112–16, 118–21, 123–5, 128, 130
Aryan race 47, 76
Ashkenazi Judaism 62
Azoulay, Ariella 123–4

Baer, James 56
Bakhtin, Mikhail Mikhaïlovich 3, 17, 18, 21, 22, 25, 53, 57
banality of evil 6, 8, 9, 13, 113, 117, 121, 122, 124
Baron, Lawrence 97
Bauman, Zygmunt 8
Berkowitz, Roger 118
Bildung (self-formation) 6, 16, 22, 25, 36, 53–6, 69, 72, 86, 112, 119, 129, 130, 133 n.2
Bildungsheld 1, 2, 4, 5, 10, 11, 13, 17, 18, 21, 30, 79
   of *The Counterfeiters* (*Die Fälscher* 2007, Ruzowitzky) 98–104
   Daniel Stein (character) as 12, 55, 60–2, 66

Sally Sorowitch (character)
   as 13, 91–2
   as violating ethical spectatorship 95–8
Blech, Benjamin 80
bonding unreliability 41, 42
Boswell, Matthew 43, 93, 95, 134 n.11
The Boy in the Striped Pyjamas (2006, Boyne) 1, 12, 71, 73, 74, 79, 84–9
Bruno (character) in 12, 13, 71, 74, 80–8
   accidental death 81
   friendship 87, 88
   innocent perspective 81, 82
   love of exploration 86
   memory of his grandmother 86
   psychological development 83
child reader 81, 88
criticism 81
Heidi (character) in 75–9, 84, 85
Kotler (character) in 84, 87
Mark (character) in 75–80, 87
online reader responses/comments 82–3
reviews 80–1
Boyne, John 72, 74, 79
Buckley, Jerome 27
Bukiet, Melvin 58, 59
Burger, Adolf 99–102, 108
Butler, Judith 49–50, 56, 60–1, 63

Castle, Gregory 87
Catholic diaspora 65
Catholic identity 12, 59
Catholicism/Christianity, conversion to 54–9, 61–4, 136 n.9
Cesarani, David 81
Chatman, Seymour 41

Chaudhuri, Shohini 96–7
child protagonist 74–5, 83, 88
Christianity
    conversion to 54–9, 61–4, 136 n.9
    Jewish 61, 63, 65–8
    Judaism and 59, 63–4
    Pauline 64, 65
Christoff, Peter 8
class system 23–6, 31, 32
communicative imperative 93
concentration camp 13, 45, 74, 76, 85, 88, 99, 100, 102, 114, 127
The Counterfeiters (*Die Fälscher* 2007, Ruzowitzky) 1, 13, 91, 97, 105–9
    Bildungsheld of 98–104
    Burger, Adolf (character) in 99, 102–7
    critics of 92, 98, 109
    Herzog, Friedrich (character) in 100–3, 105, 107
    historical Jewish experience 104–5
    Jewish diaspora 104, 105
    Sally Sorowitch (character) in 91, 92, 98, 100–7
    as *Bildungsheld* 13, 91, 92
    Wauchope's review 97–8

Dalley, Hamish 17, 104
Daniel Stein, Interpreter (2006, Ulitskaya) 12, 53
    criticism 59
        of Israeli policies 58
    Daniel Stein/Brother Daniel (character) in 12, 53–4, 56–7, 60, 62, 66–9
        anti-Semitism 58
        as a *Bildungsheld* 55, 60–2, 66
        Christian identity 65
        conversion to Catholicism/ Christianity 54–9, 61–4, 136 n.9
        diasporic Judaism 61
        divine justice 64
        Holy Land 12, 66–9
        Jerusalem syndrome 66
        Jesus Christ and 64–5

Jewish Christianity 61, 63, 65–7
Jewish identity 58, 63, 65, 136 n.7
Jewish nationality 59
Judaism 64–5
self-formation 54
as trickster translator 55
Jewish diaspora 12, 54, 56, 59–66, 68, 69
political Zionism 58, 59, 65, 66
rabbinical view 59
dehumanization 25, 26, 67, 71, 87
Der Untergang (Fest) 95
Diamond, Diana 112, 115
diaspora
    Jewish 12, 13, 50, 51, 61, 65, 92, 104–5, 136, 136 n.8
    The Counterfeiters (*Die Fälscher* 2007, Ruzowitzky) 104, 105
    Daniel Stein, Interpreter (Ulitskaya) 12, 54, 56, 59–66, 68, 69
    Judaism 61, 92
dignity 23–5, 27–9, 32–4, 36
Downfall (*Der Untergang*, 2005, Hirschbiegel) 94, 136 n.2

Eaglestone, Robert 80
Eichmann, Adolf 7–8, 11, 18, 43, 46, 49, 107, 111, 112, 115, 117–18, 121–3, 126
    trial 18, 111, 113–14, 116, 118, 120, 121, 124, 126–7
Eichmann in Jerusalem: A Report on the Banality of Evil (1963, Arendt) 8, 111, 113, 117, 121
estranging unreliability 41, 42
Esty, Jed 54, 68, 130

fascinating fascism 86
fascism 106
Fraiman, Susan 5, 31, 97, 112, 129
Franklin, Ruth 96, 120–1
French, Jackie 72, 74, 76

galut. *See* Jewish diaspora
genocide 62, 92, 94, 96, 97, 134 n.11.
　　See also Holocaust
　of Jews 13, 38, 39, 42, 43, 45, 47,
　　80, 121
　Rwandan 96
Goethe, Johann Wolfgang von 2, 4, 10
Goldstein, Jan 121
Graham, Sarah 11, 55–6

Halakhic law 59, 64
Hannah Arendt (2012, von Trotta) 1,
　13, 111
　Arendt, Hannah (character) 111–16
　　banality of evil 113, 117, 121,
　　　122, 124
　　conception of thinking
　　　(*Selbstdenken*) 13, 112–16,
　　　118–21, 123–5, 128, 130
　　and reconstruction of
　　　ethics 117–23
　　thinking on Eichmann
　　　affair 114, 118, 125
　　critics of 120–1
　　Eichmann trial 111, 113–14, 116,
　　　118, 120, 121, 123, 124,
　　　126–7
　　Heidegger, Martin (character) 13,
　　　113, 114, 119, 125–6
　　Köhler, Lotte (character) 13, 113,
　　　116, 123, 126, 128
　　screenplay of Katz, Pamela 122–3
　　spectators 124–8
Haskalah 62, 136 n.10
Herman, Linda 86, 88
hermeneutic approach 5–9
Hesse, Isabelle 51
Himmler, Heinrich 43, 45, 47, 49
Hirsch, Marianne 30, 55
Hirsch, Susan 88
Hirschbiegel, Oliver 94
historical fiction 1, 3, 6, 9, 10, 12, 17,
　18, 35, 39, 42, 93, 95, 99
　for children 71–5
　　The Boy in the Striped Pyjamas
　　　(2006, Boyne) (*see The*
　　　Boy in the Striped Pyjamas
　　　(2006, Boyne))

Hitler's Daughter (1999,
　French) 1, 12, 71, 74, 76–9,
　83–5, 87
Hitler, Adolf 38, 43, 44, 46–8, 50, 80,
　94, 95, 101
　anti-Semitism 12, 50
Hitler's Daughter (1999, French) 1, 12,
　71, 74, 76–9, 83–5, 87
Hoffman, Eva 51
Holocaust 1–3, 8, 37, 39, 40, 42, 44–6,
　48, 71, 72, 78, 80–2, 95, 98,
　107, 109, 117, 125–7, 130,
　143 n.11
　children's fiction 12, 73–4, 80
　　The Boy in the Striped Pyjamas
　　　(2006, Boyne) (*see The*
　　　Boy in the Striped Pyjamas
　　　(2006, Boyne))
　　Hitler's Daughter (1999,
　　　French) 1, 12, 71, 74, 76–9,
　　　83–5, 87
　cinema/films 91–3, 96–7, 105
　as crime against humanity 127
　imaginative fictions 92–3, 95–6
　interpretation of creative texts
　　about 94
　memorial institutions 137 n.6
　pedagogy 88
　survivor 53, 59, 99
'Holocaust etiquette' 73, 137 n.5
Honig, Bonnie 123
Hotel Rwanda (2004, Adhikari) 96
Humboldt, Wilhelm von 22
Hyvönen, Ari-Elmeri 114–15

Ishiguro, Kazuo 15, 16, 22, 46
Israel 59–61, 68
Israeli-Palestinian war 67–8

James, David 22, 28, 35
James, Henry 10, 19
Jaspers, Karl 116
Jeffers, Thomas 10, 27
Jerusalem syndrome 3, 12, 66, 116
Jewish
　assimilation 136 n.7
　Christianity 61, 63, 65–8
　Halakhic law 59

identity   12, 58, 59, 62–3, 65, 136 n.7
   conversion to Catholicism   58
   and Judaism   56
   Zionist conceptions of   92
nationality   59
suffering   58, 64
Jewish diaspora   12, 13, 50, 51, 61, 65, 92, 104–5, 136, 136 n.8
   The Counterfeiters (*Die Fälscher* 2007, Ruzowitzky)   104, 105
   Daniel Stein, Interpreter (2006, Ulitskaya)   12, 54, 56, 59–66, 68, 69
Jewish exile. *See* Jewish diaspora
Jewishness   59–61, 63
   Zionist monopoly   61
Jews
   conversion of   58–9
   genocide of   13, 38, 39, 42–3, 45, 47, 80, 121
Johnson, Patricia   35
Judaism   57–9, 63–5, 67, 68
   Ashkenazi   62
   and Christianity   59, 63–4
   diaspora   61, 92
   Jewish identity and   56
   monotheistic iconoclasm   64
   post-Haskalah   62
Judeo-Christian Western tradition   117
Jurist, Elliot   112, 115

Katz, Pamela   122–3
The Kindly Ones (2010, Littell)   1, 11–12, 37–9
   anti-Semitism   37, 44, 46, 47, 50, 51
   Aue, Maximilien (character)
      in   6, 11–12
      as disillusioned historical witness   44–6
      disillusionment   38, 46–7
      as mobile focalizer   43–4
      Nazism   43–4, 46–7
      as participant-observer of Jews' genocide   44–5
      as provocateur   48–51
      redemptive anti-Semitism   47
      transformation from blindness to insight   47–8

criticism   39–40
   as historical novel   43–4, 49
   readers of   41–2
   unreliable narration   41–2
King, Richard   121, 124
Kokkola, Lydia   73
Kristeva, Julia   37, 40
Krüger, Bernhard   100, 101, 108

LaCapra, Dominic   37, 40, 49
Landsberg, Alison   98
Langer, Lawrence   106
Levantovskaya, Margarita   55, 56, 59, 63, 64
Levi, Primo   93, 94, 98, 104, 106, 107
The Life of the Mind (1978, Arendt)   114, 119
Lima, Maria Helena   4
Littell, Jonathan   37, 39, 41, 45, 51
locus classicus   39, 136 n.7
Lodge, David   10, 16
Løvlie, Lars   35, 53
Lukács, Georg   56
Lydon, Jane   104

McCarthy, Mary   127, 128
McGlothlin, Erin   48, 134 n.11
McMullin, Irene   18
McWilliams, Ellen   11, 20, 112
Marrano Jews   63
Martin, Mary Patricia   41
Meister, Wilhelm (character)   2, 4, 10, 27
Mendelsohn, Daniel   39
Mendes-Flohr, Paul   86
Men in Dark Times (Arendt)   124–5
Michaels, Walter Benn   40
Möller, Frank   114–15
Moreau, Frédéric   27
Moretti, Franco   2, 3, 5, 22, 27, 55, 74, 98, 115, 133 n.7
Moscovici, Claudia   81
Moses, Dirk   51, 80

Nazi crimes   12, 39, 42, 44, 50
Nazism   42–4, 46–7, 64, 74, 78, 94, 108
neo-Aristotelian virtue ethics   117

Ophir, Adi   118

Palestine 51, 61, 62
Pauline Christianity 64, 65
Phelan, James 41
Pinfold, Debbie 80
political Zionism 58, 59, 65, 66
post-Haskalah Judaism 62
Prager, Brad 98
protagonist of a *Bildungsroman* 1–2

radical evil 113
Ratner, Megan 97
Rauch, Stefanie 105
The Remains of the Day (1989,
    Ishiguro) 1, 11
  Lord Darlington (character) in 15,
    16, 20, 21, 32, 35, 46, 47,
    135 n.4
  Miss Kenton (character) in 19–23,
    25, 26, 28, 31–4, 135 n.4
  political allegory and future
    horizons 35–6
  Smith, Harry (character) 34, 36
  Stevens (character) in 6, 10, 11,
    15–19, 38, 41, 42, 46, 47,
    135 n.2
    anachronistic 28, 29, 34
    awakening 19–23
    as butler 11, 15, 18, 24–6, 29, 34,
      46, 135 nn.2, 4
    dignity 24–5, 27–8, 36, 135 n.2
    as Eichmann like figure 11,
      15, 17
    father of 24–6, 135 n.4
    image of Englishness 24
    indicative important of
      travel 29–31
    journey into post-war Britain 35
    life crisis 20
    metonymic relation 24
    movement away from Darlington
      Hall 23–6, 35
    off-piste drive 11
    question of vocation 11, 26–9
    unbecoming in
      memory 17, 31–6
Rider, Ann 88
Rieff, David 120–1, 124
Robbins, Bruce 15, 18, 26, 27, 29, 32, 34

Rose, Jacqueline 60
Rosenberg, Joel 114
Rosenstone, Robert 98, 108, 109,
    136 n.3
Roth, Zoë 38, 39
Rothberg, Michael 94
Rufeisen, Oswald 53, 56, 59
Ruzowitzky, Stefan 91, 99, 100, 102,
    103, 105, 108, 109
Rwandan genocide 96

Sandberg, Eric 39, 44
Sanyal, Debarati 39, 48
Scherzinger, Karen 18, 22, 23,
    27–31
Schiller, Friedrich 4, 130
Scholem, Gershom 118, 136 n.7
Second World War 1, 3, 7, 32, 54,
    72–4, 76, 78, 92, 96, 99, 117,
    119, 130
Selbstdenken (conception of
    thinking) 112–16, 118–21,
    123–5, 128
Short, Geoffrey 72
Slaughter, Joseph 3
Sorvari, Marja 54
Speer, Albert 47
Standish, Paul 35, 53
Stangneth, Bettina 121
Stone, Dan 46, 107–8
Suleiman, Susan 42, 44
Swales, Martin 4, 10, 19, 29, 102

Teo, Hsu-Ming 77–8
Theweleit, Klaus 45, 47
*A Thousand Darknesses: Lies and Truth
    in Holocaust Fiction* (2011,
    Franklin) 96
Tripp, Valerie 73
Troupin, Orit 37, 48
tzaddik 57, 135 n.3

Ulitskaya, Ludmila 53, 54, 56–60, 62,
    136 n.9
unreliable narration 9–13, 41–2

Varnhagen, Rahel 126
Vice, Sue 2, 73, 93, 134 n.11

Vichy France   46
von Trotta, Margarethe   13, 111, 117, 118, 120–3, 126

Wajnryb, Ruth   58–9
Wall, Kathleen   41
Wauchope, Mary   97–8, 102, 103, 105
Wehrmacht   43, 45

Westerman, Molly   24
Wiesel, Elie   93

xenophobia   13, 24, 77

Yerushalmi, Yosef Hayim   92

Zionism   12, 50–1, 58–62, 65, 66, 105

www.ingramcontent.com/pod-product-compliance
Lightning Source LLC
Chambersburg PA
CBHW052050300426
44117CB00012B/2054